# *Lessons Through the Word*
# *Day by Day*

## *By*
## *Dwight Knight*

*Daily studies from every book of the Bible*

# Dedication

This book is dedicated first to my teachers: My first Sunday school teacher, Ms. Marion Love, and her wonderful husband the late Dr. Pellam Love, who taught me as much about being a husband and father as he did the bible; Dr. Charles Oliver my Sunday School teacher, and a living classroom on how to shepherd the local flock of God. And finally Dr. George Philip, the most thorough bible teacher I have ever known.

Secondly, to my babies; my grandchildren: My Nookie Nook, Anna Carr; her brother, my Chum Chum, Asa Carr; and my new Sweetie, Sophia Vasquez.

My nieces and nephews: Derek, Zachary, Christina, Madison, Daniel, Maxim, and Noah.

To four great men who over the past five years have believed in me and gone to great lengths to encourage, protect and love me; Dr. Varghese Varghese and his son Shaji (Minnesota); and Mr. George Mathew and Viji Roberts (Mississauga).

Lastly to my women: Mrs. Dorothy Knight, my mother; and my wife, my Sweetness, M'bo, Stephane Knight; you're my daily proof that God truly loves me.

Special thanks to my new son, Lear Kirkland, who patiently transcribed every word in this book. I couldn't have done it without you.

# How to use this Book

This was a work of passion. I've always wanted a book that I could use every day that would cause me to both read the work and understand what I read.

I realize that some people are not use to a daily bible study, or just unable able to study it daily, but still want to learn it systematically. So, I've tried to provide a monthly study that is project oriented.

If you can go through the book day by day, read the entire passage and work through the simple short study.

From time to time there will be Hebrew or Greek words, the definition is always given; study them and their meanings, memorize them and make notations of them in your bible.

Remember to invest in the weekly challenges that are designed to encourage lifestyle changes; please use these throughout the year.

If you are more of a monthly student, do all of the assignments, learn all the verses, be sure to take on all the challenges.

But regardless of what type of devotion you may undertake, make sure that you use one of the daily reading schedules found at the end of the book.

May the Lord bless you as you learn and grow.

Dwight Knight

Spring 2012

# *January*

## *A Time for Consecration*

*Lesson:* The Word of Faith

*"But what saith it? The word is nigh thee, even in thy mouth, and in thy heart: that is, the word of faith, which we preach"*
Romans 10:8

*T*he word of faith is the statement of Gods' given require-ments for the salvation process to be accomplished. It is God's statement of validation; better, it is Gods' self-satisfying payment for humanity's sin. Thereby, the righteousness of heaven is accurately met by the sinner. It is the only thing heaven will accept as payment, as so to eliminate the debt the sinner has incurred.

This word of faith, believed by the sinner, and confessed openly serves as the final payment the Lord requires before He applies His innocent and incorruptible blood as sacrifice for salvation. When His precious blood is accepted the righteousness of Jesus is imputed to the sinner; thus, making him a fully justified saint.

It serves as the only currency that heaven will allow for the sin of any man.

The word of faith preached and accepted, believed and confessed is God's fair market cost for me to receive full son-ship in the kingdom.

### Outline of the Passage

Verse 8 shows us four wonderful discoveries
  A.  The contract of faith – "the word of faith" v.8a
  B.  The conditions of faith – "mouth and heart" v.8b
  C.  The confession of faith – that if thou will confess with thy mouth/ believe in thine heart" v.9c
  D.  The confirmation of Faith – say and believe v.10

**Facts: The month of January, first month of the Gregorian calendar.**

It corresponds to the month of Tebeth; the tenth month of the Hebrew calendar. It was the time of year mentioned in Esther chapter 2, when the search was made for a new queen replacing Queen Vashti.

*Focus:* **Prayer and personal scrutiny.**

Use the time of this month to do personal evaluation. Ask others about areas in your life that maybe a hindrance to your testimony. Ask the Lord to open your eyes to things you may have overlooked in your life that may slow your spiritual growth.

*Assignment:* **Research**

Create a chart that records all the kings of Israel beginning with King Saul; include who the high priests were and who was the prophet of the Lord.

*Memory Work:*

**Exaltation:** Psalm 34:1

**Excellence:** Philippians 4:13

**Edification:** Jude 21

**Evangelical:** Romans 10: 9, 10

**Exhortive:** Galatians 6:14

**Educational:** Romans 1:16

*Drawing Closer*

*Consecration*

*Week One*

> *Tithe a tenth of every waking hour to prayer. Not for yourself, but for someone or something different for each hour. Use this time to talk to the Lord about a specific situation, cause or concern that will directly affect the lives of others.*

# *January 1*

*Lamentations 3:21-23*

*The Lords' Mercies*

**"This I recall to my mind, therefore have I hope.
It is of the LORD'S mercies that we are not consumed,
because his compassions fail not. They are new every
morning: great is thy faithfulness."**

*He provides for every living thing.*
*Every animal can trust that He will feed them.*
*He causes it to rain on the just and the unjust.*
*We can ask, and He will give us our daily nourishment.*
*And just as we have come to expect, He supplies all of our*
*needs according to His riches in glory by His Son Jesus.*
*There is no one like our God.*
*Every day He gives brand new mercies. Not one, or some,*
*but more than we could ever exhaust. He endears Himself*
*to us by giving when we don't ask, don't know, won't*
*acknowledge, and when we don't deserve. It's evident here,*
*that without these mercies we would be consumed.*
*We are disasters waiting to happen.*
*We are so pitiful and so helpless, that*

*God must intervene each day of our lives.*

*So don't lose sight of who you should*

*worship and focus your heart on.*

*Live by His mercies; enjoy His presence;*

*trust in His grace.*

# *January 2*

*Psalm 32*

### *Make a quick account of sin*

*"I acknowledged my sin unto thee, and mine iniquity have I not hid. I said, I will confess my transgressions unto the LORD; and thou forgavest the iniquity of my sin. Selah."*

*vs.5*

*David acknowledges that the secret to perpetual blessing from God is to have a short account of sin.*
*Those who live their lives with unconfessed sin and broken fellowship short circuit this blessing and the power of God in their day to day existence.*
*God already knows what you have done;*
*He knew before you did it.*
*To confess your sins to Him is not giving Him knowledge of a deed He was unaware of.*
*No, to confess to Him (homologeo) means,*
*I say what He has already said.*
*I am acknowledging my sin to Him (Psalm 51:3).*

*By telling God the truth from your heart you are in fact*
*removing the awful curse of guilt and retribution.*
*Do yourself the best favor possible – keep a good and short*
*account of your sin and confess.*

# *January 3*

*Genesis 1:1*

### **In the Beginning**

**"In the beginning God created the heaven and the earth."**

*The most important ten words in the Bible.*
*Pretty bold statement when you consider that*
*it contains over 100,000 verses.*
*But no doubt about it, these are the most important words*
*in the Bible; found in the most important verse in the Bible.*
*I make this statement because if this verse isn't true*
*than the rest of the Bible can't be.*
*For if He can't speak the worlds in to being;*
*He cannot rise from the dead.*
*And if He cannot create the universe from nothing;*
*then He can't not save us from our sins.*
*If this God cannot make a mature Earth capable of sustaining*
*life, then He cannot prepare us a home in glory.*
*I could go on and on.*
*This Jesus for whom and by whom all things exists*
*did all of the above and more.*

*He began the beginning with the genius of infinite*

*variety and unequaled splendor.*

*Because He is Lord and Master,*

*Creator of the natural world,*

*He deserves worship.*

*He deserves worship from everything and everyone.*

# *January 4*

*Psalm 32:7*

### *"Thou art my hiding place"*

**"Thou art my hiding place;
thou shalt preserve me from trouble;
thou shalt compass me about
with songs of deliverance. Selah."**
**vs.7**

*Anyone who has been outside on a cold windy rainy day
knows the benefit of a covert – a hiding place,
something bigger and stronger than themselves
to take the brunt of it and the elements so they
don't have to feel it.
David speaks of the Lord in exactly the same way.
The Lord covers and protects you from the powers
that would otherwise overwhelm us.
But His protection isn't just for the elements.
It's for the beating battered brunt of life's attacks and storms.
The Lord is the perfect covert for the fiercest elements
and the most ferocious enemies.*

*Despite your struggles and despite the attacks*
*that accompany the believer you can rest assured that*
*God is the perfect hiding place.*
*He is the perfect shelter in the time of storm.*
*Don't waste your time looking for someone else or*
*something else. Put all your trust in Him now.*

# *January 5*

*Judges 21:25*

*Self*

*I need a spiritual compass in my life.*
*I need someone or something else to give me*
*their perspective and direction in my life.*
*If I follow my own path, going the way I want without*
*a special standard, I will, like the man alone in the desert,*
*walk myself into a circle.*
*I cause my life to spiral into a morbid selfish,*
*self-destructive, self-gratifying pit.*
*Because Israel lived without a king, the true king;*
*Jehovah, the entire populace became selfish and unfulfilled*
*(Isaiah 53:6).*
*I need, you need, to see the importance of the*
*pre-eminence of the Lord's word in our lives;*
*I must regard the Lord's voice from all others.*
*My view of the world, the way I assess the situation*
*will never be perfectly accurate.*
*I must employ the full resources of God's word,*
*His Spirit and His people to live a life of holiness.*
*Drop your guard; stop trying to run your own life.*
*Live with the power of the Spirit as your barometer.*

*We all need outside scrutiny, for we all see*

*the world through tainted lenses.*

*Refuse to follow your own way.*

*Learn that trust in Him is the only secure path to take.*

# *January 6*

*Psalm 62*

### *Mine*

*"He only is my rock and my salvation: he is my defence;*
*I shall not be moved. In God is my salvation and my glory:*
*the rock of my strength, and my refuge, is in God."*

*vs. 6,7*

*The importance and wonder of the God of all power, majesty and might availing Himself to the affairs of people is one of the great mysteries of the universe.*

*David mentions God in the personal sense of his life over and over.*

*He makes it clear that what gave him absolute confidence was that God was his personal friend and possession. Note the terms he uses: my salvation (4 times), my rock (3 times), my refuge (2 times). It's clear that what gave him solace and steadfast security was the absolute certainty of the Lord God in his life.*

# *January 7*

*Proverbs 2*

### *Knowing God*

**"Then shalt thou understand the fear of the LORD, and find the knowledge of God. For the LORD giveth wisdom: out of his mouth cometh knowledge and understanding"**

**vs. 5,6**

*There are two great pursuits that everyone should undertake.*
*One is greater and one lesser, but are both imperative.*
*The greater: Knowing God, the lesser: Knowing ones' self.*
*There is no discovery of self without knowing God.*
*The lesser will never precede the greater.*
*David instructs his son Solomon*
*to know the Lord and to fear Him.*
*All of the quests and questions of life find their answer here.*
*and all that could be accomplished, all that might*
*could be realized is incumbent upon this fact.*
*For us he points out it is in knowing God that we find:*
*1) Vs. 8, the path of judgment and God's council.*
*2) Vs. 13, the path of uprightness.*
*3) Vs. 9, the path of good (God's standard of excellence).*
*4) Vs. 19, the path of life (not death).*

*5) Vs. 20, the path of righteousness.*

*Know God.*

*All the answers to purpose and being*

*are found in knowing Him.*

*Drawing Closer*

*Consecration*

*Week Two*

> *Start each day with the prayer: "Lord show me the areas of my life that have yet to be surrendered to you."*

# *January 8*

## *Psalm 122*

### *Fellowship of the Family in Worship*

### *"I was glad when they said unto me,*
### *Let us go into the house of the LORD."*
### *v.1*

*Everyone is looking for a way to be and stay happy*
*– David says – Let's go to Church!*
*He thinks that the greatest place to be in the universe*
*is with God's people and he's right, there is nothing better*
*than the fellowship of God and His people (1 John 1:3-4).*
*God so wants His people united in His work, that He gives the*
*church unlimited power (Matthew 16:19; 18:16-20).*
*He further added the dimension of truth and its defining*
*quality to the church (1 Timothy 3:15).*
*David wants the true worshipers to move up the holy hill in*
*praise to the Lord.*
*An isolated believer is a vulnerable believer.*
*Nowhere in the New Testament is the word saint used;*
*only saints, plural.*
*God always wants us in fellowship together.*

*I know that sometimes Christians are difficult to deal with. You can rest assured that there is no such thing as a perfect local church. But these are not reason enough to isolate yourself from the fellowship of the body. We need each other and the Lord was so ordained that we must be inter-connected if we are to grow. Drop your pride and excuses and hang out with the saints.*

# *January 9*

*Psalm 92*

### *The Best Way to Start and End Your Day*

*"It is a good thing to give thanks unto the LORD,*
*and to sing praises unto thy name, O most High:*
*To shew forth thy lovingkindness in the morning,*
*and thy faithfulness every night"*
*vs. 1,2*

*When is the cool of the day?*
*At dawn and at dusk. God would meet with Adam*
*in the cool of the day.*
*Its beginning and its end.*
*In the morning He would sanction his day*
*and in the evening He would sanctify His day.*
*In the morning He would give him his assignments*
*and in the evening His approval.*
*The psalmist makes it clear and simple what it takes*
*to make a good day before the Lord.*
*"It is a good thing to give thanks unto the Lord."*

*Loving kindness in the morning and faithfulness at night,*

*it doesn't get any better than that.*

*This is the recipe for a God honoring happy life in Christ.*

*Don't ever neglect it!*

# *January 10*

*Joshua 14:6-14*

### *Give Me This Mountain*

*A life lived on purpose.*
*There are 6 times in scripture the phrase used here*
*is found, "Wholly followed the Lord."*
*This is the absolute reason for every man's being:*
*To wholly follow the Lord.*
*No life will be complete; no life will have purpose*
*unless it is pursuing its reason for being.*
*Caleb is commended by God in the pages of scripture*
*because he is an important example of what it means*
*to honor God completely.*
*Therefore, it should be no surprise that when the children*
*of Israel received their inheritance in the promise land,*
*Caleb requested the most difficult land to conquer and possess.*
*The land that was inhabited with giants;*
*the fiercest of all the giants, the Anakims!*
*But that was not an issue. For the most important thing*
*that could ever happen to you is when you realize*
*that following Jesus completely is the only reason for existence.*

*When that happens you will begin to do things much larger than yourself; you begin to live! Live your life on purpose... honor Him.*

# *January 11*

## Psalm 3

### *Divine Favor*

**"LORD, how are they increased that trouble me! Many are they that rise up against me. Many there be which say of my soul, There is no help for him in God. Selah."**

*It really doesn't matter who is against you –*
*"The Lord" (vs. 1). It is of no consequence that people,*
*your enemies, or discouragers say about you –*
*"The Lord" (vs. 2). No matter the fights, the insults,*
*or the disappointments –*
*"The Lord" (vs. 3). Near or far, alone or in company;*
*you cannot ultimately lose –*
*"The Lord" (vs.4). Rest easy, wake up early, and totally trust –*
*"The Lord" (vs. 5). Be it one strong man, one billion,*
*or one trillion, whatever –*
*"The Lord" (vs. 6). I always win when I live for His glory,*
*it's simple, I have – "The Lord" (vs. 7).*
*"At the end of the day" as my Bermuda sister,*
*Cheryl-Ann would say, the battle is – "The Lord's" (vs. 8).*

# *January 12*

*Numbers 24*

## *The Star of Jacob*

*"He hath said, which heard the words of God, and knew the knowledge of the most High, which saw the vision of the Almighty, falling into a trance, but having his eyes open: I shall see him, but not now: I shall behold him, but not nigh: there shall come a Star out of Jacob, and a Sceptre shall rise out of Israel, and shall smite the corners of Moab, and destroy all the children of Sheth."*

*vs.16-17*

*He had set out to curse Israel.*
*He had taken money from wicked Balaam*
*to pronounce on God's people a nasty evil indictment,*
*thinking that **his** words were of the Lord.*
*His mind made up and his course laid out,*
*with absolute determination he set out to prophesy*
*ungodly words to God's people.*
*Only the intervention of a speaking donkey caused him*
*to come to his senses and there discovered that as God's prophet,*
*he had to say what only God wants said.*

*It was there in a vision God gave to him one
of the first truths in revelation about Christ.
He saw the Lord Jesus Christ as the "Star of Jacob", the glory of
God revealed through His Son would change his life forever.
Oh what wonder we would see if we would subject our hearts to
follow and know Him as He truly is!
God is waiting to reveal deeper vistas of His person if the Chris-
tian would honor Him with all his heart.*

# *January 13*

*Psalm 51*

**Lord, I Want to Come Home**

*Reflection*

Using the stories of David and Bathsheba,
the prodigal son, and several select scriptures in
the New Testament, let's take a close look at what it takes
to get back to right standing with God, His people – the Church,
and one's self. When the crisis of self rears its selfish head
demanding to be pre-eminent, the flesh provides a wide assort-
ment of dainties that seem harmless, but at the end they are
deadly and enslaving.
When we read about David's crisis in 2 Samuel 11,
we see that the unholy marriage of opportunity and
desire produced the sin that changed the course of
Israel's history. The danger of these two principles getting
lost in our circumstances will result in for trouble us
with consequences that only the Holy Spirit can repair.
So with all diligence stay alert and prepared so
that when you are challenged to fall,
you can fight back with the power of the Spirit.

# *January 14*

*Psalm 51*

### **Lord, I Want to Come Home**

*Recognition*

### ***"For I acknowledge my sin..."***

*We have become a people that have forgotten what sin truly is.*
*Sin is an affront to God.*
*Period.*
*There are no little sins or big ones.*
*No half or white lies.*
*Sin is sin, all sin is sin.*
*Gossiping is worthy of death just as much as murder;*
*lying, just as guilty as adultery.*
*All sin is sin, and if we truly desire to be forgiven,*
*there must be recognition of both the act committed*
*and the one who we've offended.*
*We must be able to see clearly what was done wrong*
*and to whom it was done against.*
*Regardless of reasons and excuses, there cannot*
*be repair without first stopping at this point of recognition.*
*If not, we'll be guilty of managing our sin instead of mastering it;*

*of becoming good at lying about our apathy,*

*excuses, and our addictions.*

*God will not accept confession without recognition.*

*If you are in this place, start first with acknowledging your sin.*

*Drawing Closer*

*Consecration*

# *Week Three*

> *Read through James 1 each morning; ask the Lord for wisdom, single mindedness and boldness to witness.*

# *January 15*

*Psalm 51*

### **Lord, I Want to Come Home**

*Regret*

**"For I will declare mine iniquity; I will be sorry for my sin."**
**Psalm 38:18**

*There cannot be true repentance without true regret.*
*When the words are singly mouthed "I am sorry", the transaction*
*is null and void, if it is not coupled with a sincere heart of regret.*
*Regret is at the tail end of recognition.*
*When we recognize the act committed, and the conviction*
*of the Holy Spirit begins to disturb us, then remorse clouds our*
*hearts and regret is born.*
*This is proof of our position in the body.*
*If we can sin repeatedly without any feeling of remorse or regret,*
*if we have no sense of a loss of fellowship with the Father, then*
*the writer of Hebrews makes a stern declaration (Hebrews 12:8).*
*This says without exception that salvation is not lost, but rather*
*that it never existed.*

*When sin appears, there may be a period of apathy,*
*but after time the wonder lust of the pleasures of sin should*
*cause a deep sense of conviction and regret.*
*Remember, God hears no act of confession without true,*
*sincere regret.*

# *January 16*

*Psalm 51*

**Lord, I Want to Come Home**

*Repentance*

**"Against thee, thee only, have I sinned,
and done this evil in thy sight: that thou mightest
be justified when thou speakest, and be clear
when thou judgest."**
**Psalm 51:4**

*As David states it here, true repentance sees the sin,
the sinner and the one offended; and the one offended
is always the same: God.
Understand, we may sin before others, but no matter the act,
God is the only one who is sinned against.
Why?
Because it is His law that has been broken,
His life violated, His name dishonored.
If you read all these stories, the scriptures mention these words;
they all say the same thing.
Here in Psalm 51, David may have had sex with Bathsheba
and had her husband killed, but verse 4 tells us
who he really sinned against.*

*Read in Genesis 39:9, Joseph tells Potiphar's wife the same thing:*

*"It's sin against God."*

*Then in Luke 15:18, the wayward son admits the same truth.*

*Once we see what we have done, showing genuine regret,*

*we can confess our sin (the act) to the one we have sinned*

*against (the offended). Then God hears and begins the process*

*of repairing our lives.*

# *January 17*

I John 1:9

### **Lord, I Want to Come Home**

*Righteousness*

*Confess (homologeo). It means "to say the same thing".*
*When we confess we are saying exactly what God*
*already knows about us.*
*It means we are agreeing with Him about every situation.*
*It is this act of full contrition that now qualifies us to receive*
*the cleansing from the Holy Spirit, the full forgiveness*
*that stays God's lawful right to judge and punish us,*
*and then most importantly, have fellowship restored*
*by having all unrighteousness removed.*
*Righteousness means "to be in right standing with".*
*It means I can stand before the holy, perfect, righteous Lord*
*without any demonstration of fear.*
*I can now relate to Him once again as clean*
*and pure as the Lord Jesus.*
*There is no better place to be than in His presence*
*uncondemned, clean, sanctified and righteous.*
*The inward work for dealing with God is all done. Abandoning*
*my sin and the process of renewed fellowship is complete.*

# *January 18*

*2 Samuel 24:1-24*

**Lord, I Want to Come Home**

*Restitution*

**"Neither will I offer... unto the Lord my God
of that which cost me nothing."**

*It is a word seldom used today.
It is almost forgotten as a concept and principle.
Most people would have a hard time explaining what it is,
but if the heart of repenting Christians is truly set to know
His forgiveness and fellowship, restitution is essential.
It is not essential for salvation, but it is essential as proof
of a fully broken heart before God.
God does not require it.
Restitution is only essential on my side.
It is essential in that I need to say by this act,
"I am acknowledging how much I have offended,
how much I have hurt our relationship."
Restitution is my offering of full disclosure, no excuses,
no justification; it is the desire of the truly repented to make
right, what he has made wrong.*

*David's statement to Araunah was borne out of*

*the heart of one who truly knew what his sin was.*

*Think on your sin and what it has cost others.*

*Think on how much it has hurt the Lord.*

*For further reading see Psalm 51:14-17.*

*What sacrifice of restitution should you bring?*

# *January 19*

*Galatians 6:1*

### *Lord, I Want to Come Home*

*Restoration*

*Restoration in two parts: Restoration of <u>what</u> was lost
and restoration of <u>who</u> was lost.*

*<u>What</u> was lost?*

*Psalm 51:12 shows us that when sin is our lifestyle,
joy is lost. And what is joy?*

*The Bible shows us that often times joy is shown as elation
or triumph of spirit, and by way of biblical definition,
Nehemiah 8:10, joy is described as strength from the Lord.
What is lost when we live in sin is the security of being at one
with Him, the wonderful sense of holiness that comes only
as we honor Him.*

*What is lost is joy that is a benefit of being in right standing
(righteousness) with Christ.*

*The other aspect is the discovery of <u>who</u> is lost.*

*The answer is obvious: the sinner.*

*Restoration is the word that is most illustrated in the
three stories of Luke 15; the stories of the lost sheep,
the lost silver and the lost son.*

*The restoration of the lost sheep, the silver and the son*

*shows that with the rekindled relationship, joy is always restored.*

*Be restored by completing the process.*

*Don't quit, don't believe the lie of embarrassment.*

# *January 20*

### **Lord, I Want to Come Home**
*Reconciliation*

*Few words in all the languages of the earth*
*carry more worth than this one, "Reconciliation".*
*The word implies "to restore back to the original relationship."*
*The blessing of this position for the Christian is to be brought*
*back to that place that was lost because of the sinful choices.*
*This wonderful word, a favored word of the book of Ephesians,*
*calls us to long for the great relationship*
*that Christ has with the Father.*
*Being in Christ Jesus, we receive the same contact*
*with the Father as Jesus, the love communication that*
*the Son has with the Father.*
*This is what God desires most.*
*He wants the relationship to always be intact.*
*That's why He instructs the Holy Spirit to convict*
*and persuade the wayward heart.*
*Nothing angers the Lord more than the child that has gone away*
*from Him in sin (Ephesians 4:30).*
*Be reconciled to Christ; brought back to Him in holy relationship.*
*Let us follow the exhortation of Paul, "Be reconciled to God".*

# *January 21*

Psalm 14:7

### **Lord, I Want to Come Home**

*Repair*

*The word restoring means repair to the original condition.*
*When sin plunges its deadly claws in the soul of the saint with*
*the delusion that nothing is lost, we need someone to not only*
*remove the objects of sins consequences in our soul, but we also*
*need a healer that can repair the scars left behind.*
*Many people may receive help in their situation, but when there*
*is no great physician to repair the damage of transgressions,*
*the scars themselves become elements of destruction; serving*
*as a constant reminder of sin and failures, of mistakes and bad*
*choices; a useful tool of the devil that he employs to keep fresh*
*the pains of past transgressions.*
*We need a rescuer who will repair us – to bring us back to a pris-*
*tine condition, totally restored, righteous and reconciled to both*
*God and His family.*
*Don't let the wicked one gain victory, seek the Lord diligently.*
*Receive His full forgiveness, pardon and repairing grace.*

*Drawing Closer*

*Consecration*

*Week Four*

> *Spend more time talking to the Lord then others. Let silence be your principle concern each day this week. Focus on hearing the Lord speak to your heart.*

# *January 22*

Psalm 51:8

### Lord, I Want to Come Home

*Rejoicing*

**"I say unto you, that likewise joy shall be in heaven over one sinner that repenteth, more than over ninety and nine just persons, which need no repentance."** Luke 15:7

**"For this my son was dead, and is alive again; he was lost, and is found. And they began to be merry."**

*If there ever was a time for singing, dancing and adulation, it would be now. The lost has been found!*
*The wanderer has come home!*
*The backslider has come to himself and has returned to the loving embrace of a waiting Father.*
*This is the message Jesus was trying to convey to the hard-hearted religious Pharisees. They had lost sight of the soul by over magnifying the sin. God does not rejoice when a wayward person strays; no God is brokenhearted and compassionate; doing what He can to woo His loved one home.*

*And on that day, when finally the world has done all of its damage, after the taste of sin has turned rancid and sour, and the prodigal comes home, there should be a shout of joy and worship!*
*There should be tears of joy and warm embraces!*
*Don't become like that older brother who had no right to be offended or cruel.*
*Rejoice with heaven and welcome the loved one home.*

# *January 23*

*Numbers 6*

### *A Benediction of Blessing, Bounty, Benefits and Benevolence*

**"The LORD bless thee, and keep thee: The LORD make his face shine upon thee, and be gracious unto thee: The LORD lift up his countenance upon thee, and give thee peace."**
**vs.24-26**

*What more could be said?*
*Everything you could ever imagine has been laid out to and for every man, woman, boy and girl in Israel.*
*This wonderful covenant keeping God has guaranteed the blessing from heaven to the descendants of Abraham.*
*These words are just the expression of what God promises to Abraham in Genesis 15, right before He made His historic covenant with him: "I am thy shield and I am thy exceeding great reward."*
*In those two statements, God made Abraham the most wealthy and powerful man on earth.*
*He gave to him the American Express Platinum card of the universe.*
*He thus also assigned him the Elite Royal Guards of Glory, the sinless sons of splendor; angels.*

*Then if that were not enough, He went on and promised
that his seed would be cared for in like manner.
Now, that was all before Calvary, we have even
greater benefit because of Christ.
We have even more exclusive benefits in Jesus.
Ours is more than earthly things, we have been given the riches
in glory by Christ Jesus.
Saint, be blessed and enjoy the bounty of heaven
that your Father has provided.*

# *January 24*

Psalm 63

**Mercy**

**"Because thy lovingkindness is better than life,**

**my lips shall praise thee."**

**vs. 3**

*"Loving-kindness" – It is always in the present tense*

*when it comes to God.*

*It has to be – if you are still alive, you are experiencing His*

*loving-kindness. "Loving" and "kindness" two of the most beau-*

*tiful words are spoken, and they come only from God.*

*The Holy Spirit, in His genius, reserved the words for only the Old*

*Testament, only towards those whom God favors, only 26 times,*

*only used once in a verse, and only about God. He alone can show*

*unearned loving kindness, and it can only be said about Him, the*

*one who is absolutely faultless and infinite.*

*It is reserved or someone who can lovingly consider the plight of*

*the helpless and meet their every need:* **only God.**

# *January 25*

*Leviticus 10*

### *Strange*

*"And Nadab and Abihu, the sons of Aaron,*
*took either of them his censer, and put fire therein,*
*and put incense thereon, and offered strange fire*
*before the LORD, which he commanded them not."*
*vs.1*

*The Hebrew word for 'strange' is "zur",*
*it means "to commit adultery" or "profane".*
*God had commanded the priesthood*
*to never offer a "strange fire" before the Lord.*
*The implications are far reaching, but very easy to understand.*
*God had already made it clear what type of animals, age, gender*
*and purity for the offerings that He would accept. There are no*
*doubts as to what were His instructions on this matter.*
*No room for error, no room for mistakes.*
*So it would not be the sacrifice of animals*
*that would make the offering "strange".*
*The animals could not be guilty of anything*
*that resembled an act of sexual impurity.*

*No, it had to be the men themselves*

*that had sexually defiled the offering.*

*It was Aaron's sons' responsibility to be as pure*

*as the sacrifices of animals they offered to the Lord.*

*Now, as believers we must come before Him daily,*

*clean, pure and sanctified.*

*Our God is holy, and His holiness must be revered.*

# *January 26*

## *Psalm 93*

### *Majesty Enthroned*

*"The Lord reigneth, he is clothed with majesty; the Lord is clothed with strength, wherewith he hath girded himself: the world also is stablished, that it cannot be moved."*

*vs. 10*

*The Bible speaks several times and
in many ways as to how God is "clothed".
Majesty and strength are the unique terms
used by the Holy Spirit.
What could be more suiting to the only one in the universe who
needs nothing to be totally satisfied with Himself.
He can be nothing else but majestic.
He can be nothing else but all powerful.
He is God.
It is so pathetic that the world has minimized the word "God".
It becomes oxymoronic to say "gods"
when the word by definition means "supreme".
Anything or anyone ceases to be supreme if there is any opportu-
nity for there to be an equal, a rival to their power and authority.*

*God is not just a title, much more than that.*

*It is a declaration of singular power and might.*

*Only He is God!*

# *January 27*

*Exodus 3*

### **God Shows Up**

*"And the LORD said, I have surely seen the affliction of my people which are in Egypt, and have heard their cry by reason of their taskmasters; for I know their sorrows; And I am come down to deliver them out of the hand of the Egyptians"*

*vs.7-8*

*God says 4 important statements to His servant Moses:*

*1). "I have surely seen the affliction".*

*Sometimes in our pain and suffering we actually think that God is looking in the other direction, often we mistake His silence as apathy.*

*Nothing could be further from the truth.*

*He sees.*

*2). "I have heard their cry".*

*The prayer of slaves is probably the most sincere there is. When someone that has no one, no prospect in sight and no advocate and yet they pray, you can be sure that their prayer is genuine.*

*He hears.*

3). *"For I know their sorrows".*

It was impossible for anyone who would just notice, to see how horribly the Israelites were being treated. God intimates Himself with Israel's pain by using the Hebrew word "yada"; it means to become intimately acquainted. God entered into their pain, and that's why number 4 is so powerful.

He knows.

4). *"and I am come down".*

When you are in your worst position, He sees, He hears, He knows and greatest of all... He shows up.

# *January 28*

## *Exodus 3*

### *The Picture Moses Saw*

*"Now Moses kept the flock of Jethro his father in law, the priest of Midian: and he led the flock to the backside of the desert, and came to the mountain of God, even to Horeb. And the angel of the LORD appeared unto him in a flame of fire out of the midst of a bush: and he looked, and, behold, the bush burned with fire, and the bush was not consumed. And Moses said, I will now turn aside, and see this great sight, why the bush is not burnt."*

*vs.1-3*

*It was a bush on a mountain; a place obscure.*
*Not public, but off in the desert, where no one else could see it,*
*verify it, or make a shrine of it, for as with most things with God*
*and man, this was private.*
*It was meant for Moses alone.*
*He tells the story and with the many other things that would*
*happen to him, people would have no problem believing it.*
*This would be the first of untold myriad*
*of such encounters with God.*

*God would pull him aside for days, weeks,*

*and even months at a time.*

*He would put him through*

*a 40 year doctorate course on humility.*

*You see, for 40 years Moses had been educated in the Egyptian*

*culture and university of secular knowledge, and at the end of*

*that time, the best the world could make him was a murderer.*

*But God would take him through His school of learning on the*

*backside of a desert, and in 40 years with God, a murderer*

*became meek; the meekest man on earth.*

# *Drawing Closer*

## *Consecration*

## *Week Five*

> *Meditate on the word of the Lord each day this week. Read Matthew 5:3 – 11 each morning and ask God to strengthen you in the areas where you are weakest.*

# *January 29*

*Exodus 3*

### *Why a Burning Bush?*

**"And Moses said, I will now turn aside, and see this great**
**sight, why the bush is not burnt."**

**vs.3**

*On fire but not consumed, totally ablaze but not destroyed.*
*What could possibly be the point of a burning bush*
*that was in the desert?*
*The aspects of the illustration are blatantly clear.*
*A burning bush in the desert that was not consumed was to be a*
*life illustrating, three dimensional image of what God does in the*
*heart and life of His faithful servants.*
*The bush was the container of God's presence,*
*but not the sustainer or source of God's power.*
*It was a vessel through which God's glory would be seen,*
*but had the element to be worshipped.*
*God did not need the energy of the bush to keep His fire ablaze.*
*So what was the point that God was making with Moses?*
*He would be the vessel, but there would be no need for him to*
*expend his might, ability, or control to do God's work. That's why*

*at the end of his life nothing had aged on him or been depleted*

*(Deuteronomy 34:7).*

*God wants to do the same for you.*

*He wants you to be a conduit for His power and glory*

*(2 Corinthians 4:7); His power, not yours.*

# *January 30*

*Exodus 2*

## *He Hears*

**"And it came to pass in process of time, that the king of Egypt died: and the children of Israel sighed by reason of the bondage, and they cried, and their cry came up unto God by reason of the bondage." vs.23**

God heard the cries of Israel for over 400 years.
Their moans of oppression echoed the
hallowed halls of heaven for centuries.
Like no other, Israel suffered not because of sin,
not theirs anyway.
Not because of military conquest, nor for the reason
of a debt that could not be paid.
No, Israel suffered under the cruel, wicked lash of
Egypt's whip because of the word: grace.
"For the iniquity of the Amorites is not yet full". God had fore-
warned Abraham that his seed <u>must</u> suffer in this manner
because they would be God's instrument of grace for a people
that would not honor Him.
God's plan to extend grace and blessing to a godless world of men
must be given at the cost of the lives of the saints.

*The pain of your life might very well be the cost of
providing God's grace to someone who may never choose Him;
only His divine eternal wisdom knows.
What He asks of me is just to trust Him completely.*

# *January 31*

*Exodus 3:7, 8*

### *God Showed Up*

*In chapter 2 verses 23 through 25, we see how God responded*
*to Israel's cries, He remembered His promise to Abraham; He*
*regarded the pain of their oppression and respected the sacrifice*
*they had made for over 400 years.*
*This God of Abraham, Israel and Jacob had no spoken prophet,*
*preacher, prince, patriarch or priest for centuries. All they had*
*was the promise He gave to Abraham.*
*There were no miracles, no Bible, no signs;*
*Just one small paragraph that gave a time.*
*Many of the Jews by this time had died off; having never realized*
*the truth of God's promise.*
*So they may have even forgotten who He was.*
*It's possible that some even blasphemed His holy name, but God*
*had not forgotten.*
*Your back may be up against the wall, all of your resources*
*depleted; whatever is happening to you and around you, don't*
*you ever lose heart.*
*God knows and He hears your every groan.*
*Trust Him through all the pain.*

# *February*

## *A Time for Reflection*

**Lesson:** The Word of the Lord

> *"For from you sounded out the word of the Lord*
> *not only in Macedonia and Achaia, but also*
> *in every place your faith to God-ward is spread*
> *abroad; so that we need not to speak anything."*
> I Thess. 1:18

Paul's commendation to the church at Thessalonica was filled with great pride and joy. On their own they gave to the Christian world an example of great faithfulness and love for both the Lord and His people the church. This local body of believers is part of a very small fraternity of churches that Paul had nothing negative to share. His encouragement to look for the Lords' coming is found in every chapter of both of his letters to them.

Here in this verse Paul's compliments to them reveals joy over the fact that they "sounded out the **word of the Lord**". No greater statement could be made to a group of saints in the local church. The phrase "sounded out" conveys that they "*echoed forth*", in other words, **resounded** the truth of the Lord, i.e., the preached word was so prevalent in their community, it was being repeated by others and repeated with accuracy.

There is no greater truth than "**the word of the Lord**". If there is anything we the church should be known for it should be for preaching His word.

The word of the Lord is that direct communiqué from the heart of God to His creation.

It is at once the most tremendous and the most terrifying.

To the lost seeker, the loyal saint, or the lonely soul it is a drink of cool refreshing water.

To the defiant sinner or the deluded skeptic it is a terrifying indictment of certain judgment.

### Outline of the Passage

A. They received the Word of the Lord and followed – v.6a – Trusting the provision of God's word

B. They relied on the Word of the Lord in much affliction –
v.6b – Showing the power of God's word

C. They rested in the Word of the Lord and the joy it bestows
– v.6c – Revealing the proof of God's word

*Facts:* **The month of February, second month of the Gregorian calendar.**

It corresponds to the month of Sebat; the eleventh month of the Hebrew calendar. It was the time of year that most likely Moses died.

*Focus:* **Prayer and contrition.**

Use the time of this month to consider areas in your life that may be weights; There may be repeating obstacles that cause you to stumble.

*Assignment:* **Research**

Create a calendar of the feasts and holidays.

*Memory Work:*

**Exaltation:** Jude 24

**Excellence:** I Corinthians 10:31

**Edification:** Phillipians 2:12

**Evangelical:** Romans 6:23

**Exhortive:** I Thessalonians 5:16

**Educational:** James 1:17

*Looking Inward*

*Reflection*

## Week Six

*The theme of the book of Deu-
teronomy is "remember". Read
through the book this week.
Learn what God told to His
people to be the diligent about.
Take special note of the many
times they were instructed to
"love" Him.*

# *February 1*

*Psalm 4*

## *Gladness of Heart*

**"Thou hast put gladness in my heart, more than in the time
that their corn and their wine increased."
vs. 7.**

*Gladness of heart is the state of a soul
that is totally content and satisfied.
The person who is glad in heart is never
the victim of circumstances.
The entire spectrum of their world is yielding
nothing but bountiful harvest.
A person who is in this state is hitting on all cylinders;
bad news is never bad news because God has yet to speak.
The unexpected is only an earthly occurrence that is never
more powerful than the will of God.
Someone who is glad at heart cannot get depressed or discouraged because they see from the vantage point of the Spirit.
Take the Spirit route; don't get stuck in
the quagmire of apathy and despair.
Learn to look ever to Jesus; He'll give you the gladness of heart
you need to make it each day.*

# *February 2*

Genesis 6

### Grace

**"But Noah found grace in the eyes of the LORD."**

**vs.8**

*It was the worst time in man's history.*
*A time that would be remembered and repeated four more time*
*in scripture (Matthew 24:37-38; Hebrews 11:7;*
*1 Peter 3:20; 2 Peter 2:5).*
*It was a horrid pornographic time that marked the end*
*of the spiritual, righteous line of Seth and the beginning*
*of an apostasy that would only to be rivaled during*
*the last hours of the Church age.*
*Each period imaged the out pouring of God's*
*lovingly subdued wrath.*
*In all of this heated, sexually charged day of evil,*
*the flow of deserved wrath and destruction was interrupted*
*by one merciful sentence: "But Noah found grace..."*
*He was only one among millions.*
*The ever promised remnant that God the Father*
*keeps in reserve for Himself.*

*This faithful man looked past the temptations to be like everyone else, to instead be God's man. You have that choice and chance every day. Will you be that godly remnant?*

# *February 3*

*Genesis 6:8*

### *Grace*

*"Grace".*

*What is that word doing there?*

*That's a New Testament word.*

*It's used only a handful of times in the Old Testament,*

*less than forty, and the majority of the time it is used to*

*show favor from person to person.*

*Only five times is it used the way we've come to know it:*

*as God's unmerited favor.*

*This word is reserved for the special treatment God gives*

*to the body over 125 times in the New Testament,*

*reflecting God's gift to His blood bought family.*

*But here in Genesis, it's used for the first time.*

*The great grace of God.*

*His favorite act, for His favored people.*

*Grace as some have defined it "God's righteousness*

*at Christ's expense."*

*This is what Noah found.*

*His heart still had an area reserved for holiness*
*that God could claim as His own.*
*Here, God could hang the notice: "Mine, and mine alone."*
*This is God's man and God's great favor would be seen in his life*
*as a permanent testimony forever!*

# February 4

## Psalm 34

### My Soul Will Boast

**"My soul shall make her boast in the LORD:**
**the humble shall hear thereof, and be glad."**
**vs.2**

*My God, how great you are!*
*Blessing the Lord at all times means praying,*
*worshipping, extoling, exalting, and magnifying Him anywhere,*
*anytime and in any situation because there is so much to say*
*and so little time (eternally) to do it.*
*As I live out everlasting life, each day,*
*if I am willing to see clearly, is filled with multiple displays*
*of His greatness, goodness, love, mercy, and grace.*
*If I love Him, I will purposefully construct each day*
*with deliberate "God sightings."*
*Then I'll have more to bless, praise, worship Him, and love Him.*
*Let me testify!!*
*My soul, will boast in my God!*

# *February 5*

*Mark 1:35*

### *Jesus and Prayer*

### *Priorities*

*The Imperatives of the Master*

*The cool of the day.*

*It is not just the time before noon.*

*The Spirit says that it was "a great while before day",*

*this implies long before sunrise.*

*This the time when all of the distractions are still asleep; a time*

*when there is no one who needs healing, advice or consoling.*

*It is a time when most people would never even consider rising.*

*The very mention of the word "rising" shows that*

*He was not up all night unable to sleep, but rather that*

*He deliberately shook off the delightful embrace of slumber*

*to do something more important.*

*He took the time to consider all that His responsibilities were,*

*all the people who hung on His every word;*

*He knew that war with the satanic is not fought and*

*won by lying in bed or being prayerlessly unprepared.*

*No, He thought of the power that comes from sacrifice.*

*And with the thought in mind, He rose to pray.*

# *February 6*

*Mark 1:35*

### *Jesus and Prayer*

### *Privacy:*

### *The Importance of the Morning*

**"And in the morning, rising up a great while before day,**
**he went out, and departed into a solitary place,**
**and there prayed."**

*Why the morning?*
*Why not the night before, what gives more power,*
*insight or anointing in the morning?*
*Isn't any other time just as good?*
*The purpose of the morning is scripturally clear;*
*it is a time for the benefits of God.*
*Notice, the Bible teaches that God has ordained mercies*
*new for us "every morning"*
*(Lamentations 3:23).*
*Whatever blessing God set out for us in the way of mercies,*
*are found in the morning.*
*So it is only wise to appropriate what He is giving to us,*
*at the time He has divinely made available.*

*You'll remember that when the nation of Israel was out in the
desert, the only time to receive manna was in the morning.
If they waited until later in the day, the food would spoil. The
morning was the time God set aside for man to spend with Him
alone, a time when all others were distant and unprepared.
It is the hour for the faithful to give their hearts
in surrender to Him.
Rise up early, receive what rich eternal treasure
He has for you.*

# February 7

## Mark 1:35

### Preparation

### The Importance of the Morning

We've discovered that the morning is the time of spiritual solitude, the opportunity for the Spirit of God to catch the diligent
heart away from the distractions of the world, and steal away to
"the secret place of the most high."
It is the hour of blessing and benefit,
the time of surrender and sacrifice in solitude.
These are the benefits of the Spirit,
but there is another reason why Christ arose early to pray.
For while the benefits and blessings of the Spirit
are there and evident, there is also the battle in the Spirit
that must be addressed.
Matthew 6:34 warns that each day of our existence
is assigned evil from the forces of darkness.
There is enough evil in one day that requires that
the saints of God must fortify themselves to be able to survive it.
Therein is the reason why so many believers are both weak and
anemic in their walk.

*The very things they need to accomplish the work*

*of the walk are found by meeting with Him early.*

*(Isaiah 26:9)*

*Discipline yourself.*

*Get up each day early and meet with God to prepare for battle.*

# *Looking Inward*

## *Reflection*

# *Week Seven*

*Compare your life now
to this time last year.
What differences do you see?
Each morning add reading
Psalm 15 to your devotion time.*

# *February 8*

*Mark 1:35*

### **Passion**

### **The Intimacy of the Moment**

*His Father; the first revealed person of the Godhead, He is the*
*grand orchestrator of the entire event of creation.*
*The wonders of His incredible love are evident by the presence of*
*His only Son on earth; the offering for sin.*
*For Jesus, the time alone with His Father was not just essential,*
*it was imperative.*
*There was nothing of this world, its people or its pleasures that*
*could be of greater value than His time with the Father.*
*He is allowed precious few moments alone, and whenever He*
*could be alone, wherever He could be alone, whether awake or*
*asleep, His thoughts were to fulfill His Father's will, nothing more*
*consumed His passion.*
*Jesus loved mankind, because it pleased His Father. Jesus suffered*
*shame and ridicule because it was the Father's plan.*
*All that He was and all that He did was inundated with the pas-*
*sion of pleasing His Father.*
*Now, what about you?*
*Why do you do what you do?*
*Is your heart set on that one goal... how to please Him?*

# *February 9*

*Mark 1:35*

### *Principles*

### *The Integrity of the Man*

*Jesus set aside the very early part of the morning*
*to commune with the Father.*
*The time He spent alone with Him constituted an executive*
*council meeting in the High chambers of Heaven.*
*God's man on earth was not there as a spy or correspondent.*
*He was not sent to be an ambassador or a courier.*
*He had a singular mission: to be the God-man.*
*The God who would interact as promised (Isaiah 7:14)*
*with the seed of Abraham and as the perfect sinless man, to offer*
*His life as the sin payment for lost creation.*
*So when the opportunity came to be alone with the Godhead,*
*other issues and matters would not be discussed,*
*only that which pleased His Father; doing exactly as He wanted*
*was always the agenda.*
*It was probably at times like this the Lazarus project*
*was revealed (John 11:41-42).*
*Such were the contents that would fill His prayer time,*
*the eternal business of the Kingdom.*
*Now, when you pray, what is your agenda?*

# *February 10*

*Mark 1:35*

**Prayer**

**His Intent and Motive**

**"Thy kingdom come, thy will be done".**

*Prayer.*
*The most important means of bridging the finite*
*to the infinite; the holy highway between heaven and earth;*
*the only way the sinner can always and in any way*
*touch the Sovereign, the reason for Christ's early rising: Prayer.*
*The Greek word, "prosueche" is defined as "with the soul".*
*The soul is the absolute person of our being,*
*it is the way we recognize our personhood.*
*This is what is required when one says they need to approach*
*God in prayer; the element of our being. When He rose early each*
*morning, Jesus' sole intent was to speak person to person with*
*the Father, to hear and to be heard at the level of perfect divinity.*
*He gave Himself over to emptying all that was in His heart to the*
*Father. And make no common assumption, He was not relieving*
*His soul of heartaches or confessing sins, NO! He was doing as He*
*instructed in the Lord's Prayer... His Fathers will. He listened to*
*the heart of His Father and lived every moment to fulfill it.*

*When you pray, stand before your Father and listen.*

*Then rise to do all that His will requires.*

# *February 11*

*Mark 1:36*

### *The Impact of the Meeting*

*He was always being watched.*

*Every day, morning noon or night; whether by the disciples,*

*the religious sects, the poor, the needy, the sick or the devils;*

*He has always being watched.*

*That's why He could make the statement,*

*"Which of you convinces me of sin?"*

*He was the most popular man in all of existence.*

*He was and is the central person of history!*

*Everyone watched Him.*

*So it is no surprise that when He stirs from the very few hours*

*of sleep, those with Him take notice as He steals away in silence,*

*mindful of their need to rest, those who eagerly hang onto His*

*every act and His every word, cannot risk missing even one*

*moment of His life.*

*They have always been of the heart and mind to do whatever He*

*does, to go wherever He goes, to hear whatever He says.*

*The impact of finding time to talk with the Father*

*is too precious a moment to miss:*

*For Him and for us.*

*Someone is watching you,*

*they want to do what you do,*

*see what you see.*

*What are you showing them?*

# *February 12*

### Psalm 64

### **The Battle is His**

**"And all men shall fear, and shall declare the work of God;**
**for they shall wisely consider of his doing. The righteous**
**shall be glad in the LORD, and shall trust in him;**
**and all the upright in heart shall glory."**
**vs. 9, 10**

*David does not ask for the ability to vanquish his enemies.*
*He relies on the power of God to deal with his*
*adversaries as only God can.*
*God always knows the perfect way to confront,*
*disarm, challenge or if necessary destroy our enemies.*
*He sees what we cannot see.*
*Often our way is to confront and/or conquer.*
*God's way is to love and show grace and mercy.*
*On whatever manner God chooses, we can trust Him*
*to be Master and do what only He can do.*
*And whatever it is, we can be sure it will accomplish two things*
*perfectly: It will be for our good, and His glory.*

# February 13

*Proverbs 4*

**Guard Your Heart**

**"Keep thy heart with all diligence;**

**for out of it are the issues of life."**

**vs. 23.**

*The word "keep" is the same word we see in Jude 21 "tereo" –*

*guard, protect, and put in safety, to secure.*

*The heart of man is a very vulnerable and at the same time a*

*dangerous thing (Jeremiah 17:9).*

*The heart is to be protected from your enemies, and restrained*

*from allowing your flesh to do its will.*

*The heart is the part of us that emotes as well as schemes.*

*It plans and perverts.*

*It is the area that Christ wants to reside and rule, but Satan*

*wants to corrupt and conquer.*

*This is a matter of absolute importance.*

*David warns Solomon to be careful with his heart, or else it*

*would be the means of his destruction.*

*Did he do as his father said?*

*Sadly no (I Kings 11:1-9).*

*Guard your heart; protect it for the Lord*

*only and from the desires of the world.*

# February 14

## Habakkuk
### The Prophet with a Problem

*Chapter 1 – It doesn't seem fair does it?*

*That God will allow the heathen to prosper?*

*But then God allows the unrighteous to prosper*

*at the expense of the righteous.*

*But even more, it just doesn't seem fair that the heathen would*

*be used by God to punish the saint, to be God's ordained instru-*

*ment of chastening of His people!*

*Where is the right in that?*

*God seems to be unjust when the wicked prosper; they prosper*

*over us; they prosper from us; and horror of horrors, they*

*prosper and are used to punish us!*

*How can God expect us to still praise and magnify and honor Him*

*in situations like this?*

*Even in the most adverse situations that we may never under-*

*stand, He wants us to trust Him.*

*He expects us to be the servant and He the Lord.*

*He deserves to be trusted. He demands to be trusted.*

*He deserves to be trusted.*

*It may not appear to be right, but it will always be right.*
*Whatever you are going through, as hard as it may be,*
*give Him your worries, fears and even complaints;*
*trust always that Heaven will be faithful.*

# *Looking Inward*

## *Reflection*

# *Week Eight*

> *Psalm 90 is a prayer of Moses, the man of God. Read through it each morning and take notice of the content of the prayer. Then detail in your bible the requests that Moses makes to the Lord. Then ask the Lord to show you where you are lacking in those areas.*

# *February 15*

*Habakkuk*

**The Prophets' Prophesy**

*Chapter 2 – "Keep your eyes on me".*
*The surreal experience of living in a physical world, yet*
*depending on a spiritual source can be very hard.*
*The physical events around us try hard to qualify themselves*
*through our senses, and thereby war against trusting the unseen*
*world and the bridge to it: God's word.*
*Where we have our biggest attacks are not with the world and*
*the devil, but with the evidence of a natural world around us.*
*God, however, demands that we ignore the facades of the physical*
*world and live only by faith; not mostly, not greatly, but exclu-*
*sively, with no other options, no other choices.*
*As a matter of fact, to live, with even a partial faith*
*is to have no faith at all.*
*Faith must be total, or it's not faith.*
*The only way to have the pure benefits of this life*
*is to live absolutely by faith.*
*To trust the world, the flesh and/or the devil in any way; in part*
*or completely will never yield the benefits and promises of God*
*(Revelation 11:6).*

# *February 16*

## *Habakkuk*
### *The Prophet's Prayer*

**"A prayer of Habakkuk the prophet upon Shigionoth. O LORD, I have heard thy speech, and was afraid: O LORD, revive thy work in the midst of the years, in the midst of the years make known; in wrath remember mercy."**

**3:1, 2**

*Let's face it.*

*We all have blown it.*

*Anyone who isn't willing to admit that is a fool.*

*We all are victims of our own self-deception; believing over and over again that we can effectively run our lives, and can effectively win the battle with our flesh and sin.*

*The prophet's prayer is a prayer of surrender and sacrifice; a petition of contrition and confession.*

*He teaches us that God was again, as always, absolutely right.*

*He knows the future and what's best.*

*We'll always make a devastating ruin of our world and will again need Him to heal, rescue, and correct us.*

*This is an hour of destiny that we must declare our undying trust*

*in Him and His word, and ultimately His plan for us. Our suc-*

*cesses and happiness is incumbent upon our surrender.*

*We cannot run our lives; we do not know what we're doing.*

*There is no way but His way.*

*It's time to give up to His sovereign will.*

*It's time to agree to His terms and let Him be master.*

# February 17

*Habakkuk*

**The Prophet's Praise**

*"Although the fig tree shall not blossom, neither shall fruit be in the vines; the labour of the olive shall fail, and the fields shall yield no meat; the flock shall be cut off from the fold, and there shall be no herd in the stalls: Yet I will rejoice in the LORD, I will joy in the God of my salvation. The LORD God is my strength, and he will make my feet like hinds' feet, and he will make me to walk upon mine high places."*

*3:17-19*

*It just doesn't matter.*
*Whether I get the job or not.*
*It just doesn't matter.*
*It is of no consequence at all if I get married or not,*
*nothing is going to change.*
*It does not affect me in any way whatsoever if I get healed or not;*
*the outcome of whatever I am going through right now will not*
*change my mind or my heart.*
*I am going to praise Him, regardless of my pain or heartache.*
*I am going to lift Him up despite all of the negatives that have*
*been presented to me.*

*I have determined that the balance sheet of my life will always*
*show that I am in the black because of who I live to honor,*
*and who it is that honors me.*
*I will praise Him, I will trust Him, I will glorify Him;*
*I will depend solely on Him!*
*Whatever state I find myself at any time and place,*
*I will find myself worshipping Him!*

# February 18

## Psalm 5

### Balance

**"But let all those that put their trust in thee rejoice: let them ever shout for joy, because thou defendest them: let them also that love thy name be joyful in thee."**
**vs. 11.**

*Rejoicing is the result of promises made and promises met.*
*The ledger balances – "But let all those that put their trust in thee rejoice... because".*
*The rest is wonderful – Every time He reveals another aspect of His character and nature by the use of a different name, i.e. Jehovah Nissi, Jehovah Rohi, etc.*
*It is because He has performed greatly, and provided wonderfully.*
*He has given another cause for rejoicing.*
*The balance that God brings to every situation is promises made and promises kept.*
*It is no wonder that David starts the psalm with the acknowledgment of God as his King and his God.*
*He has experienced God as his sovereign and his source.*
*Balance provides the reason to rejoice!*

# *February 19*

Psalm 119

### *I Know Him for Myself*

### *"For I trust in thy word"*
### *vs.42*

*I have known Him now for nearly fifty years.*
*I accepted Him as my King when I was just 4 years old.*
*My soul has known no other master.*
*Sure, there have been temptations, other voices that sounded so*
*sweet and sincere, but none has been willing to back everything*
*they say with the certainty of eternity.*
*Simply, no other has been absolutely right every single time.*
*I have seen His word work.*
*As a boy; in that He lovingly and miraculously cared*
*for our fatherless family.*
*I've seen His incredible protection guarding me from*
*the skillful temptations of adolescence.*
*As a man, He provided a career that would not compromise*
*my standards, and then gave me a wife*
*that could only come from heaven.*

*All along the way it was His word that was*
*the constant reminder of who was on my side.*
*Don't ever forget His word.*
*You can always trust it in every facet of life.*

# *February 20*

*Psalm 119*

### *The Terror of Night*

***"I have remembered thy name, O LORD,
in the night, and have kept thy law."***

**vs.55**

*The psalmist says that terror travels by night (Psalm 91:5).
David reminds us that weeping endures at night (Psalm 30:5).
It seems that Satan and his minions take great pleasure
and go to great lengths to haunt and attack the believer
during the nocturnal hours.
They feed into already mounting insecurities from the uncertainties of the unknown and with the cloak of darkness to accent our
fears. But as always, God as the loving Father, has supplied for
the saint His blessed word..
No fear can overcome the heart that will put trust in His holy
name and His flawless word.
The night has terrors and dangers; but we have Him.
The dark may hold uncertainties, but these are no reason to fear,
when we trust in His name and rely on His word.*

# *February 21*

*Psalm 119*

### *Staying Faithful*

*So many in the walk have found it difficult to be faithful and
anyone who touts that the life of Christ is an easy one is just not
being truthful. To wrestle with the world and the wicked one are
fights that will endure until He comes or takes us home.
These matters will be a constant reminder that
this is an evil world and it has an evil master,
but even in this, our greatest enemy is not the world outside
or the enemy above, but the sin – within. Our flesh will always
outdo Satan and the world as our most dangerous foe.
The prophet sets a method, a spiritual standard for us
that attempts to remind us how important it is
to be faithful to the Lord and His word.
We must make demands on ourselves,
if we have any desire to remain pure and live faithfully.
The Lord is our life; His word is our portion.
Hold onto these and the faithful life will be yours.*

# *Looking Inward*

## *Reflection*

# *Week Nine*

*Hebrews 12:1 speaks about "weights and sins". Can you do a self evaluation and uncover what maybe weighing you down? If you, can write a "no more" contract to yourself this week, highlighting a different weight and/or sin that you will fight to be free of forever.*

# *February 22*

*Psalm 35*

### *All You'll Ever Need*

**"Take hold of shield and buckler,**
**and stand up for mine help"**
*v.2*

*For most of the 28 verses in this psalm David*
*is recounting all the things the world,*
*evil men and the ungodly have made up about him.*
*He even provides a messianic statement prophesying*
*what would indeed happen to Christ (vs. 11).*
*His pain and frustration is not over sin or faults.*
*But rather that those who hate him do so*
*for no righteous reason at all. To this he does not fight back*
*in the conventional way, instead he prays.*
*He says Father "Stand up for me" (vs. 2).*
*We can always take solace in this – He is always on the side of the*
*innocent, the righteous and the needy.*
*He is more than just a good friend, He is the gracious Father.*
*You can try to fight this battle, but it's so much better if He does.*
*He is all you need.*

# *February 23*

*Romans 8*

### *For We Know*

**"And we know that all things work together**

**for good to them that love God,**

**to them who are the called**

**according to his purpose."**

**vs.28**

*Three of the great words in the Bible; not what we hope,*

*not what we think, but what we know.*

*Paul is speaking from the dual aspect of absolute proof,*

*and from apostolic authority.*

*Absolute proof that comes from being in the truth;*

*he knows unlike any other that God is the perfect keeper*

*of promises. He has been where no other has been, he's able to*

*speak from the aspect of experience, and he shares the validation*

*with the Church universal, by using the words: "we know".*

*This shows us for sure that this is a promise that the whole*

*Church may benefit; Christian by Christian.*

*This is a promise we must claim.*

*Not just because of its worth, but also because*

*it is further evidence of His faithfulness.*

*Then lastly, because he is one of the writing apostles, he can*

*speak with the apostolic authority of the word of God.*

*It is more than a promise to claim, but a heaven based,*

*guaranteed benefit to every believer.*

*We know. We know.*

# February 24

*Romans 8*

### *All Means ALL*

**"And we know that all things work together for good to them that love God, to them who are the called according to his purpose."**

**vs.28**

*Small word, big package.*
*To quote my very dear friend, Dr. James Ford,*
*"All means all, and that's all, all, means."*
*God has given to the saints one of the greatest assurances in all*
*of scripture: "All things work together for GOOD".*
*The blessed blend of the hardships and pains, the tears*
*and the fears, joys and elations that intersect with the daily exis-*
*tence of the child of God will end up being for the good for all*
*those that qualify by loving Him.*
*No matter the crisis, no matter the cost,*
*He promises that our eternity will be good. GOOD.*
*That's God's standard for excellence; and it will be realized in the*
*life of everyone who surrenders their love to Him.*
*The future is sometimes foreboding with uncertainty and fears.*
*The evil one is always trying to discourage; don't let him.*

*Keep your heart on the promise.*

*Remember Him and His promised love reward.*

*In all that you do, know His heart, and His work in your life will work toward His purpose and your good.*

# *February 25*

Psalm 65

### He Can Do Nothing Wrong

**"Praise waiteth for thee, O God, in Sion:
and unto thee shall the vow be performed."
vs.1**

What a powerful testament to the nature of God.
The psalmist pauses outside the palace
to survey a panoramic view of Zion.
Everywhere he looks he sees the infinite power
and majesty of the great God.
His heart becomes so full because God
has proven Himself in every aspect of creation.
From sunrise to sunset, there is always something new that displays God's incredible power and unfathomable genius.
God has proven His greatness over and over in David's life, but
here David looks outside his needs and circumstances and just
praises God for being Master and Lord.
God has overwhelmed him with the greatness of His control
and concern for His creation.
So it is only right, that our praise should rise to the heavens.
Praise your Lord, He can do nothing wrong!!!

# February 26

*Philippians 4*

**Prayer**

**"Be careful for nothing; but in everything by prayer
and supplication with thanksgiving let your requests
be made known unto God."**

**vs.4**

*The Greek word is "proseuche", meaning "with the soul". When we
pray, we're to bring the matters of our soul into the presence of
God our Father in Jesus name.
All the things that matter to us, matter to God.
He wants us to bring the issues that concern us; things that
would cause us to fear, worry or doubt.
We can confess to Him our sins and
bring to Him the desires we have.
Anything that comes to mind that is
beyond our capabilities He wants us to share.
But prayer is also to be that quiet place of communion
where we can just meditate on Him, praise Him,
tell Him of our love for Him.*

*It's a place of solace; away from the hectic pace*
*of the outside world, meeting with Him alone.*
*This is the agenda of the holy place; the arena of spirits,*
*where no one else is allowed.*
*Go there, stay there, don't be in a hurry; pray.*

# *February 27*

*Philippians 4*

## *The Path to Answered Prayer*

**"Be careful for nothing; but in everything by prayer
and supplication with thanksgiving let your requests
be made known unto God."**

**vs.6**

*1). "Be careful for nothing" – Prepare Completely. To prepare for
prayer means to do whatever it takes to remove doubt from your
heart. God will not keep company with doubters (Hebrews 11:6).
This means reading your Bible to fortify your heart and thinking
before you go to your prayer closet.*

*2). "In everything by prayer" – Pray Correctly. Pray only God's
will. A Dwightism here: "God always answers the prayers He
composes." Stand on the word and pray the promises of God
(II Corinthians 1:20).*

*3). "And supplication" – Persist Constantly. To supplicate means
to struggle, engage, fight with winning in mind. Don't let failure
be an option, go to God realizing your enemy does not want you
to hear from God, and certainly doesn't want you to trust Him.*

*4). "With thanksgiving" – Praise Continually. Worship and praise
must be part of your time alone with Him.*

*5). "Let your request be made known" – <u>Petition Confidently</u>. You can absolutely tell Him what's on your heart, you're ready now, your heart is now at the place where you can accurately commune with the Father.*

# February 28

## Philippians 4
### The Peace of God

**"And the peace of God, which passeth all understanding,
shall keep your hearts and minds through Christ Jesus."**
**vs. 7**

*The Greek word is "eirene", it means "eye of the storm".
The world foolishly thinks that peace is the absence of conflict;
that when all things are quiet than all things are right.
Nothing could be further from the truth.
Jesus said "my peace give I unto you,
not the peace the world gives."
Jesus is making it clear that the peace He gives is a place of pure
safety and security, where everything there is in my favor.
The world will never be at true rest.
There will always be turmoil, if not always visible,
it will always be in trouble spiritually.
In Christ, we are safe in the storm.
When the weather patterns around us are in whirlwinds of hell,
we are safe in the eye; in the eye of the storm.*

*The things around us are in severe danger,*

*but in the middle of the eye there is nothing*

*but serenity and sweet peace; His joy and safety.*

# March

## A Time for Research

**Lesson:** The Word of the Righteousness

*"For every one that useth milk is unskillful in the word of righteousness: for he is a babe." Hebrews 5:13*

The word "righteousness means to be "in right standing". The word of righteousness is communicated message of God for all who would desire to have His righteousness imputed on their behalf.

The word of righteousness encompasses the eternal truth of the gospel and all matters of eternity.

It is the full contract from God to saint, guaranteeing the eternal security of this salvation life. Nothing is more permanent and secure than this divine edict.

Nothing is more glorious than the word of righteousness. Therefore there should be no wonder that it is the target of every cult, critic, and skeptic.

There are no facts of truth more hated by the forces of darkness.

No one in the body who seeks to grow will mature to "full age" who has not fully embraced and follow the righteous declarations of God's truth.

### Outline of the Passage

We see in vs. 5:12 – 6:1:

    A.  The first principles – v.12

    B.  The full principles – v.14

    C.  The foundation principles – 6:1

**Facts: The month of March, third month of the Gregorian calendar.**

It corresponds to the month of Adar; the twelfth month of the Hebrew calendar. It was the time of year that held the feast of Purim. It was month the second temple was completed.

*Focus:* **Prayer and study.**

Projects and research assignments are best accomplished with reasonable goals and accurate detailed notation. Use a good journal and document your studies in the New Testament.

*Assignment:* **Research**

Create a chart of all the Hebrew names of God in the Old Testament.

*Memory Work:*

**Exaltation:** Psalm 103:1

**Excellence:** Isaiah 26:3

**Edification:** Revelation 1:3

**Evangelical:** Isaiah 12:3

**Exhortive:** II Corinthians 5:17

**Educational:** Hebrews 11:1

# Going Deeper

## Research

# Week Ten

> When the Lord calls a person by their name twice, it shows Gods' Fatherly attention and a special love for them. Search through the scriptures and find all those whom the Lord calls their name twice.

# *March 1*

*Proverbs 3*

### *The Believers Contract*

**"Trust in the LORD with all thine heart;**
**and lean not unto thine own understanding."**

**v. 5**

*If you trust Him completely, He promised that*
*He would direct your path – your life will never,*
*ever go in the wrong direction or astray.*
*You will live out the purposes for which you were created –*
*I swear this is the strategy for happiness.*
*Give Him only what He deserves and you receive*
*what only He can give; absolute contentment,*
*satisfaction, fulfillment, and purpose.*
*He obligates Himself to those who surrender*
*their love, life and longing to Him.*
*He has never broken a promise, and will never,*
*ever remove His love.*

# *March 2*

*Psalm 123*

### *Absolute Assurance*

*"Behold, as the eyes of servants look unto the hand
of their masters, and as the eyes of a maiden unto the hand
of her mistress; so our eyes wait upon the LORD our God,
until that he have mercy upon us."*

*v.2*

*I have no one else but God.*
*Not because my options have run out.*
*But because in an impossible situation,*
*there is only one option; an impossible answer: God.*
*The Lord should always be sought: forget all else; trust God.*
*One of the most heretical and useless statements ever penned by
man is "When all else fails, try God."*
*It is: 1) a waste of time – your situation must be: a) not urgent if
you have time to look elsewhere b) unimportant if you are in a
situation where failure is not fatal.*
*2) To "try God" is an affront to Him and will yield negative
results; Hebrews 11:6 – trust God from the very first and wholly
watch what only He can do!*

# *March 3*

*Philippians 4*

### *Complete Rest*

### *"...that passes all understanding*
### *shall keep your hearts and minds"*
### *vs.7*

*"...that passes all understanding*
*shall keep your hearts and minds".*
*It is completely human to want to understand*
*what's going on when crisis arise.*
*It is not sinful, it's not faithless; it's human.*
*So quite naturally when the hard facts of life invade our world,*
*it's easy to turn toward heaven and ask God*
*to help us understand.*
*So often the saints have prayed, "If you can't tell me why, won't*
*you please help me understand?"*
*The truth of the matter is that God knows that most often the*
*whys' and hows' are often more difficult than we can bear.*
*The full knowledge of what may be happening beyond the phys-*
*ical veil is greater than our ability to handle.*
*But if we pray, He promises that His peace*
*will surpass our need to understand.*

*<u>His</u> peace will step in and calm our humanity, and give us that heavenly solace; the godly ability to endure.*

*So pray.*

*Let His peace give you more than the need to understand.*

# *March 4*

*Philippians 4*

### *Peace of Heart, Peace of Mind*

**"And the peace of God, which passeth all understanding,
shall keep your hearts and minds through Christ Jesus."**

**vs. 7**

*Heart – the seat of our emotions. Mind – the seat of our intellect.
The two unpredictable and often mischievous children that most
often get us into trouble.
Those areas that we've come to trust more than anything else.
More than facts and reason; more than our family and friends;
more that truth and proof; more than even God and His word.
So much can be said about the heart and mind.
Sometimes they're in conflict, sometimes they are cohorts. But is
there any time they can be trusted?
The Holy Spirit never wants us to have to make that decision.
What is going on in the world around us is happening much too
fast and the stakes are much too high to depend on and to wait
on what our hearts and minds will conclude.
God substitutes His voice, the voice of the Holy Spirit,
and the truth of this fact; His word is all that is necessary in the
matters of this life.*

*Every time we choose to ignore His voice and the certainty of His*
*word, the results will ultimately be disastrous.*
*Give Him the rule over your life; He's never wrong.*

# *March 5*

*Psalm 95*

### *Worship*

*"O come, let us sing unto the LORD:*
*let us make a joyful noise to the rock of our salvation.*
*Let us come before his presence with thanksgiving,*
*and make a joyful noise unto him with psalms."*

**vs.1, 2**

*Worship, the act, is not just saying the right words*
*to and about God.*
*Worship in truth is the exercise of the entire being.*
*With the Spirit, man is to come to God on His terms, His way*
*(John 4:24).*
*With the soul, that part of us that makes us self-aware, we are to*
*yield and surrender all of our intellect, imagination, emotions,*
*and will to the direction of Him.*
*And with our bodies, we are to position ourselves physically in*
*whatever manner that would negate any pleasure or comfort,*
*(vs. 6) because He is God.*
*He is like no other, He is never to be compared to*
*or measured by anything else.*

*Worship must be the exclusive right of God.*

*It is on this fact we assign our hearts, our souls and all our ability to the project of loving Him with all we are and have.*

# March 6

*Ephesians 6*
### Flaming Arrows vs. Long Knife

**"Above all, taking the shield of faith,**
**wherewith ye shall be able to quench**
**all the fiery darts of the wicked. And take the helmet**
**of salvation, and the sword of the Spirit,**
**which is the word of God"**
**vs.16-17**

*The rules of modern warfare prove that "he that has the stron-*
*gest weapon will win the day."*
*Whether it's guns against bows and arrows; tanks against*
*horses; camouflage against bright uniforms; deep cover over*
*open ground; the best position, plans, preparation and parapher-*
*nalia will always win the day.*
*So as it is in the natural world, so is it also in the spiritual. For*
*while we do not fight a fleshly fight; we are still at war and must*
*fight with wisdom, strategy and purpose.*
*God has given to us the task of engaging the enemy and com-*
*manded us to defeat him in every engagement, but our weaponry*
*seems inadequate for the task.*
*We seem to be ill-equipped for the conflict.*

*Satan, after all, has fiery arrows, a distant weapon*

*that can mow us down from afar.*

*We have a long knife (machaira),*

*an intimate weapon used for close conflict.*

*What kind of general is God?*

*Why are we not better equipped?*

*Your perspective is all wrong, we have the superior weapon.*

*Ours is not to be a distant fight with Satan, we are to engage up*

*close, where his weapon is ineffective; we are to get in his face*

*and attack him on his ground and win the day!*

*We have the perfect weapon for this war; so let's seize the oppor-*

*tunity and engage the enemy with no fear of defeat.*

# *March 7*

*Psalm 125*

### *Live Right!!*

**"For the rod of the wicked shall not rest upon
the lot of the righteous; lest the righteous
put forth their hands unto iniquity."**

*v.3*

*Different from everyone else, the Christian sins and
receives the consequences of their sin, not because they have to,
but because they choose to.
Before the saving experience of the cross, I sinned
because I could not help myself.
Everything I did was an affront to God
(Psalm 7:11; Proverbs 21:41; Romans 14:23).
But now as the saints of God we need never fear the judgment of
God in our lives, unless we decide to live as the ungodly.
I have encountered so many believers who are unhappy.
This is a contradiction to salvation.
The only justifiable reason to live under the judgment of God
is because we refuse to live for Him.*

*Privilege and contentment are the purview of the redeemed!*
*If your life is questionable, do the obvious, repent,*
*live right, and honor Him.*

*Going Deeper*

*Research*

## *Week Eleven*

*The books of Ephesians and Colossians are called the twin epistles; On alternating days read through each book. Contrast and compare the two books, noting specific similarities in the two and the exact statements found in each.*

## *March 8*

*I Corinthians 15*

### *Stick with It*

*"Therefore, my beloved brethren, be ye stedfast, unmoveable, always abounding in the work of the Lord, forasmuch as ye know that your labour is not in vain in the Lord."*

*vs.58*

*It is all based on the resurrection.*
*Paul's instruction that the work that we are doing got the Lord is*
*one of eternal worth because Jesus conquered the grave.*
*He spends the greater part of the chapter giving*
*a surgical argument for the truth and proof of*
*the bodily resurrection of the Lord Jesus.*
*He gives sound logic, spiritual and personal evidence*
*as to the wonderful fact of the most incredible fact*
*and important event in all history.*
*The hope of our resurrection and glory is secured*
*in the fact of His resurrection.*
*That puts an end to the skeptics and unbelievers*
*conclusion of a totally naturalistic world.*
*There is a life beyond the flesh.*
*There is hope of a bodily resurrection.*

*The Church will be caught up to meet Him in the air!*
*So don't lose sight of your goal.*
*Keep the promise you made to Him to be faithful*
*despite the world's opinion of you.*
*Your work is not in vain in the Lord!*

# March 9

*II Timothy 4:19*

### Hollow Victories

**"For Demas hath forsaken me,**
**having loved this present world,**
**and is departed unto Thessalonica;**
**Crescens to Galatia, Titus unto Dalmatia"**
**vs. 19**

*"Thessalonica" – We know the Greek word*
*"nike" from the enormously successful sports brand.*
*It means simply: victory.*
*A great incentive and goal to set your course by; to win.*
*Anyone who engages in the world of competition does so with the*
*intent of winning; honestly and fairly, I hope.*
*But the first part of the word tells a different story of their city*
*from ancient times is the word "thessalos".*
*It means – hollow, empty or vain.*
*Amazing isn't it?*
*Here is a man that had experiences*
*we all wish we could have known.*
*A man that had seen the great power of God and has been a wit-*
*ness of His Spirit in the presence of Paul the apostle;*

*He has an observer to the incredible matchless proof of the resur-rected Christ lived before him.*

*But with all of that he fell in love with "this present world" and went to a place of "hollow victories".*

*Now stop.*

*What world are you living for?*

*This one offers a chance for "hollow victories".*

*In others words, an opportunity to enjoy "beautiful nothing-ness"... still want it?*

# March 10

## Philippians 1:6

### *I Haven't Forgotten You*

*Behind the scenes of the veil of flesh, God is doing the impossible. Obscured from the weakness of our humanity He is working out in eternity that which shall have infinite worth in time. It is the concerted effort of the forces of darkness to keep your focus on the things that are temporal. The moment by moment aspects of this world are but a façade of the failings that lost creation has come to believe in. Don't be focused on the hopelessness you see in the universe around you. Our God, the master designer is doing something in your life that can only be performed in the Spirit, and when it is in His time, it will be revealed in the miraculous majesty of His divine will. Don't see things around you as the end all and be all of life. God has not forgotten you, He's perfecting that good work using the pressures of time and patience to create the person that you were meant to be.*

# *March 11*

*Proverbs 5*

**The Strange Woman**

**"And why wilt thou, my son, be ravished with a strange woman, and embrace the bosom of a stranger?"**

**vs. 20**

*This is a phrase repeated often in the Old Testament.*
*It is used to describe the female whose sole intent is to lure the saint away from all that is familiar and righteous in his life.*
*Using the bait of unhindered sex and wild life fulfillment and fantasy, she attracts him away from the confines of holy desires and pleasures found in a godly wife, and seeks to pleasure him with sex without guilt and false love without responsibility.*
*This is something that should be easy to remedy with simple logic.*
*But such is not the case.*
*So many men and women are trapped by their own cravings for that which is not and can never be truly theirs.*
*Be wise, be holy, beware, and be warned.*

# *March 12*

*Psalm 6*

### *Confession and Accountability*

**"O LORD, rebuke me not in thine anger, neither chasten me in thy hot displeasure. Have mercy upon me, O LORD; for I am weak: O LORD, heal me; for my bones are vexed."**

**vs.1, 2**

*The very fact that God does not consume us*
*each time we sin shows His immense love.*
*Only those who have drawn near to His secret presence*
*understand how much it is an abomination to God*
*to see us covered with sin.*
*His divine holiness repeatedly adjusts to the wickedness of men,*
*by suspending judgment through the provision of grace.*
*David's confessions are passionate, sincere, and thorough.*
*He knows both the act and the consequences of his sin and*
*because of the unique wonder of his relationship to God, he is*
*driven to confess, repent, and regret his transgressions.*
*It is not the deed done that hurts God so; but rather it is the fel-*
*lowship broken. And God wants that relationship restored.*

*This alone should be enough to drive us to our knees and beg for the great mercy from heaven.*

*Whatever you've done, get right before God, and return to the fellowship that you've known before.*

# *March 13*

*Psalm 8*

### *How Excellent is Thy Name!!!*

### *"O LORD our Lord, how excellent*
### *is thy name in all the earth!"*
### *vs.1 and 9*

*Oh Jehovah (the covenant name of a promise keeping God)*
*our Adonai! (master ruler, sovereign); These are some*
*of the great names and titles of a Great God.*
*He is the wonderful one, the glory of the universe,*
*unparalleled in the entire universe.*
*He is the matchless one; He spoke the worlds into existence*
*and holds all things under His control.*
*By His great power, seas are held back from the land;*
*the seasons keep their place and the storms do His bidding,*
*as to maintain His divine order.*
*Yet, in all of this, the most appreciable aspect*
*that warrants our attention today is the three letter word*
*between the two great names of God; "our".*
*"Oh LORD **our** Lord".*

*Nothing warms the heart more that the realization*

*that He, the awesome, uncreated, self-sufficient,*

*self-satisfying Lord of all, is **ours**!!!*

*We, who have come to know Him by faith, have been given legal*

*authority by the high counsel of the Godhead to claim Him.*

*He's your God, my God, and our God!*

# *March 14*

*Psalm 8*

### *Failed*

*The most glorious opportunity afforded*
*to all creation was given to humanity; and we failed.*
*Take a look at verse 6.*
*God gave to His man control of a vast paradise,*
*one where there was no lack, no crisis or conflict;*
*where everything obeyed his will.*
*There were no restrictions or restraints*
*to his ability, and only one rule: to obey.*
*Just that: <u>obey</u>, and we failed, yes, **WE** failed.*
*Don't chide Adam, for if you were in the garden*
*you would have done the same.*
***WE** failed.*
*Had Adam obeyed God and been found faithful with the duties of*
*the garden, God would have given him the globe (Psalm 115:16),*
*and had he been found faithful over the globe, God would have*
*given him the galaxy (Psalm 8:6), and had he been trustworthy of*
*all these, God would have rewarded him with glory (John 17:22).*
*All things were put under his feet and **WE** failed!*
*Thank God the story doesn't end there, because one man,*
*not of Adam's ruined race, but the Lord of Glory came as a man;*

*and He was found faithful and all things are given to Him,*

*and He reigns forever!*

*He never fails!!*

*Going Deeper*

*Research*

## Week Twelve

*The Philistines were a constant enemy to the nation of Israel. Their wickedness and idolatry were an affront to Jehovah. Trace the origins of this ancient and ungodly adversary and research their eventual end.*

# *March 15*

*Psalm 3*

### *The Privilege of the Righteous*

*"I laid me down and slept; I awaked; for the LORD sustained me. I will not be afraid of ten thousands of people, which have set themselves against me round about. Arise, O LORD; save me, O my God: for thou hast smitten all mine enemies upon the cheek bone; thou hast broken the teeth of the ungodly. Salvation belongeth unto the LORD: thy blessing is upon thy people. Selah."*

### *vs. 5 – 9*

*The redeemed family of God glories in His favor, His love, His blessing, His provision, but also in the company of His greatness. The prophet David is given, through the Spirit, a glimpse of the glory of Heaven and the kingdom for the benefit of the righteous. God gives him a chance to express as much as humanly possible, the blessed truth of the divine life as well as the divine lifestyle and blessing that come with it.*

*From the wonderful splendor of His glorious throne, to the incredible beauty of the divine encounter with Him, God is never separate from His nature.*

*And it is from that nature flow all that is magnificent
and miraculous.
Oh wonder of wonders that we are blessed
to be a part of the family of God.*

# March 16

*Deuteronomy 5*

### Learn the Law

**"And Moses called all Israel, and said unto them,**
**Hear, O Israel, the statutes and judgments which**
**I speak in your ears this day, that ye may learn them,**
**and keep, and do them."**

**vs.1**

*There are myriad verses in the bible*
*that extol the virtues of knowing God's word.*
*In fact, the entire chapter of Psalm 119, the longest chapter in*
*the bible, is given to that one aspect.*
*The power of God's word in action*
*is the greatest force knowable to mankind.*
*For anyone who would avail themselves to intimately know Him*
*through His word, God has committed Himself to*
*blessings of enriched and full life.*
*God's instruction to the people of Israel is clear and absolute:*
*Learn the word!*
*Know it within the depths of your heart.*
*Keep the word, that means to be loyal to it*
*daily without compromise.*

*Then finally, <u>Do the word</u>.*

*That means to live it; give your life*

*to the sole exercise of practicing what God has said.*

*Now this is not a suggestion, it is a command.*

*The promised power of God is available to all and for all those*

*who would learn, keep and do His word.*

*Change your life forever; learn, keep and do Hus word!!*

# *March 17*

*Deuteronomy 5*

### *Live the Life*

**"O that there were such an heart in them, that they would fear me, and keep all my commandments always, that it might be well with them, and with their children forever!"**

**vs.29**

*The men of Israel had so many chances to get it right.*

*So many opportunities to have God's favor blessing and presence;*

*like no other time in all the history of humanity the people were given an open door to know Him.*

*Can't you hear the lamenting cry of God when He cries, "Oh that there were such an heart in them..."*

*The anguish He feels for a people who don't realize the opportunity they had thrown away.*

*The enormous blessings they would never come to share; the person of God the Almighty that they would never encounter.*

*What an invitation!*

*To know God, to have the awesome presence of God and not to be condemned; it can't be any better!*

*What have you done with the invitation God has given to you?*

*Do you push it aside and long for other things*

*that can never satisfy?*

*Have you set your world around another love that promises*

*everything, but can deliver nothing?*

*Or will you take up the most wonderful opportunity there is:*

*to walk with the eternal?*

*Where is your heart?*

# *March 18*

*Deuteronomy 6*

**Love the Lord**

**"And thou shalt love the LORD thy God with all thine heart,**
**and with all thy soul, and with all thy might."**
**vs.5**

*Had Israel kept any law of God at all,*
*it should have been this one.*
*Jesus said that upon this commandment and to love you neighbor*
*as yourself, hangs all the law and the prophets.*
*In the book of Deuteronomy alone, God tells this nation to love*
*Him over 10 times.*
*It is the most repeated command God uses.*
*He is making it quite obvious that if one would love Him with*
*everything within them, then benefits of life would be incredible.*
*Divine favor, divine access, divine blessing.*
*The rewards would be untold! There would be joy unspeakable;*
*life to the fullest and peace of heart and mind*
*that could never be imagined.*
*Loving Him would open every door.*
*It would provide protection from every adversary and every*
*adversity; there can be nothing greater.*

*Now, the question is turned to us.*
*Do we love Him with all that we are and have?*
*Love the Lord you saint of God.*
*Love Him with every fiber of your being.*
*Love Him and watch with wonder His love in you.*

# *March 19*

*Deuteronomy 6*

### *Leave a Legacy*

**"And these words, which I command thee this day, shall be in thine heart: And thou shalt teach them diligently unto thy children, and shalt talk of them when thou sittest in thine house, and when thou walkest by the way, and when thou liest down, and when thou risest up." vs.6-7**

*The next generation must know.*
*They were not there when He parted the waters,*
*but they must know.*
*They never felt the pain of the whips or the restriction of chains*
*and fetters, but they must know.*
*The hunger of slavery; the hunger for freedom, mercifully they*
*had never experienced.*
*Spared were they from the agony of oppression and fear,*
*so they must know.*
*They must be told of the God who heard*
*the cries of their fathers and mothers.*
*This wonderful Lord who kept His promise to Abraham,*
*Isaac and Jacob was always there.*
*And they must know.*

*You, like the patriarchs of Israel, have known of the pains of many heartaches and disappointments.*

*You've felt the hurt and sting of loneliness and despair; and cried out for the mercy of God during the difficult times, and found Him to be true to His word.*

*You must give to the next generation your testimony, and teach them about the God of truth and His awesome word.*

# *March 20*

## *Psalm 66*

### *He Listens to ME!*

**"But verily God hath heard me;**
**he hath attended to the voice of my prayer."**

*Blessed be God, which hath not turned away my prayer.*
*Of course He hears!*
*He is God, He hears everything. Nothing escapes Him.*
*Of course He listens!*
*He is God, He knows intently every word ever uttered.*
*But He listens to ME!*
*This implies more than just a working knowledge of facts. It*
*means He has already foreknown what is on my heart and mind.*
*He has prepared the only God honoring path and solution, but He*
*still wants for me to voice my flawed and feeble words, so that I*
*can take part in the relationship; so that I can boast about Him.*
*He does not lead me around as a drone, mindless and numb.*
*He wants for me to speak and listen even though He knows.*
*Do you understand now why we love Him so?*
*He Listens.*

# *March 21*

*Matthew 11:28*

### *Come*

*It is the Lord's favorite word.*
*It is used as the principle word of instruction*
*in the very first invitation in the Bible (Genesis 7:1),*
*and the very last (Revelation 22:17).*
*It is the opportunity from God*
*to every man, woman, boy and girl.*
*It separates pretentious zeal from actual faith;*
*a four letter word that if ignored,*
*will mean the difference between Heaven and Hell.*
*It is the word "come".*
*It is the intimate word that God*
*uses to activate the human heart to trust Him by faith.*
*Whether it is the call of the Spirit to consider God's offer of spiritual cleansing (Isaiah 1:8), or His invite to exchange burdens*
*(Matthew 11:28).*
*This precious little word produces enough sustaining power of*
*God to do anything.*
*All we need do is follow its direction and "come".*
*Would you accept His offer now?*

*Come with any burden, come with any concern, come with every question, come at any time and see what the amazing power of a loving Father will do.*

*Going Deeper*

*Research*

## *Week Thirteen*

*In Revelation 7
twelve tribes of Israel are listed.
However this list is different
from the list in Genesis 49; two
names are missing and have
been replaced. Research the
difference and the explanation
of the change.*

# *March 22*

*Psalm 96*

### *The Beauty of Holiness*

*"O worship the LORD in the beauty of holiness:*
*fear before him, all the earth."*
*vs. 9.*

*Only three times in the sacred writ does the Holy Spirit allow the prophet to use this phrase: "the beauty of holiness". The statement is to communicate three things: "the sanctuary for man", "the sanctuary of man", and "the sanctuary in man".*
*The first in Psalm 27:4 describes the sanctuary for man: The temple, the physical place God demanded would be made under His strict design and orders.*
*The sanctuary of man: Man is to be the dwelling place of God (John 14:17).*
*He is to have the person and presence of God living inside of Him.*
*The last is the sanctuary in man: His spirit (I Corinthians 6:17).*
*This is the holiest of holies.*
*The spirit of man is to be exclusive to and for God.*
*No one else, nothing else can ever occupy that place.*
*It is to be the beauty of holiness where God alone must dwell.*

173

# *March 23*

Psalm 30

### *Fulfilling My Purpose*

**"To the end that my glory may sing praise to thee,
and not be silent. O LORD my God,
I will give thanks unto thee forever."
vs.11-12**

*Because I was created to glorify Him.
That's the answer to why He delivers me; for His glory and honor.
Yes, He delivers me because I need help; I am once again taken
over by evil and wicked intentions.
Yes, He sees that my enemy, who outnumbers me exponentially,
and He knows I cannot win on my own, so He rescues me.
Yes, He knows I am weak and unprepared so He makes up the
difference so that I am not consumed, but these, while they are
noble and wonderful, loving, kind actions of the Lord toward His
loved ones, His motives have nothing to do with any of this.
No, He does all things for the sake of His glory.
My reason for being is to, with my life and deeds,
be a glory and a praise to Him.
David shows this is why God has placed him
in the position he lives in.*

*All of us live for one end: to give Him honor.*
*The key of true holiness, true happiness, true honor,*
*is to live your life to glorify Him.*
*This should be our only pursuit.*

## March 24

*Psalm 126*

### *Let the Heathen Testify*

**"Then was our mouth filled with laughter,
and our tongue with singing: then said they among
the heathen, The LORD hath done great things for them."**

**vs. 2**

*"Let your light so shine before men that they might see..."*
*It has always been the responsibility of the righteous to live a*
*life, whether it's pain or pleasure, affluence or affliction that the*
*unredeemed would observe and testify of the greatness of God.*
*The blessings on the saints is to be of such obvious magnitude,*
*the world cannot ignore it and must testify of it.*
*"The Lord has done great things for them".*
*It should be the exclamation of every critic, skeptic and atheist.*
*For no matter how clever the banter or reasoning the unbe-*
*liever may present, nothing stuns their rhetoric like the miracle*
*working power of our faithful God.*

# March 25

*Psalm 27*
### Why?

Why do we give up all the pleasures
and opportunities that we are offered just in daily living?
Why do we abandon the cravings and appetites we have
that are normal and won't hurt anyone?
We are certainly the most puzzling people
to the world around us.
I mean, they are prospering without
following the Bible's teaching.
They live just as long as we do, they have successes,
they have set backs; there seems to be no disadvantage
for being a "normal" person.
So why do we afflict ourselves, why do we restrict ourselves,
why do we ignore all of the base, simple things?
Well, the answers to all those questions are found
in verses 5 through 10.
When the entire world has no way, no answers,
when all that they have come to trust in fails there will be
nothing. But we will always have Him.
He hides us in trouble (vs.5),
He honors us above our enemies (vs.6);

*He hears us when we pray (vs.7);*

*He helps us (vs.9);*

*He holds us (vs.10).*

*The world can feel confident in their moments of success, but over the course of life they all will fade away.*

*Not so with us; problems will come and go, situations rise and threaten, but through it all, we will always have Jesus.*

# *March 26*

*Proverbs 6*

### *It Doesn't Take Long*

*"Yet a little sleep, a little slumber, a little folding of the hands to sleep: So shall thy poverty come as one that travelleth, and thy want as an armed man."*

**vs. 10-11**

*These two verses are used once again in Proverbs 24.*
*I believe that Solomon quotes David his father for a good reason.*
*When a man refuses to take his God assigned place in the world*
*around him, he leaves unattended the areas of his influence*
*unprotected and vulnerable.*
*Every horrendous act perpetuated by wicked hands succeeds*
*only because the righteous decided not to live the life God*
*intended for them.*
*As a result the areas that should have been subdued*
*are now in jeopardy.*
*It takes so little time for the enemy to work harm and damage.*
*If a man of honor would stand in his rightful place and be on*
*guard for his duties the foe would have no opportunity to work*
*his evil in society.*

*Beware precious one; it doesn't take long to lose*
*all that you have worked to accomplish.*
*Be steadfast and vigilant.*

# *March 27*

*Psalm 119*

### *Lord, Help Me to Live for You*

**"Teach me, O LORD, the way of thy statutes;**
**and I shall keep it unto the end. Give me understanding,**
**and I shall keep thy law; yea, I shall observe it with my**
**whole heart. Make me to go in the path of thy command-**
**ments; for therein do I delight."**
**vs.33-35**

*"Teach me, oh Lord – Give me understanding – Make me to go."*
*These simple statements encompass the great need*
*of the human soul.*
*I need God to instruct me, first, give me didactic reasoning*
*(instruction that is logical, clear and personal),*
*God's own truth that is pure and inerrant,*
*but that I cannot, on my own, follow accurately.*
*I need God to give me understanding beyond*
*my sinful perceptions.*
*I need wisdom to grasp His great truths*
*and powerful wonders that He wants to give me.*

*Yet, even though I have been through His word*
*and have received His instruction, my sinful heart, my wicked*
*nature, must have divine intervention.*
*He still needs to make me take the path of righteousness. I know*
*what is right, I know what He has is best for me, but even in all of*
*that I cannot choose the good thing without Him.*
*Make your prayer for today these 3 things:*
*Teach me, Give me, Make me.*

# *March 28*

*Psalm 7*

**If I have rewarded evil unto him that was at peace with me; (yea, I have delivered him that without cause is mine enemy:) Let the enemy persecute my soul, and take it; yea, let him tread down my life upon the earth, and lay mine honor in the dust. Selah.**
**vs. 4-5**

*It's not very easy to look at yourself with complete objectivity.*
*To divorce yourself from your intentions and motives enough to accurately assess things about you and see yourself as others see you it's well, difficult at best.*
*Quite frankly, it's probably impossible;*
*only the deluded think otherwise.*
*But there is someone who knows us and can righteously analyze our motives and our true intentions: The Lord God.*
*I admire David for speaking forth rightly and submitting himself to the only righteous Judge.*
*A saint that refuses to avail their life to continuous criticism is blind to think that the world sees them flawless.*
*Part of our daily prayer should be,*
*"O Lord my God, if I have done this…"*

*Going Deeper*

*Research*

## *Week Fourteen*

> *There are several names of God in the bible, each reflecting a different aspect of His character. Research each of the following in scripture and their meanings: El, El Shaddai, Elohim, El Elyon, and El Gabor.*

# March 29

*Psalm 27*

### *Fully Covered*

*When one looks at this song, you cannot help but be amazed at how much truth, encouragement, power, blessing, promise and doctrine David presents to us.*

*If we just look at the first 3 verses, we see David jam-packing so much information that you need to stop and take a break and catch your breath.*

*He gives us two covenant names of God and their importance and the promises found in each one.*

***Jehovah Ore** (My light) and **Jehovah Ma'oz** (My fortress; my rock) With Him being my light, He secures my salvation; as my strength, He secures my soul.*

*He proves once again that He is always concerned about me and my welfare.*

*He puts Himself in the place where I am most vulnerable and insecure and fortifies my position.*

*His forward thinking and personal involvement with me is a constant reminder of how much He really loves me!*

*I cannot look elsewhere for this kind of loving tenderness. My King and my God has so provisioned His love and care so that for all my life He will be my everything.*

# *March 30*

*Psalm 24*

## *Selah*

*Pause, take a moment, and think about what has just been said.*
*Don't go any further.*
*Pull over and park here for a while.*
*That's the essence of what the word "Selah" means.*
*It is a music instruction to the choral conductor as well as to the*
*choir; the orchestra leader as well as the listeners.*
*It means God has just said something so powerful we should just*
*sit quietly and let it soak in.*
*The Holy Spirit was uses the psalm as one*
*of the weapons in His multiple arsenal to speak clearly*
*to the heart of fallen, lost humanity.*
*Here, as He does often in the hymn book, He instructs the reader*
*to heart-fully and wisely consider what was just said.*
*The instruction or wisdom that was just conveyed is too heavy*
*and too important to just skip over.*
*These breaks in the song allow for the reader*
*to meditate, to ponder deeply, both the instruction,*
*and the importance of the song.*
*You take time now and pause; think on what He is saying to you.*
*Selah.*

# March 31

*John 19:30*

### *It Is Finished*

*Tetelestai - it is finished.*
*The mighty words from the cross. Jesus' final statement*
*was not to man, but for man.*
*Heralding to the entire universe that*
*the most wonderful thing has happened.*
*All the unseen forces of the spirit world watch in awe at the*
*incredible work of the Savior.*
*The angels of God – ready to rush into the natural sphere*
*of man that has been wrecked and ruined by sin;*
*ready to destroy all of the world ruled by flesh gratifying sinners,*
*for daring to touch, to offend, to torture and condemn to the*
*cross the high Lord of Heaven.*
*The hell condemned devils of Satan watch in anticipation*
*thinking in their deception that they have killed the Christ!*
*But the Godhead was intimately involved with this*
*fantastic plan, and He is the only one who knows*
*completely what was happening.*
*Every ear should these three wonderful words - "It is finished!"*
*And behold with eternal awe the wonder of God!!!*

# *April*

## *A Time for Discovery*

**Lesson:** The Word of the Life

*"That which was from the beginning, which we have heard, which we have seen with our eyes, which we have looked upon, and our hands have handled, of the Word of life"* I John 1:1

" **J**ohn, the aged apostle, loved the phrase "in the beginning".

He constantly reminds the world that He – Jesus, is the author of time and creation.

Using the same words as Moses in Genesis, he establishes Christ rightful position in the Godhead, giving Him divine honors as the second revealed person of the trinity.

He is the Word of God made manifest in time and history, heir to the privileged throne of His Father God – eternal deity, and the promised throne of His father David – earthly dominion.

The phrase "Word of Life" introduces both Gods' purpose and Person.

The direct communications from heaven provide us with all that is necessary for fallen man to have the life of God.

God has given His orders to humanity, simply stated: Choose this and live.

His **purpose** for this is He wants man to have not just *bios*, that is **terminal** life, life that has beginning and ending.

His purpose includes *zoe*, that is **true** life, life as God intended. This means life for all creation.

This can only be achieved by the **person** of the Word of Life – Jesus, Gods' only Son.

As we said before in the introduction of this section, the word of God is heavens mandated means of communicating with His creation. And thus verse is no exception to the way in which the wonders of heaven come to Mankind.

John gives just a peak into hallowed halls of heaven, to see what he saw during his time with Christ.

a.) "that which was from the beginning" – **The deity of Christ**

b.) "which we have heard" – **The declaration of Christ**

c.) "which we have seen with our eyes" – **The dynamics of Christ**

d.) "which we have looked upon" – **The description of Christ**

e.) "and our hands have handled" – **The definition of Christ**

*Facts:* **The month of April, fourth month of the Gregorian calendar.**

It corresponds to the month of Abib; the first month of the Hebrew calendar. It was the time of year that held the feast of Passover. It was month that Christ was crucified.

*Focus:* **Prayer and revelation.**

Revelation happens when we are yielded to be filled with the Holy Spirit. Shut out any other media and spend time alone with God and His word.

*Assignment:* **Research**

List all the Christophanies in the Old Testament.

*Memory Work:*

**Exaltation:** Revelation 4:11

**Excellence:** Psalm 19:14

**Edification:** Hebrews 6:10

**Evangelical:** Romans 5:8

**Exhortive:** I Corinthians 10:13

**Educational:** Isaiah 53:5

# *Seeing Clearer*

## *Discovery*

## *Week Fifteen*

*This week learn of a family that may be going through a difficult time and love them as Christ loves and do what you can to help them through it.*

# *April 1*

*It Is Finished!*

### *The Payment for Sin*

*John 19:30*

*"Tetelestai". The word was used often*
*in the ancient Roman Empire.*
*It was used as an official decree*
*for many important transactions.*
*It was used as an official statement that a financial debt was*
*paid; whether for services rendered or a loan from a creditor.*
*It was also used to signify full purchase of a loan*
*or the payment of taxes to the government. It was the proof*
*of release from indentured servanthood;*
*the seven years of agreed laboring was completed*
*and there were no more obligations to his former master.*
*But most of all, it was used when a man had paid the full price in*
*prison for crimes committed against the state.*
*Jesus cried, "Paid in full" from the cross,*
*the sentence has been met.*
*The price paid.*
*The debt is over, the term is fulfilled.*
*Jesus has paid it all!*
*It is finished!*

# *April 2*

*John 19:30*

*It Is Finished!*

### *The Problem of Sin*

*"Guilty, vile and helpless we, spotless Lamb of God was He."*

*The hymn writer stated perfectly our situation.*

*Guilty!*

*Vile!*

*Helpless!*

*That is the problem with sin.*

*The sinner has found out that the passion and craving for what is*

*an affront to God, has grave and fatal consequences.*

*All that we, the fallen have trusted in*

*to make our situation better has failed.*

*There is no way out and time is slowly wearing away at our lives.*

*Hurting, hopeless, helpless; this is the reason God implored the*

*nation of Israel to obey His commandments and live.*

*Sin is deadly, all sin; all the time.*

*While it promises absolute pleasure and gratification, it never*

*remedies the true needs of the heart.*

*Sin at its best is death.*

*Mankind needs a genuine encounter;*

*one that satisfies and is guiltless.*

*David found it, "In thy presence is fullness of joy, at thy right hand*

*there are pleasures forever more!"*

# *April 3*

*John 19:30*

*It Is Finished*

### *The Presence of Sin*

*I travel extensively.*

*I am usually on the road hundreds of days a year.*

*I have been on several continents,*

*dozens of countries and every state.*

*I have seen most of the major cities of the world*

*and visited more islands than I can count.*

*And with every mile I travel; every step I make, I am accompa-*

*nied with the most evil person I know.*

*Everywhere I have gone, he has been there with me.*

*I cannot avoid him, and I have been convinced that despite what I*

*do, he'll be with me until the day I die.*

*I sleep with this person every night and whenever I look in the*

*mirror he stares back at me.*

*I am of course talking about myself.*

*The presence of sin is resident in me the sinner.*

*Paul enlarged on it like this, "... when I would do good, evil is*

*present with me."*

*I need someone who knows my state and can remedy it.*

*To this Paul gives the answer,*

*"I thank God through Jesus Christ our Lord".*

*I no longer have to answer the call of my flesh. I am no more*

*forced to live a helpless life.*

*I am free because Jesus paid it all.*

*It is finished!!*

# *April 4*

### *A View of Calvary*

*Matthew, Mark, Luke, John.*

*These gospels all tell the story.*

*Each of the four gospels reports on the events of Calvary.*

*All of the evangelists report the story of what happened on that most important "good Friday".*

*Each gives an accurate rendering of what happened there, but, with individual perspective, each share what they saw.*

*It then requires that all four authors' reports be given full scrutiny,*

*In order to have a complete picture of that fateful day.*

*We will take a look at all four accounts and highlight the specific details unique to each gospel.*

*From Matthew, we will take a look at the crowd. Mark will show us a view of the cost.*

*Luke's eye takes in a view of the cross.*

*Finally, John, the beloved, will give us a look at the Christ.*

*Together, they provide not only an accurate view of the crucifixion, but also an adequate one. So, let's look to see what the word tells us about God's Son and His love gift to the world.*

# *April 5*

*Matthew 27:27-54*

**A View of Calvary**

*The View of the Crowd*

*It is the gospel book written to the Jews.*
*There are more quotes from the Old Testament found here than*
*in the rest of the New Testament combined.*
*Matthew is trying to convince a Jewish world that Jesus indeed is*
*the promised messiah.*
*With the reporting skills of a present day investigative reporter,*
*Matthew draws attention away from the Christ*
*to focus in on the crowd.*
*For, the word "they" is used over 30 times, whereas "Christ is*
*mentioned merely 9 times.*
*The intent of Matthew is to show us the extremely low position*
*man has sunk to.*
*He gives clear evidence that if there was ever a need for a savior,*
*it is now; and Jesus is the man.*
*Take the time now and underline in your copy of the Bible each*
*time the word "they" is used, and do a study of the progression of*
*man's descent, debauchery, and finally his deliverance.*

# *April 6*

*Mark 15*

### *A View of Calvary*

*A View of the Cost*

*The book of Mark is the fastest paced book in the entire Bible,*
*with the use of such words as "immediately"*
*and "straightway" and "suddenly".*
*The evangelist takes off running with barely time*
*to stop and take a breath.*
*The reason is simple; he's writing his story with*
*the Roman citizen in mind.*
*The Romans were people of action;*
*they wanted to live life on the edge.*
*Every moment of their existence was to be*
*an expression of indulgence.*
*That is why Mark focuses on the cost. Mark's assessment of the*
*cost of Calvary shows all that Christ sacrificed for our salvation.*
*Verses 2 through 5 reveal the cost of providing no self-defense.*
*Jesus would not answer in trial before Pilate*
*anything that could free Him.*
*In verses 16 through 20, He endured mock-worship under the*
*cruelty of the soldiers.*

*Verse 23 shows that He would take no relief from the pain when they offered Him a stupefying drink to drug Him.*

*Then lastly, when they beckoned Him to come down from the cross to save Himself, He would not*

*(although He could have... easily).*

*This is the view of what it cost to save the world.*

# April 7

*Luke 23:33*

**A View of Calvary**

*The View of the Cross*

*The university trained physician, Luke.*
*The man who would write two gospels; one*
*showing the actions of the Savior, and the other revealing the*
*actions of the saints. With His trained eye, Luke turns our atten-*
*tion to a view of the cross. "There they crucified Him". "There" –*
*The place. The name Calvary means in Latin, "the skull", a rocky*
*outcropping of stores, a granite mount that made up a hill for all*
*to look upon. For this was sport to them.*
*"They" – all the people groups were there: The Romans, the Jews,*
*the Greeks and us. Yes, we were there too, maybe not in person,*
*but definitely in heart. In the heart of the savior.*
*"Crucified" – The worst form of punishment that man could ever*
*receive; the most agonizing death one could die!*
*"Him" – The Lord of all creation, there is no one greater.*
*"There" – The place! The cross of redemption is also a cross of*
*remembrance. What happened there will never be forgotten.*
*"They" – The people! The very ones He came to save,*
*slaughtered Him.*
*All of mankind; past, present and future, represented.*

*"Crucified" – The penalty! The only payment the Godhead would accept. For the wickedness of man's sin no other death would satisfy.*

*"Him" – The Person! Jesus. Sweet, sweet Jesus.*

*Seeing Clearer*

*Discovery*

## *Week Sixteen*

*The bible warns of "a root of bitterness"; it is a deadly condition that many are not even aware of about themselves. Pray each day this week for discernment and ask the Holy Spirit to reveal things in your life that maybe hidden under the surface and ask for the Lord's help to correct, forgive and surrender to Him.*

# *April 8*

John 19:25-30
### *A View of Calvary*
A View of the Christ

While Matthew's book was written to the Jew,
Mark to the Roman and Luke to the Greek, John's
book was written to the Church.
John's assignment was to explain to the Church and the world the
power of the Savior; His motives and His ministry.
He was to report the mysteries of the Christ.
So he does not expend the energy required
to discuss the birth or lineage of Jesus.
He simply explains that He was God,
is God and always will be God.
So when it comes to discussing the details of Calvary –
he shows us the Christ.
In verse 25, he talks about Christ's care.
He leaves His earthly mother
in the care of the author of this book.
Then in verse 28, he speaks of His cost, by suffering what every
human since the fall has suffered, thirst of the soul.
Then finally, he speaks of His commitment in verse 30.

*Tetelestai – it is finished. Christ fully committed Himself to work of salvation until the full price was paid.*

*No wonder He is rightly called the center focus of all humanity.*

# *April 9*

*Psalm 68*

### *More than Enough*

**"Blessed be the Lord, who daily loadeth us with benefits,
even the God of our salvation. Selah."**

**vs.19**

*The name El Shaddai, "the almighty breasty one",
He is also referred to as the God that is "more than enough."
In this passage again we see the wonderful benevolence of God as
He "daily loads us with benefits".
Let's look as a few of them.
We see His new mercies every morning
(Lamentations 3:22-23), our daily bread (Matthew 6:11).
Even here the psalmist craftfully uses
the unique word "loadeth." It is in the continual tense
of the Hebrew, implying that it never ends.
The God that is more than enough bestows His excellent life, love,
and living on the redeemed, and does so daily!!!
The most wonderful person in the Universe whose splendor
and excellence surpass our most elaborate dreams,
positions Himself to be generous to the most unworthy.*

*This is the Father we have; the Lord we serve.*

*"Let God Arise!"*

# *April 10*

*Psalm 98*

### *He has Made Known His Salvation*

**"The LORD hath made known his salvation: his righteous-**
**ness hath he openly shewed in the sight of the heathen."**
**vs.2**

*The psalmist's quote is adamant in regards to the*
*Lord receiving the honor and the glory due Him.*
*He commands the heavenly and the celestial choirs to prepare*
*their anthems and he conducts them with the skill of a maestro*
*to give of their best with a joyful sound.*
*Why?*
*It's Quite simple, because "The Lord has*
*made known His salvation!"*
*The most wonderful news fallen humanity will ever hear.*
*The Lord God has opened the doors of heaven*
*to the lost, the poor and the needy.*
*He has opened His heart of compassion*
*and poured out from His coffers the flood of His love.*
*And the wonders of eternal life have been realized by man,*
*appreciated by man, and received by man.*
*Let all that know and believe on Him, REJOICE!!!*

# *April 11*

Psalm 128

### How to be Happy

**"For thou shalt eat the labour of thine hands:**
**happy shalt thou be, and it shall be well with thee."**
**vs.2**

*It is the most elusive element on Earth: Happiness. People steal,*
*kill, cheat, lie, spend, destroy, manipulate and deceive whatever*
*they think is necessary to be happy.*
*Sad, but the key to lifelong happiness is found*
*right here in two short statements.*
*Sure the words may be easy to say, but the direction they give,*
*well, it's not so easy to live.*
*Here they are:*

### 1.)  Fear the Lord

### 2.)  Walk in His ways

*These two directives require giving up*
*all you previously loved and held dear.*
*But let's be honest; isn't that a lot less than*
*pursuing everything else with all you have for your entire life*
*and at the end of it all you come up empty?*

***"His yoke is easy, and His burden is light".***

*All that man craves is found in these two truths.*

*If happiness is your aim, fear Him and follow Him.*

# *April 12*

*Proverbs 8*

**Wisdom**

**"For wisdom is better than rubies"**

**v.11**

**Wisdom** – *The best friend of the learning soul.*
*"Wisdom".*
*Godly wisdom, that is, is not just pithy sayings that sound witty,*
*intelligent and provocative.*
*Wisdom is the God given understanding of things*
*that can affect our quality of life.*
*It cannot be mainly conventional insight as*
*a greater moral imperative.*
*Wisdom is the ability to rightly decide and righteously*
*apply the good, and godly.*
*By wisdom, the scripture says, God formed the natural world.*
*By wisdom God confounds the mighty.*
*Godly wisdom is the element that will continually make the dif-*
*ference between life and death.*
*If you lack it, the promise of scripture is, all you need do is ask.*

*Don't allow your life to be absent of wisdom.*
*Ask God for it and let it permeate your heart,*
*order your steps and change your life.*

# April 13

*Psalm 9*

### He Reigns Supreme

**"For thou hast maintained my right and my cause;**
**thou [art seated on] the throne judging right."**
**vs.4**

He can maintain any cause, because He judges right.
He can judge correctly and righteously because
He sits on the throne.
The wonderful glory of this life is that the one
who gives it made the universe.
The chief reason David had such a praise filled life was because
he was thoroughly convinced that the Lord God Jehovah, his God
and King, sat on the throne, judging right. Your God and King
sits on the throne of all creation, He judges rightly and always in
your eventual favor, and always for His glory.
What your enemies plan and scheme mean nothing.
The devices of Satan and the evil of this world system can do
nothing to alter His will and plans for you.

# *April 14*

*Psalm 39*

### *Personal Responsibility*

**"I said, I will take heed to my ways,**
**that I sin not with my tongue: I will keep my mouth**
**with a bridle, while the wicked is before me."**
**vs.1**

*Many set unrealistic goals and plans that cannot consistently be accomplished. Learning to first master our own selfish desires is the most intensely difficult undertaking ever.*

*David has assessed himself, his most deadly enemy, and realized that a diligent plan was needed if he ever wanted to meet his goal of honoring God with his life.*

*To honestly expect a consistent life change, one where we begin to love the things we once loathed, and to now loathe the things we once loved; there must be an honest assessment of our world.*

*A genuine manageable evaluation based on truth.*

*In no way can we expect God to work in us or instead of us.*

*We are working together with Him.*

*And His greatest work is to have our will conform to His through sacrifice and surrender.*

*Drawing Closer*

*Discovery*

## *Week Seventeen*

*The Lord Jesus offers us His perfect rest in Matthew 11:28-30; compare this with the passage in Hebrews 4:1-11. Discover what being in His rest means.*

# *April 15*

*Psalm 69*

### **Wrongfully Accused**

**"Because for thy sake I have borne reproach; shame hath covered my face. I am become a stranger unto my brethren, and an alien unto my mother's children. For the zeal of thine house hath eaten me up; and the reproaches of them that reproached thee are fallen upon me."**

**vs. 7 - 9**

*In this messianic psalm, David is living out*
*the full generalization of the psalmist.*
*The task of the psalmist is to be the living example*
*of what it means to die to oneself for the sake of the Kingdom.*
*The psalmist is especially anointed by God to go through every*
*challenge of the righteous man and report his pain and his pas-*
*sions, his hurts and hopes, his troubles and triumphs as well as*
*his problems and pleasures.*
*The psalmist must be able to speak in the middle of his heart-*
*ache; he must record his prayer when his soul wants to complain.*
*He must know, at least in part,*
*what the coming Savior must endure.*

*Each of us will one day be called upon to be the psalmist;*

*that is if we walk righteously.*

*It is here we are evidence of God's greatness and His deliverance.*

*It is here we hear His voice speaking lovingly even in silence.*

# *April 16*

*Psalm 99*

**Holy**

**"Let them praise thy great and terrible name; for it is holy."**

**vs.3**

*Holy is His name.*

*The roll call of His matchless deeds is ever true and righteous.*

*Holy is every act of His.*

*The world wants to view God as all loving only.*

*And therefore in a fleshly perspective, He must be all accepting.*

*However, the more accurate descriptive would be He is holy,*

*and all those who would draw near to Him*

*must approach Him as such. His name is holy!*

*Vs.5 – His nature is holy. He does everything according to the*

*pure character of His being.*

*He follows the qualities of His nature.*

*He is not driven nor influenced by anything*

*other than the qualities of His own character.*

*He is holy.*

*Vs.9 – He is Lord of a holy nation.*

*All things about Him, around Him, accepted by Him are holy.*

*He dwells only in the midst of that*
*which is sanctified by His holy presence.*
*His name, His hill is holy!*

# *April 17*

Psalm 129

**The God Haters**

**"Let them all be confounded and**
**turned back that hate Zion."**
**vs.5**

*The saint is often the target of many unwarranted attacks.*
*As time progresses, ever more will the saints find themselves vic-*
*tims of mankind's hate for God.*
*Yet because man, like Cain, he cannot in his*
*fury strike God, he'll lash out to what he can touch;*
*the ones whom God has shown favor.*
*Jesus said* **"He that hates me, hates my Father also... now**
**have they both seen and hated both me and my Father."**
*(John 15:23-24).*
*As the world draws closer to its goal; that of an existence without*
*God, the more its hatred of God will be felt by the righteous.*
*The prophet's prayer is one for the vengeance of God against all*
*that truly hate Him but attack His people.*
*Don't be weary with doing right. Honor Him, stand up for Him*
*and His name, and remember:*
**"Many are the afflictions of the righteous, but the Lord..."**

# *April 18*

*Proverbs 9*

### *The Tale of Two Women*

*The faithful or the foolish, within the context of life,*

*mankind must choose one or the other: the life of faith,*

*or the life of the fool.*

*Despite past histories and/or glories, the nature of one's inten-*

*tions will be borne out eventually as one or the other.*

*If the heart changes to be faithful, God has promised*

*His blessing and approval.*

*If the opposite is chosen than the end result will be the sad song*

*of the ages bearing out the promise of Proverbs 29:1.*

*The immediate gratification found in the instant*

*and alluring lifestyle of fools is quickly soured when all of the*

*negatives of that choice begin to bear fruit.*

*Do yourself a favor; follow the wise,*

*forsake the foolish. Honor God.*

*Wisdom disciples (vs.3), it declares (vs.4-5), it discerns (vs.6).*

*But foolishness is ignorant (vs.13), it is idle (vs.14),*

*it is inviting (vs.15), it is insolent (vs.17), it is iniquitous (vs.18).*

*And it will eventually destroy.*

# *April 19*

*Psalm 10*

### **The Lord is King Forever**

*It seems so often that the sinners prosper*
*and the righteous suffer.*
*The sinner has all the fun, wild sexual encounters*
*and seemingly endless money; while the saints seem*
*to deal with all the responsible godly decisions.*
*It doesn't feel right nor does it seem fair*
*while Christians try to lead a holy*
*God honoring life, the world spins out of control with fleshly*
*desires, selfish pursuits, and immoral and ungodly acts.*
*Our peace rests in this fact: The Lord is King.*
*One dear friend of mine always admonished us this way.*
*"The wheels of divine judgment turn exceeding slow,*
*but grind exceeding fine."*
*The Lord knows, and in this life we will see the reward of the*
*right and the judgment of evil doers.*
*Don't lose heart; God is judge and He sees all.*

# *April 20*

*Psalm 40*

### *What God Really Wants*

*Throughout his psalms, David will remind us*
*of what God really wants.*
*God is not impressed with or in need of animal sacrifices.*
*What God has always been after is the heart of man willing and*
*wanting to serve Him alone.*
*God wants the person who wants Him.*
*Not out of terror of obligation, He's looking for those*
*who long to know Him.*
*He is looking for the heart that has decided to follow Him*
*without any regard to what He can give or do.*
*What God wants is that person who looks beyond His ability to*
*bless, and sees Him as a person to know.*
*David had surpassed the futile, vain attempts at happiness by*
*pursuing things – he had found the true love of life in discovering*
*the heart of God.*

# *April 21*

## Psalm 70

## *He Answers Prayer*

*God answers every prayer of the righteous.*

*Make no mistake; every prayer uttered to Him*

*by the redeemed gets His attention and gets His answer;*

*always in accordance with His will.*

*Where we miss the mark is that we think because*

*God does not respond to us verbally He has not answered at all.*

*Nothing could be further from the truth.*

*God answers every prayer.*

*His favorite method to do so is from*

*His word and the witness of His Spirit that lives within us*

*(I Corinthians 2:13). God will use His word to determine*

*the bounds of our understanding about Him and unveil*

*what can be ours through the promises of His word.*

*Don't let the crisis you're in convince you*

*that God has forgotten you; He hasn't.*

*Get deep in His word and speak with Him often.*

*Seeing Clearer*

*Discovery*

*Week Eighteen*

> *Look around your church*
> *this week and find areas that*
> *require attention, replacement*
> *or repair. As much as possible*
> *and inoffensive do what you*
> *can to correct the situation*
> *without anyone discovering*
> *who did it.*

## *April 22*

*Psalm 100*

**With**

**"Serve the LORD with gladness: come before his presence with singing. Know ye that the LORD he is God: it is he that hath made us, and not we ourselves; we are his people, and the sheep of his pasture. Enter into his gates with thanksgiving, and into his courts with praise: be thankful unto him, and bless his name."**

**vs.2-4**

*The presence of God cannot be breached without a sacrifice. To enter into His presence God demands and deserves tribute. It is not a tribute of money or gifts of lands; God's tribute is praise, His sacrificial price is singing, worship and honor. He wants our adoration not our avarice.*
*Praise is the sacrifice of the heart that will allow us into the high throne room of God.*
*God has never rejected the heart that is willing to adore Him correctly.*
*The best way to get both His attention and His affection is to praise Him.*

*God loves the sincere heart that comes to Him*

*with worship in mind (John 4:23-24).*

*Prepare your gift; what do you have to give to Him?*

*How will you honor and adore Him?*

# *April 23*

*Psalm 130*

### *Blessed Forgiveness*

**"If thou, LORD, shouldest mark iniquities,
O Lord, who shall stand?"**

**vs.3**

*He forgives, and He forgets.*
*His love knows when the truly repentant has come trembling,*
*not out of fear, but out of regretful shame.*
*It's not the God we're afraid of that evokes the shame,*
*but the Father wronged.*
*This same Father knows us and our propensity*
*to fall away and chase the most ridiculous bobbles.*
*He watches, not with disappointment, but with care. He is totally*
*aware and concerned about the sin committed, but more impor-*
*tantly, the soul of His child.*
*This Father of ours; this wonderful compassionate Father,*
*loves beyond our comprehension, and loves beyond*
*our ability to understand.*
*Don't run away from his forgiveness, go to Him quickly,*
*restore that wonderful love relationship again*
*and be refreshed in His presence.*

# *April 24*

*Proverbs 10*

### *No Baggage*

**"The blessing of the LORD, it maketh rich,**
**and he addeth no sorrow with it."**

**vs.22**

*How can you tell when a medicine is good for you?*
*No side effects.*
*How can you be sure of the quality of pure*
*and fresh milk? No after-taste.*
*How can you be sure that it is God that has blessed you*
*and that it is not just another trick of Satan?*
*No baggage, no blackmail.*
*God gives and there are no strings attached.*
*He's not hiding something sneaky or painful in His love gifts*
*to us; His blessings are full of His personhood*
*and replete with His great plan.*
*The Lord adds His promise to us with every blessing He gives*
*(James 1:17).*
*He will never change what He gives because*
*His love will never be taken away.*

*God gives and loves as only He can.*

*Follow Him totally and watch how*

*He proves His everlasting love*

*again and again.*

# *April 25*

*Psalm 11*

### *What Really Matters*

### *"If the foundations be destroyed,*
### *what can the righteous do?"*
### *vs.3*

*Every day the position of our faith and the practice of our life-
style are challenged. Continually we are challenged to compromise our beliefs in order to "fit in", but this must not happen.
Our righteous lifestyle is predicated on essentials
that are non-negotiable.
I call them the "to die for" issues.
Without the foundation of the pillars of biblical absolutes,
there is no basis upon which we live by faith.
The "to die for" matters have become more and more
of a problem for the world; but that is no reason why
the church and the Christian should change.
Do you know what the essentials are?
Have you decided to make a stand on the virgin birth, the incorruptible blood of Jesus, the deity of Christ, the infallibility of the
word, etc.? What are your "to die for" issues?*

# *April 26*

## Psalm 41
### *Self Examination*

*Only when I see myself <u>honestly</u> can I see myself <u>clearly</u>. David's psalm here balances what he sees about himself and what his enemies say about him.*

*Because he can be honest enough to see his own flaws he can assess his enemies' taunts.*

*Wherever I am willing to submit myself to the pure eyes of God and avail myself to His righteous gaze can I expect to be objective when valuing what others may say or see.*

*We all have enemies of one sort or another; whether we want to admit it or not; God has never promised that we will have an existence without them.*

*But regardless of whatever people may hold in their thoughts about us, we must see ourselves as clearly as we can, and remain humble in the process to ensure constant growth.*

# *April 27*

*Psalm 71*

### **Passing the Baton**

**"Now also when I am old and grayheaded, O God, forsake me not; until I have shewed thy strength unto this generation, and thy power to everyone that is to come."**

**vs.18**

*We were never called on by God to be "Christians".*
*That is a moniker given to us by the world. We were never asked to be right wing conservatives, abortion clinic protesters, and anti-gay right advocates.*
*We are not ordained by God to be talk show hosts or guests.*
*We are only commanded by God to go into all the world and make disciples.*
*God has called us to reproduce the life of Christ in others; and to be witnesses of His matchless grace to a lost world. We are His light of salvation, His life line to a dead culture. David's plea at the end of his life is exactly that.*
*His desire is to be the bridge to the next generation. Our passion should be exactly the same.*
*We should accurately present Jesus to a culture gone mad.*
*It starts first at home then flows forward fueled by His grace.*

# *April 28*

*Psalm 101*

### *Living Right*

*The Ten Commandments (Exodus 20:3 – 17):*
*the personal model of the holy (Psalm 15),*
*the qualifications of the true servant of God (Psalm 24:3-4),*
*the requirements essential for pleasing God (Micah 6:8),*
*and here David's 7 declarations for personal Holiness..*
*Each list is a forerunner for getting it right.*
*Attention to the detail of life in areas specific*
*to every saint while still being unique to each situation.*
*In some of those scriptures you'll find what it takes to enjoy righ-*
*teous fellowship, in another, what is true evil before God.*
*But David records 7 mandates as personal parameters designed*
*to keep him and anyone from getting too close to the edge; from*
*dropping his guard.*
*These declarations serve as the fence we must put around*
*ourselves, fences to keep out the world and keep in*
*the pursuits of our flesh.*
*Your desire and mine should be to please Him in every area.*
*So what are you going to do?*
*What is your fence?*

# April 29

## Psalm 131
### Be Humble

It's not about the wicked, nor the enemies of the righteous.

It has nothing to do with the devil and his wicked

hordes of demons.

It's about me.

Here I need to maintain holiness at all cost.

The desperate need to perform humble self-evaluation that keeps

me from becoming lifted up in pride and arrogance. It's so easy

to forget that He is the only one who should be glorified.

The Lord is the one that should always get the credit

and attention.

Humbly David puts the eternal pen to eternal paper

and speaks in the first person about his need to remain

on guard against his own pride.

God cannot be honored and enthroned when we are.

God help us to reign in our egos

and lift Him up higher and higher.

# *April 30*

*Proverbs 11*

### *Accountability*

**"By the blessing of the upright the city is exalted: but it is
overthrown by the mouth of the wicked."**

**vs.11**

*No one has it all right and is never wrong.*

*No one is even right the majority of the time,*

*not without help and counsel.*

*Solomon's advice here is very sound indeed.*

*We would love to see ourselves as rugged individualists; people*

*that need nothing or no one but Christ to make it.*

*Well, if that were true there would be no need for the family,*

*the body of Christ.*

*We have been given each other for this very purpose;*

*We cannot make it alone.*

*The situations that we face in life require that we employ all of*

*our assets and advantages to survive. Accountability means that*

*the areas of my life that are blind to me can be exposed and pro-*

*tected by employing the great network of believers.*

*God wants us to fellowship and depend on each other. This is the*

*quality that proves us as a family.*

# *May*

## *A Time for Decision*

**Lesson:** The Word of the Grace

*"And now, brethren, I commend you to God, and to the word of his grace, which is able to build you up, and to give you an inheritance among all them which are sanctified."* Acts 20:32

Some theologians concluded the acronym that grace is "God's riches at Christ expense". That's pretty good. I like instead "God's righteousness at Christ expense".

When I was a kid, the teacher's at our church would say that grace was "Gods' unmerited favor".

All of these express the true intention of God's most extravagant act of love. Simply saying that He gave to us what we didn't deserve. It is the first principle numbered in the trinity of necessities; first grace then justification and finally righteousness.

These three comprise the essentials for the act of salvation to be complete.

Grace spearheads the act by supplying guilty humanity everything it has no right to expect. The great demand from heaven has been

### Outline of the Passage

Romans 10:8-10 show us four wonderful discoveries

    A. The contract of faith – "the word of faith" v.8a

    B. The conditions of faith – "mouth and heart" v.8b

    C. The confession of faith – that is thou will confess with thy mouth/ believe in thine heart" v.8c

    D. The confirmation of Faith – say and believe v.9

**Facts: The month of May, fifth month of the Gregorian calendar.**

It corresponds to the month of Zif; the second month of the Hebrew calendar. This was the month that construction on the temple began.

**Focus: Prayer and obedience.**

It may be that you have been hesitant about doing something that the Holy Spirit has been compelling you to do. Now is the time to undertake the Spirit's challenge and do Gods' will.

*Assignment:* **Research**

Make a list of at least 20 Old Testament Messianic prophecies.

*Memory Work:*

**Exaltation:** Ephesians 3:20, 21

**Excellence:** Hebrews 10:35, 36

**Edification:** Romans 10:17

**Evangelical:** John 3:16, 17

**Exhortive:** James 1:12

**Educational:** Acts 10:38

## Going Further

## Decision

## Week Nineteen

> Fast something you really love this week. It may be food, a hobby, an event, or a possession. Take the time you would have spent enjoying it and go to the Lord in prayer. During this time ask Him to help you see the things around you that need attention and that you may have neglected. As He reveals those things to you, ask for His power to help you make the right choices concerning each of them and strength to accomplish what you have determined may be lacking.

# May 1

## Psalm 31

### *The Covert in Times of Trouble*

*When I am overwhelmed on every side by forces too great for me,*
*the good news is that God is my refuge.*
*Never failing always there, all powerful King,*
*the true lover of my soul.*
*God has anticipated my needs and has assessed my situation.*
*He loves me so much that He is acutely aware*
*of the troubles that are ahead.*
*This calming information causes me*
*to rest easy at night and live confidently.*
*He has placed in my world everything I need to see*
*His hand at work.*
*Obstacles, enemies, setbacks, temptations, giants and impassable*
*walls; these all He has constructed and assigned to me so that*
*when each impossible crisis appears, I'll rest completely in Him,*
*and observe as He does wonders!*

# *May 2*

*Psalm 61*

**Bigger Than Me**

**"From the end of the earth will I cry unto thee,
when my heart is overwhelmed: lead me to the rock
that is higher than I."**
**vs.2**

*At all times we are confronted with concerns*
*that make us feel so small.*
*They don't have to be enemies or problems,*
*sometimes it's just life.*
*So many things are happening all at once; one situation*
*encroaching on another. More to be done on the "to do" list than*
*there is time to do it in.*
*Some things are perpetual. They will never go away or get easier.*
*In some cases they can never be completed; life just goes on.*
*Aren't you glad this isn't all there is?*
*Aren't you glad that life is not measured*
*by successes and failures?*

*Grace and mercy has provided an answer*
*to all of these challenges and every other.*
*Aren't you glad the Lord is our reason*
*for being and that He is always there?*

## *May 3*

*Psalm 91*

### *The Best Place to Be*

*The pre-eminent psalm; a psalm of psalms; it's the psalm that promises almost everything and delivers in all points. Like nowhere else in the scripture do we see the perfect blend and balance of Lord and servant, the faithfulness of the Father, and the absolute assurance the redeemed have in Him.*
*It shows us the relationship mechanics beyond the veil;*
*it reveals the work of the Spirit in the life of the Christian;*
*it gives us a glimpse into the secret place.*
*It's the psalm of dual authorship. In the first 13 verses, the psalm is in the voice of Jesus speaking about the work and works of the Father; all the promises He has made for His child.*
*Then in the last 3 verses, it is the Father speaking for Himself; explaining His reason and purpose for His actions.*
*It is the blessed record of the Holy Spirit as He tells of the great love the Father has for the Son and the great joy of being in His presence.*
*This psalm is ours to claim.*

*We can enjoy this encounter too. Because verse one invites all who would, to enter in. This holy of holies is available to us today!*

*This is God as His best.*

*It don't get no better than this!*

# *May 4*

## *Psalm 121*
### *My Help*

**"I will lift up mine eyes unto the hills, from whence cometh my help? My help cometh from the Lord." vs.1-2**

*It really is a question you know.*

*Those who do not know David, or the Lord he serves, have every right to question the source of his strength. After all, David is a mere man, barely a man, really, yet there is some unseen force that seems to always help him. What or who is it?*

*This is one of the sweetest, and most consoling of the 150 songs written.*

*The dialogue is so precious; extolling the absolute assurance that David, a man of might and war, has in his God.*

*He speaks with the confidence of a seasoned soldier trusting perfectly in his great, undefeated Commander.*

*Absolutely sure, that, by virtue of His past victories, his Lord will get him home.*

*It's more personal here than in most other comfort psalms.*

*The rhetoric here is about the solitary soldier and his thoughts about what lies ahead.*

*Others may fear, but because the Lord watches over him,*

*fear is not part of the equation;*

*the Lord is on his side.*

# *May 5*

*Proverbs 1*

### *The Fear of the Lord*

*"The fear of the LORD is the beginning of knowledge:*
*but fools despise wisdom and instruction."*
*vs.7*

*The fear of the Lord is the whole duty of man.*
*The Holy Spirit rightly dedicates 10 verses extolling*
*the virtue of fearing the Lord.*
*The instructions of a righteous life begin right here.*
*He admonishes us to fear the Lord by serving, honoring,*
*reverencing, and exalting Him.*
*It is the greatest pursuit anyone could have.*
*The ongoing benefit of having a righteous fear of God will only*
*enhance life and all things concerning it.*
*The fear of the Lord will set a path*
*of dependent loyalty and admiration.*
*The fear of the Lord does not mean terror, or horror.*
*It means respect, awe, and reverence.*
*We approach Him with clear understanding of who He is.*

*This should cause us to be careful in our actions*

*and pure in our motives.*

*Have a biblical fear of Him.*

*It is the only pathway to blessing.*

# *May 6*

*Psalm 12*

### *"I've got this"*

*During a showdown between two rivals,*

*the odds on favorite sent their best player in attempts*

*to intimidate the other team's (the underdog) player.*

*When the smaller team saw who was next to play – well,*

*needless to say – the plan worked, everyone shook in their boots,*

*everyone except the team captain.*

*He went and stood next to the scheduled player on his team*

*and said simply "I've got this".*

*That's what God says in the crises of life that are too big for us.*

*"I've got this".*

*In this, one of the many psalms written as prayers*

*to the Lord when the enemy is too great for us,*

*we see our God stand as our captain; never intimidated,*

*always victorious. He positions Himself to vanquish the rival*

*opposition with His righteous fervor. Do not wallow in fear and*

*despair. Look to your Lord and don't worry;*

*He's got this!*

# *May 7*

## Psalm 42

### **God Cure for Depression**

**"Why art thou cast down, O my soul? and why art thou disquieted in me? hope thou in God: for I shall yet praise him for the help of his countenance."**

**vs.5**

*Real depression is a real problem that cannot be waved away and dismissed with clichéd banter, like "You just need to trust God", "You must have sin in your life" or "Just let go and let God".*
*I wish it was that simple.*
*We have been indoctrinated, intimidated, deceived, and manipulated to view life through lens of hopelessness. We've been taught to believe that things can and will only get worse.*
*Listen my friend; the truth of the scripture is that when the lights have gone out all over the rest of the world, God is still on the throne.*
*When fear grips your heart, don't look around or down, LOOK UP! He is the Master. Talk to your soul, give it the heavenly update, God is King, and hope in Him. He's never lost a battle and He's never lost a saint.*
*Hope thou in God.*

# *Going Further*

## *Decision*

# *Week Twenty*

> *Make a list of your favorite pos-sessions, passions and people. Then ask the Lord if any of them is in contention with your time with Him. Make the right decision about those that are in competition with your time with Him.*

# *May 8*

*Psalm 72*

### *What Only God Can Do*

**"Blessed be the LORD God, the God of Israel,**

**who only doeth wondrous things."**

**vs.18**

*I learned just recently that with all the accolades that are said*

*about God; His great power, amazing wisdom, and incredible*

*love, that they all prove something quite simple;*

*God can only do one thing.*

*I know it sounds limiting, but in truth*

*He has said it about Himself.*

*God can only do but one thing; do you know*

*what that one thing is?*

*He can only do: the impossible.*

*That's it, that's all. Whatever is possible,*

*He has given to man to accomplish.*

*His matchless greatness and overwhelming deity make it so that*

*He can only do what only God can do.*

*You want to know the reason why so many prayers*

*seem to go unanswered?*

*Because they most often times*

*are accomplished through human means and efforts.*

*God shows up to do what we <u>cannot</u>.*

*And when that interaction takes place,*

*the miracles of God invade the environs of man.*

*And the impossible happens.*

## May 9

*Psalm 102*

### *Ever Near*

*There are times when things look so bad and enemies seem so*
*many that it appears as though even God is against you.*
*He seems to sit silent when everyone else berates you.*
*He seems unmoved by the things that break your heart*
*and bring you to tears.*
*And when you need Him to show His mighty power*
*on your behalf, well, He seems like the dad that*
*never came to one of your games.*
*The illusion is a lie. God can't show up, when will we see that? He*
*can't appear just when we need Him. Why not? He has never **left**!*
*He has never drifted away to take care of something more*
*pressing. He has always stayed by you. He has heard every*
*prayer, noticed every tear.*
*This is our God, the ever faithful. He deserves our worship*
*because He is everything He said He would be.*
*Talk to Him right now. Let your soul bask in His parental care*
*and never, ever lose heart; for*
*He is always there.*

# *May 10*

*Psalm 132*

### *The Sanctuary*

*Have you prepared Him a place? Have you prepared a place for Him? Not a shrine in your house or car, but within your heart, in your life does He have a place?*

*Let me give you some details of how it should be.*

*It should be clean, holy and blameless; sin should be an infrequent, unwanted visitor.*

*It's kept immaculate by the cleansing power of the word; adorned with praises on every wall and the sounds that emanate from it are the language of a soul set free; godly music that give attention to His majesty.*

*It needs to be spacious and unencumbered.*

*This place also has a throne and an altar; a place for the sovereign and a place for the sacrifice.*

*It's peaceful and holy. There's only room for two, for Him and for you. No one else is invited!*

*But again the query is made: Do you have a place prepared for Him?*

*Not a place set aside. But a kingdom, where He rules you absolutely, and you surrender completely.*

# *May 11*

*Proverbs 12*

### *The Life of the Diligent*

*Maintenance is essential in nearly every area. Regardless of how well something is made, it will eventually break down and stop working if it is not maintained; so also it is with life. Routine maintenance is an absolute. The Bible calls it, diligence. There are six non-negotiable rules of diligence that we must employ if we ever plan to be consistent in our lifestyle.*

***Rule 1:*** *Proverbs 10:4 takes on the issue of personal finance.*

***Rule 2:*** *Proverbs 11:27 teaches us to keep a health handle on our integrity.*

***Rule 3:*** *Proverbs 12:24 gives us insight into our responsibility as leaders.*

***Rule 4:*** *Proverbs 12:27 shows the heart of the diligent and how he handles his possessions.*

***Rule 5:*** *Proverbs 13:4 shows us the prosperity of the diligent with respect to his personal life*

***Rule 6:*** *Hebrews 11:6, the most important, shows us how to walk with God and receive His favor. Strive to be diligent in these areas, develop yourself to greatness, honor and blessing.*

# *May 12*

Psalm 13

### **Thank God for David**

*I praise God for David.*

*If it were not for him, I wouldn't know how to talk to God. David is able to emote and speak to God from his heart without losing his respect and reverence of Him.*

*He can tell God exactly what he feels honestly. So often people are afraid to convey vocally and verbally, what's "on their mind" because they feel if it is never spoken, God will never know.*

*Of course that's not true. God wants us to tell Him **exactly** what we think. He wants us to know that honesty is not the enemy to reverence and respect.*

*We can come to Him expressing how we see things as long as we never forget that honesty is not irreverence and the freedom to speak freely is not license to be disrespectful. Talk to Him, tell Him what's on your heart and mind.*

*Learn what it means to be conversational with God.*

# *May 13*

*Psalm 43*

### *The Solemn Protector*

*Another part of living righteously is living for the right cause.*

*Having an absolute assurance that what we're involved in is the right place and the right reason.*

*When we ask God to act on our behalf, the audacity to do so is because of the clear and ordered life we have imaged before Him and He has blessed it.*

*So when the enemies of our cause oppress, criticize and attack us because of our stand, we have every reason to expect Him to come to our aid righteously.*

*Our position is not our own.*

*He has taken us into His Kingdom agenda and ordered our worldview to that of the Kingdom.*

*Therefore our prayer is not one of selfish pride, but one of righteous indignation.*

*"God, these are your people coming under attack; this is your will being approved. This is your child they seek to destroy. Hear our plea and rescue us."*

# *May 14*

*Psalm 73*

### *It Will All Balance Eventually*

*No, sometimes it's not easy watching the ungodly excel
and get ahead. The forces of evil appear to have all the advantages and opportunities. The sexually immoral seem to have all
that their flesh craves and by and large for the most part, never
appear to have a down side to it. The life of the committed is
fraught with lackluster, drab, colorless tedium, as well as an
often boring, mundane, predictable existence.
Worst of all, God knows all this yet nothing seems to change.
There seems to be very little to cheer for.
There should be something, anything that encourages
us to believe we are doing the right thing.
Take heart pilgrim; not only does He see, He knows.
God is working amidst all the din and noise of the
wicked world around us and has the best news to give us:
We'll see His will triumph over evil;
we'll see His mighty hand at work.
His grace demands that He give things that appear
to be wicked their moment in the sun. Take heart,
we'll understand it better, real soon.*

*Remember, He is the righteous judge, He knows.*

*He's working all things out for the good.*

*Going Further*

*Decision*

## *Week Twenty-One*

> *Assess your occupation:*
> *Is it God honoring? If not, ask*
> *the Lord for help deciding*
> *how His will may be seen in all*
> *that you do there. If it is God*
> *honoring ask for His aid in*
> *becoming a greater witness to*
> *those around you.*

# *May 15*

*Psalm 103*

### *The Benefits of Blessing Him*

**Bless the LORD, O my soul, and forget not all his benefits**
**vs.2**

*He loves us far more than we could ever love ourselves.*
*He is always thinking of me. My best outcome is part*
*of His wonderful plan.*
*In verse 3 He **repeals** all the charges against me by*
*forgiving me. He heals my illnesses brought on by*
*my bad decision making and (refreshes) me anew.*
*In verse 4 He **redeems** my life from destruction, and then*
***rewards** me with the splendor of his loving-kindness.*
*In verse 5 He feeds me with the best of His bounty*
*and **refreshes** me, even to the depths of my soul.*
*He keeps close watch on my personal world so that I can be ever*
*protected. Just like a father understands the needs of his children,*
*God understands me and my pain.*
*Each area that concerns me and*
*my welfare is a priority with Him.*
*There is no part of my world that He doesn't view*
*as essential and important.*

*So never under estimate the love of your God and Father. Your every thought is on His mind and your every cry He hears and has comfort in mind for you.*

# *May 16*

*Psalm 133*

## *Together in the Spirit*

*Unity among the believers is essential and imperative. When we*
*are on one accord, Jesus said the church is invincible.*
*All the power if heaven is unleashed and at the disposal of the*
*church of Christ when it is of one heart.*
*Notice that the birth of the church happened*
*when it was in one accord.*
*The power of God was evident when Peter was imprisoned and*
*that power brought about his miraculous deliverance.*
*Jesus said that when we agree touching anything, anything on*
*earth, it would happen just as we ask.*
*The gates of hell are defeated when the church*
*has one mind and one heart.*
*The place of unity is bounded by love,*
*fueled by faith and acted on by prayer.*
*Here is where God commands a blessing.*
*Here is where God commands life and unity.*
*Even two can bring about the impossible, if they act together on*
*one accord in Jesus name and for His glory.*

# *May 17*

Proverbs 13

### *Only Pride Will Cause a Fight*

**"Only by pride cometh contention:**
**but with the well advised is wisdom."**
**vs.10**

When there is a fight, it is because someone

or everyone has an ego problem.

Don't blame me, I didn't say it;

**He did.**

Whether it is as small as two friends, a married couple, or as

major as a world war; conflict only arises because of pride.

The Holy Spirit opens up the intents and motives of the psyche to

show us where our pride will lead us.

It is a biblical absolute: only by pride will contentions come.

The reason Jesus never lost an argument with His enemies; He

showed that He had no personal animus.

He never needed to defend His position. He remained totally

objective because He never once did anything for Himself.

His ambition was always the will of the Father, His motives

always the Kingdom.

*His love was never self-focused; His heart only saw others. How could He then lose? He never had to fight; His enemies were destroyed just because of their own pride.*

*You don't have to have everything your way. Sometimes it's better to yield and learn to be patient.*

*And in those moments when there can be no compromise, ask the Holy Spirit to teach you how to stand firm without ego or pride. You'll find that you'll get much more accomplished in peace than by war.*

# *May 18*

## *Psalm 15*
### *His Tabernacle, His Holy Hill*

*Fellowship with God: nothing on earth compares to it.*
*The question David asks is a challenge as much*
*for himself as for others.*
*He is examining his own hand and life;*
*he questions his own integrity and qualifications.*
*This long list of requirements challenges his holiness and purity.*
*God is holy and righteous.*
*To fellowship with Him requires not absolute perfection, but*
*instead purely absolute consecration.*
*This is obtained by someone who is determined*
*to live an exemplary life; someone who constantly assesses*
*the integrity of their lifestyle.*
*The heart of this man is set and determined to keep as close to*
*the Lord as possible by honoring Him with a holy life.*
*This psalm should be one that is in*
*the constant memory of every believer.*
*When we remember all that He is and has given to us, the ques-*
*tion of personal dedication to Him should be answered with*
*adoring love and obedience.*

# *May 19*

## Psalm 14
### *There Really is a God*

**"The fool hath said in his heart, There is no God."**

**vs.1**

In the original Hebrew text, the words "there is" cannot be found.
The fool has not said "God does not exist" he has said instead,
"No" to the God he knows exists.
He has defiantly said to the Lord of Creation, "I refuse to obey
you", "I will never serve you."
The reason why the prophet refers to him a fool is because this
man knows who God is, knows that He is all powerful and knows
personally that God is the judge of all the earth.
This can only mean that one day God will call him to account and
on the day of judgment he will confess that He **is** God Almighty
and King of kings and Lord of lords (Philippians 2:11).
This is non-negotiable and an absolute fact, he will own God
as Jehovah – not because he wants to, not even because
he is forced to, he will because the universal law of
God's majesty will compel him.
Fool or saint, all will confess Him as Lord and God.

# *May 20*

## *Psalm 44*

### *The Only True God*

**"Through thee will we push down our enemies: through thy name will we tread them under that rise up against us. For I will not trust in my bow, neither shall my sword save me. But thou hast saved us from our enemies, and hast put them to shame that hated us. In God we boast all the day long, and praise thy name for ever. Selah."**

**vs. 5-8**

*It is a sad faith or religion that follows a god that must fight his battles by using children as bombs.*
*It is a pitiful teaching when a deity requires its followers to kill its enemies.*
*Poorly conceived is the myth of a god that requires his followers to hate his enemies.*
*Our God, the Lord God Almighty, demands in Christ, that we must love our enemies.*
*Pray for those who would abuse you and for the one who would otherwise seek to destroy you.*

*We may boast in our Lord, for He brings us into the battle only to observe the conflict and return to tell the story of the victory (Psalm 91:8).*

*God can assign us the task of living out this life before others by doing good, thereby bringing about great glory to Him.*

*The battle is the Lord's.*

*Don't you ever forget that.*

*And we who love Him love to show the truth of His mighty wonders and the amazing depths of His great love.*

***He is the only true God!!***

# *May 21*

## Psalm 45
### *He is High and Lifted Up*

*This mesmerizing Psalm discovers for us the glorious majesty
and deity of Jesus – high and lifted up.*
*The Holy Spirit, for the first time in scripture, gives us a glimpse
in the high throne room of glory.*
*There we see the coronation scene of eternity. How we see the
2nd person of the Godhead being crowned with the diadem, the
multifaceted crown, reflecting the kingdoms He has conquered,
revealing the kings that must bow before Him. He has been
handed the scepter of righteousness, because He is the rightful
sovereign of the universe.*
*He is anointed with the oil of gladness because
He has eliminated sorrow.*
*He is robed with the ephod of glory, for He is the King of glory.*
*Oh, what a wonder it will be to see Him
given all that He deserves.*
*This King is not just to be obeyed, He is to be worshipped (vs.11),
adored, magnified and praised.*
*We'll be there, observing it all around the throne,
worshipping Him in glory!*

*Going Further*

*Decision*

## *Week Twenty-Two*

> *It is time for spring cleaning.*
> *Not your home but your heart.*
> *Look into those places where*
> *you may have become compla-*
> *cent, apathetic, or lazy. Open*
> *the closed closets and dark*
> *corners of your soul; stretch the*
> *lax muscles of your person and*
> *move toward the Lord in each*
> *of those areas.*

## *May 22*

*Psalm 74*

### *Don't Give Up!*

*It is hard to yield to the Spirit of God when He asks us to lay our
weapons down and let the enemy win the battle.*
*It is extremely difficult to submit to God's will and allow the
enemy to seemingly win the conflict.*
*To place our future into the Lord's hand, knowing that He expects
us to submit to the will of the wicked.*
*All too often, God's plan to judge the wicked must take
the path of grace first.*
*God wants every person to be given the option to choose Him.*
*Maximizing grace and its power, sometimes means that the hea-
then must be given power over God's people (Genesis 15:13-16).*
*Being a willing servant of the King often means that we may
never understand what God is doing, but trust Him that what He
is doing will bring about His will. The admonishment is simple
from the pen of the apostle Paul "Be not weary of well doing"
(Galatians 6:9).*
*God's plan brings Him great glory.*
*Don't be discouraged pilgrim; we will reap, if we faint not.*

# *May 23*

*Psalm 75*

**God is the Judge**

**"For promotion cometh neither from the east, nor from the west, nor from the south. But God is the judge: he putteth down one, and setteth up another."**

***vs.6-7***

*No one can stop you when God has set your path.*

*The will of the King has been set, no one can stop it.*

*Every person that declares Him King and Lord is set in a position*

*that's set in Christ – and was part of His will before the world*

*began; before it was planned and ordained.*

*To the heaven above, and the earth below, God has declared that*

*His counsel will stand; no one can pervert His will.*

*No government or power; secular, satanic,*

*or social can alter His will.*

*Listen Christian, rest in the peace that God created you*

*with a divine and specific plan that will be accomplished*

*no matter what.*

*Stand and live in the truth that His divine purpose will come to*

*pass, no one can stop it and He, as always, will bring about His*

*glory in your life.*

*Don't worry about circumstances or the powers*
*that are around you; God is the judge.*
*And because He is also King He'll move the entire world,*
*if necessary, to bring about His plan for you.*

# *May 24*

*Psalm 104*

**Think On Jesus**

**"My meditation of him shall be sweet:**
**I will be glad in the LORD."**
**vs.34**

*There are 7 things that are the basics to maintaining*
*a health spiritual life.*
*The first is **prayer** – talking to God is a must and the Holy Spirit,*
*through the hand of Paul, says we should do it without ceasing*
*(I Thessalonians 5:17).*
*The second is **praise** – the fruit of my lips regaling to God all that*
*He is to me, and extolling my love for Him.*
*Remember the Holy Spirit admonishes that praise should be a*
*constant in life (Psalm 34:1).*
*Then there is **worship** – the fruit of my being; a God honoring life*
*that is proven and perpetuated by my absolute obedience to Him*
*in every area of my walk, and saying to Him everything He has*
*said about Himself.*
*Then there is **study** – projects in His word that cause me to trust*
*and know Him better.*

*Then, as is mentioned here (vs.34),* **meditation** *–*

*thinking on Him and the Kingdom in my quiet time, allowing Him*

*to inundate my heart and thoughts,*

*Then there must be* **fellowship** *with His people around His word*

*(I John 1:3).*

*Then lastly,* **witnessing** *– sharing my life in Christ with others.*

*These 7 things will yield a healthy and holy life in Him.*

*A life that will be full and satisfying.*

# *May 25*

*Psalm 105*

### *Seek the Lord*

***"Seek the LORD, and his strength: seek his face evermore."***

***vs.4***

*There are two pursuits that every person must have.*
*First is to know God and the second, much less important,*
*is to know oneself.*
*To know God, the apostle Paul reveals to us, is worth more*
*than any other possession in the world.*
*The Psalmist instructs us to get to know Him by three means.*
*Seek the Lord – get to know the person of the Lord. This means*
*intimating with Him not only as Father, but also as friend. Con-*
*fide in Him in all areas of life. Give Him that secret place that is*
*meant only for Him, and allow your heart to fall in love with Him.*
*Second, seek His power – Learn what it means to be empowered*
*by Him to do His service.*
*There is amazing joy and fulfillment in doing His perfect will.*
*Finally, seek His presence – Get to know*
*the intimate nature of God.*

*Learn what it means to know God's heart.*

*He pleads with us to come before Him,*

*and to know His heart, and seek His face.*

# *May 26*

## Psalm 144
## **The Perfect Society**

*"I will sing a new song unto thee, O God:
upon a psaltery and an instrument of ten strings will I sing
praises unto thee. It is he that giveth salvation unto kings:
who delivereth David his servant from the hurtful sword.
Rid me, and deliver me from the hand of strange children,
whose mouth speaketh vanity, and their right hand is a
right hand of falsehood: That our sons may be as plants
grown up in their youth; that our daughters may be as
corner stones, polished after the similitude of a palace: That
our garners may be full, affording all manner of store: that
our sheep may bring forth thousands and ten thousands
in our streets: That our oxen may be strong to labour; that
there be no breaking in, nor going out; that there be no complaining in our streets. Happy is that people, that is in such
a case: yea, happy is that people, whose God is the LORD."*
*vs.9-15*

*A perfect world is possible; a world where happiness is the rule
not the exception.*

*A community of life where children are protected*
*and families are a safe haven.*
*The Kingdom agenda allows only for a perfect society.*
*Not a near perfect society, but a true perfect society.*
*One where the benefits of the family are a true witness*
*to the world of the God we love.*
*This is not another worldview philosophy;*
*this is achievable and possible now.*
*How?*
*David says, when I order my lifestyle to be one of worship*
*and praise, and as I acknowledge my God as King,*
*His righteous plan will take control and will work out all the*
*knots that cause pain and confusion.*
*When He is given rightful place all the forces of heaven enforce*
*His will against the enemies of the Kingdom.*
*No one, not one thing can lay challenge to His authority.*
*This is a biblical absolute, our sons and our daughters,*
*and the prosperity of our homes will flow with divine power,*
*honor and purpose.*
*In this perfect society every promise of God*
*will be realized in our lives.*

# *May 27*

*Psalm 145*

### *The Benefits of Divine Favor*

*"He will fulfil the desire of them that fear him: he also will hear their cry, and will save them."*

*vs.19*

*It is amazing that God is willing to make such an outlandish promise, "He will fulfill the desire".*
*At first glance that appears to be a God sanctioned license to anything/everything.*
*It seems that God is opening an enormous door that lets all of man's fleshly passions to be expressed and pursued with impartiality.*
*This is so not like God.*
*Why would God give fallen man, no matter how holy he tries to be, why would He let the flood gates of man's nature open without restraint to do whatever it wants?*
*The answer is simple: God gives this promise only to those who*
### *Fear Him!*
*God gives His blessing of pleasure to the heart that is yielded and that is humble and surrendered.*

*He knows that when we honor Him in His holiness, we will not, cannot turn to dishonor Him at the same time.*

*Do you want that world where God feels free to fulfill your desires? "Fear the Lord all ye His saints" Watch what will happen to him whom He chooses to bless.*

# *May 28*

*Proverbs 14*

### *A Message from Mess*

**"Where no oxen are, the crib is clean:**

**but much increase is by the strength of the ox."**

**vs.4**

*A biblical lesson from manure;*

*Can wisdom, I mean wisdom from God, come from noting the*

*amount of manure that comes from a bull?*

*Absolutely.*

*We have in many cases become small groups of people who*

*refuse to fully fellowship in community and brotherhood because*

*of the fear of conflict.*

*We have shamed accountability and confession;*

*we have avoided "iron sharpening iron" because of fear of hurt*

*feelings, and betrayal.*

*So the things that are imperative and*

*essential for our growth as a family never happen.*

*Solomon explains simply, where there are individuals there will*

*be things that happen that aren't pleasant and even smell!*

*But those are not reasons to avoid the effort.*

*Just the opposite; it is all the more reason to risk interaction.*

*We need each other; we need to risk hurt feelings and conflict. We are to be engaged in the lives of the people around us, the impact is worth it, because the results and rewards are a family that has learned the hard way to love.*

# *May 29*

*Proverbs 15*

### *Rise Above It*

**"The way of life is above to the wise,**
**that he may depart from hell beneath"**
**vs.24**

The eagle is the only bird that is not affected
negatively by a bad storm.
The storm never impedes the eagle and his journey.
When storms gather, the eagle, instead of hiding, rises above the
clouds and rain; he mounts up to higher jet streams and uses the
power of the winds to help move him on his way.
This should be the mindset of the believer.
Despite the powerful storms, we are given the ability to "mount
up with wings as the eagle".
Ours is the heights of glory not the depths of despair.
Don't you dare allow circumstances around impede your growth
in Christ. Survive believer!
Employ the full blessings and promises of God and rise above all
that would hold you back!

*As this passage says, "the way of life is above to the wise",*

*rise up believer and live to honor Him every day*

*with your praise and worship!!*

# *May 30*

*Psalm 8*

**Why God, why?**

**"What is man, that thou art mindful of him?**
**And the son of man, that thou visitest him?"**

**vs.4**

*I guess from our vantage point it is ridiculous to question God as*
*to the reasons and motives of His divine grace and amazing love.*
*We benefit so greatly by receiving the bounty of His kingdom,*
*being elevated to the highest position obtainable by mortal man:*
*Heirs of God and joint heirs with Jesus Christ (Romans 8:17).*
*But how does it benefit Him?*
*What does a high and holy God get for taking sinful, traitorous*
*humanity into His bosom and sacrificing the life of His son Jesus?*
*So matchless and infinite His actions, one would assume so must*
*His reasons and motives must be.*
*What is man?*
*Why are you mindful of him?*
*Why do you come down to love and save him?*
*Why send and give your only son?*

*Only God knows, He alone can justify His actions; only He is com-*

*pletely satisfied with His plan to redeem the saints.*

*We may never know, He may never decide to tell us.*

*But let us worship and adore Him.*

*Let's honor His love-gift by living exclusively for Him.*

# *May 31*

## Psalm 16

### *The Path of Life*

**"Thou wilt shew me the path of life: in thy presence
is fulness of joy; at thy right hand there are
pleasures for evermore." vs.11**

*Where are we going?*

*When will we get there?*

*How many parents have heard those questions*

*from the backseat of the car?*

*I have counseled many people who want*

*those same answers about life.*

*"If God would just tell me where He is taking me, or when I'll*

*finally get there, then I could be at peace and I wouldn't find*

*myself making so many bad choices."*

*But that's just it, isn't it? God will show us where we are heading*

*and what we are to be doing along the way.*

*David says the answers are obvious.*

*They are all revealed in His presence.*

*They are all appropriated at His right hand.*

*God wants us to relate before He will reveal.*

*Two of the most wonderful words in all creation are used here.*

*These two words are the most sought after*

*experiences in all humanity.*

*People pay massive amounts of money for them, yet they are only*

*found here: in His presence – joy, at His right hand – pleasure.*

# *June*

## *A Time for Implementation*

**Lesson:** The Word of the God

**"For it is sanctified by the word of God and prayer."**

I Timothy 4:5

*T*he only way anyone or anything can be sanctified is by the **Word of God**.

God Himself must validate and authenticate every transaction before it can be deemed, "holy".

Religious legalists were trying in Timothy's day to compromise the true work of the Spirit by placing unrealistic and unreasonable conditions for salvation. The life of the believers at Ephesus was difficult enough for them given the fact of persecution from the Jews and the Romans; as well as from the many and varied cults that enslaved that city. But for there to be further afflictions from within, claiming that the true work of the Spirit was incomplete strained the believers there beyond reason.

Paul warns Timothy that the practices of the legalists were more unholy than the actions they were seeking to condemn.

The danger of legalism has existed from the beginning. There will always be those who seek to validate their holiness by comparisons and criticisms.

Paul gives his disciple clear instructions on how to handle this situation in a God honoring way.

Only the **Word of God** can determine holiness and genuine heart intent.

People are not given the right to pronounce divine honors or declare judgment without the Holy Spirits' absolute authority.

Gods' word has not been placed in the hands of a few. He alone grants the acceptance or rejection of all things.

Jesus on several occasions placed the entire weight of truth on Gods' word (John 17:17). He shouldered all the power of life there also (John 6:63b). There is no power in all creation that can come close to the power in the word of God.

*Outline of the Passage*

    A.  A truly grateful heart seeks to glorify God

    B.  A tender godly heart sees only a good God

    C.  A trusting gracious heart senses the glory of God

*Facts:* **The month of June, sixth month of the Gregorian calendar.**

It corresponds to the month of Sivan; the third month of the Hebrew calendar. Asa causes Israel to repent and recommit to the covenant with God.

*Focus:* **Prayer and planning.**

Forward thinking and planning is strategic in our personal warfare. If we plan for the attacks of the wicked one, he will not be able to get advantage.

*Assignment:* **Research**

Make a list of all the offerings and sacrifices.

*Memory Work:*

**Exaltation:** Psalm 34:3

**Excellence:** Psalm 1:1

**Edification:** Psalm 34:8

**Evangelical:** John 14:6

**Exhortive:** Proverbs 3:5, 6

**Educational:** Colossians 2:9

*Getting it Done*

*Implementation*

## *Week Twenty-Three*

---

*You have been thinking about witnessing to someone you know; do it.*

---

# *June 1*

## Psalm 46

### *Be Still and Know*

**"Be still, and know that I am God: I will be exalted among the heathen, I will be exalted in the earth." vs. 10**

*There's always a way.*
*Sennacherib had surrounded the city of Jerusalem.*
*As a conquering king, he had many great empires that had fallen*
*under his boot. There seemed to be no way out and the city was*
*cut off from the water it needed to survive.*
*All hope was gone.*
*With his enemies outside the gate Hezekiah*
*could have been discouraged and given up,*
*instead he did what we all should do when the enemy*
*sets up camp around us and has plans to wipe us out.*
*Employ the God factor. Do what Hezekiah did.*
*He prayed. Then the prophet prophesied, and the Lord moved, a*
*way was found that no one had ever considered; the way that the*
*Lord had made before there ever was a problem.*
*God wants to be God in every area of our world.*
*To "be still and see" the faith that is required here is based on the*
*facts of God's past dealings with Israel.*

*The heart that is afraid need only look back at a loving Father
who is faithful, a good God that is supportive and kind.
Bring Him all your problems, let Him be God; be still and know...*

# *June 2*

*Psalm 76*

### *Let's Talk About a Good God*

*It is important to list all the wonderful attributes
and works of God. Never would there be enough time to tell all
the story of our God and His goodness.
There would never be enough computer space; there could never
be enough libraries to house the information. But that doesn't
mean we shouldn't try.
Let's talk about His goodness, let's brag about His power, let's
regale His deeds of might and glory; let's say to the world what
our God has done.
Let's pull up the chairs around the table and speak one by one
about all the Lord has done for us.
Let's write down the things that could only be done by God.
Forever let us compare Him to the idols
that cannot love or speak.
Let us interview those who have no hope
and hear their despair, then let us give them the news about the
living God who can only do great things!*

# *June 3*

## *Psalm 106*
### *Don't Ever Forget*

*Sometimes it's very healthy to reflect; recall what your life has been about, both the good and the bad.*
*When things seemed to go astray and when things all seemed to work, the highs and the lows.*
*The psalmist does that here, he gives all the news; Israel in her glory, Israel in her shame.*
*He lays bare all the dirty laundry and gives no excuses, but is honest about the things the Jews should be ashamed of. But also he is careful and clear to report the constant that God was always there.*
*Sometimes He delivered them from an enemy that was too great for them, sometimes He was empowering their enemies to overcome them because of their sins against Him, but regardless of what God did, he reports fairly why God did what He did.*
*It was always for Israel's best and His glory. Every person in the body has a history with God; good times and bad times, but God has always been there.*
*Please don't ever forget that.*

# *June 4*

## Psalm 136
### **His Mercy Endures**

*Mercy is the compassion shown on one that is either
less than you or in a situation that places them in jeopardy
and puts them in a position of need that you have the power
and resources to correct.*

*The Holy Spirit often uses the word "loving-kindness" to reveal
not only the act shown, but the heart of the one showing it.*

*Here the prophet does just that, He remembers the acts of God in
Israel's history but most importantly he reminds us of His heart.*

*God is **so** good and His nature and character act out His goodness among the people He loves in so many ways. Sometimes it is
seen in His provision, oftentimes in His deliverance.*

*Yes and sometimes we see His great love through His chastening.
But it is always from the love of His heart.*

*Pull back, reflect, and remember, He is your great God, despite
what has happened in your life, His mercy endures.*

# *June 5*

*Proverbs 16*

### *How to Live Your Dreams*

**"Commit thy works unto the LORD,**
**and thy thoughts shall be established."**
**vs.3**

*Psalm 37:4 says* **"Delight thyself also in the Lord, and He will**
**give you the desires of thine heart."**

*The meaning is a little deep.*
*He's saying that if we delight in the Lord,*
*He will not give us our own hearts' desire, no;*
*He will give our hearts the desires to desire.*
*The same is the point here, if we commit our works to Him,*
*to His will and purpose, never taking control again, He will cause*
*the dreams and ideas in our hearts to happen.*
*Why?*
*Because with Him in control of our lives, the very things we*
*pursue will be for His glory, and His kingdom agenda will per-*
*meate every thought we have.*

*The tainted easily influenced thoughts we have apart*
*from His way will only stall and short circuit true purpose*
*and godly accomplishments.*
*Commit yourself to Him and His will, you'll find out how great He*
*truly is and how much more satisfying your life could be.*

# *June 6*

*Psalm 17*

### *The Apple of His Eye*

### *"Keep me as the apple of the eye,*
### *hide me under the shadow of thy wings"*
### *vs.8*

*Physically there is nothing more sensitive than the human eye.*
*The smallest invasion will interrupt whatever we're involved in*
*to investigate and correct the problem.*
*It's amazing isn't it that the problem could be caused by some-*
*thing nearly microscopic, but no matter what it is, the eye and its*
*comfort must be secure at nearly all costs.*
*The point that the Holy Spirit illustrates is blatantly clear.*
*God places us in care and is so sensitive about what happens to*
*us, the only human point of comparison is the understanding of*
*how it feels to have something in your eyes.*
*We have the security of a Father who is so acutely aware of our*
*situation, that like as a foreign object has violated our eyes, so is*
*He aware of anything that might jeopardize our wellbeing and*
*with even greater passion, He will come to our aid and lovingly*
*make things right.*

# *June 7*

*Psalm 18*

### *My (x8)*

*"I will love thee, O LORD, my strength. The LORD is my rock, and my fortress, and my deliverer; my God, my strength, in whom I will trust; my buckler, and the horn of my salvation, and my high tower."*

*vs.1-2*

*My strength – Who can overpower me? My rock – Who can overcome me? My Fortress – Who can outflank me?*
*My deliverer – Who can oppress me? My God – Who can overwhelm me? My buckler – Who can oppose me? My salvation – Who can offend me? My high tower – Who can overtake me?*
*These are the eight declarations of a secure man.*
*Each area of his life that was before vulnerable, God has secured.*
*Everyone knows that in the field of battle, the most coveted position is the high ground.*
*Well, in Christ we have taken the high ground, we have the high ground, and we'll keep the high ground.*
*He is everything we need.*
*He is not a mere ally; one that fights with us because we share the same enemy.*

*No, He is the Captain of the Lord's Host,*

*He it is that fights the battle.*

*He is best at waging and winning the war.*

*The Lord God of Hosts (Jehovah-Sabboath) is His warrior name,*

*and He is mighty to save, regardless of the conflict.*

*Getting it Done*

*Implementation*

## *Week Twenty-Four*

*There is a matter
that you've been struggling
with for too long now; come up
with a plan and attack it before
it is too late!*

# *June 8*

*Psalm 47*

### *Sing Praises (x4)*

**"Sing praises to God, sing praises: sing praises unto our King, sing praises. For God is the King of all the earth: sing ye praises with understanding."**

**vs.6-7**

*Four times in two verses the psalmist commands "sing praises". The point seems to be extremely important to him. Praise is the offering of our lips, produced from the overflow of our grateful hearts.*

*When praise is commanded it is always because of the truth that God has done exactly what He said.*

*He continually keeps His word. Every one of His assurances and promises has a flawless track record. God not only commands that we praise Him, He demands that we praise Him.*

*But He shouldn't have to demand that we praise Him, because quite simply He deserves it.*

*After all He has done and with what great love He has shown to us in every situation, praise from us should be spontaneous.*

*Despite our constant sin and high treason against Him,*
*He deserves the praise of our lips and the true adoration*
*of our hearts.*
*Make it a priority in your day to pause several times and deliber-*
*ately offer Him the gift of your praise.*

# June 9

### Psalm 48
### The City of God

**"Great is the LORD, and greatly to be praised in the city of our God, in the mountain of his holiness. Beautiful for situation, the joy of the whole earth, is mount Zion, on the sides of the north, the city of the great King."**
***vs.1-2***

*It is glorious and magnificent, high and holy, the city of our God;*
*not to be compared with anything in all of creation.*
*This prepared place, this home in heaven, the new Jerusalem,*
*fixed and fitted to be the high home of the Universe's King!*
*The place of His dwelling, the celestial dwelling*
*of the family of God! This perfect place is described so perfectly*
*here; the sing-song method the sons of Korah use helps us to*
*understand the great feeling of celebration that comes only from*
*the residents of righteousness.*
*God has crafted this wonderful place after the architecture of His*
*divine holiness. The perfection of His planning is so structurally*
*sound it will continually echo His praises. What a sight! What*
*sounds! It is the apex of all visible, vocal and victorious worship.*

*Any human construction wouldn't be able*
*to handle the sounds alone. Rejoice!*
*Soon and very soon, we are going to see the King!*
*Hallelujah!*

# June 10

*Psalm 77*

### Remember

*There are 8 types of psalms: psalms of rejoicing – Psalm 136, psalms of rescue – Psalm 18, psalms of return – Psalm 126, psalms of repentance – Psalm 51, psalms of revenge – Psalm 69, psalms of relief – Psalm 55, psalms of restoration – Psalm 67, and psalms of remembrance – Psalm 78.*

*This psalm was written to remind Israel that despite the many hardships it has suffered, the people of God have endured.*

*This is a call to remember the great provision God has made for Israel throughout His long relationship with them and because He loves them dearly.*

*His care and kindness is replete throughout their years. Often it is easy to forget just how great our God is. If there isn't a concerted effort to recall all that God has done, we'll permanently forget all that He is, and all that He will do.*

*Don't ever allow yourself to forget.*

# June 11

*Psalm 78*

### *Be Careful What You Ask For*

*It is a wonder to think that God would give to mankind the very
things that he wants, knowing that it will eventually destroy him.
Israel pressed God and begged God to give them things that could
only hurt them in the long run.*

*God knows that by begging to be like other nations, they would
become just that, like other nations!*

*The allure of the world is so strong because the world cun-
ningly masks all the consequences of its lifestyle, never honestly
showing that "the wages of sin is death". Advertisers never show
the cancer wards filled with people who have smoked all their
lives, casinos never report the number of people who've lost their
homes and gone bankrupt.*

*Beer ads never show what it means to live in an
abusive household because of parents that have gone mad
from a lifetime of drinking.*

*God still, in His great love, knows what will happen if we're
allowed to go our way, yet He sometimes needs to give us what
we want to show us what we truly need.*

# *June 12*

*Psalm 107*

**Soul Talk**

*Four times in this chapter, God shows the desperate condition*
*man puts himself into and the consequence and the result of very*
*bad decisions and lifestyle.*
*Four times the writer implores mankind*
*to be humble and contrite.*
*He wants us to stop and assess the past, look at all the things God*
*has done, to look and see clearly how good God has been.*
*He begs us to consolidate our thinking toward*
*knowing Him by living righteously, because,*
*as is mentioned in verse 9; God satisfies.*
*Absolutely and completely, never once does God offer man any-*
*thing that would harm or destroy him.*
*His great love permeates every action*
*and His grace is on every gift.*
*If you are really interested in the real life,*
*follow the instructions of this psalm.*
*Worship Him.*
*In this small and simple chapter you'll uncover the vast wisdom*
*and glory of the happy life.*

# June 13

*Psalm 108*

### The Lord's Right Hand

**"That thy beloved may be delivered:**
**save with thy right hand, and answer me."**
**vs.6**

*In the scriptures, the right hand signified*
*the area of a man's strength.*
*As the most people born are right handed, the analogy here is*
*that the strong position to take is the one of the right hand, the*
*side of strength and the side of battle.*
*The greatest complement to a fellow soldier was to say to him:*
*"You're my right-hand man" i.e., you're the one I rely on.*
*For strength and skill David says to the Lord,*
*"Do what only you can do".*
*"Use the strength of your greatness*
*and power to make my situation right."*
*Over and over in the psalms, David asks for God's help*
*and deliverance, knowing that no one could ever defeat His Lord.*
*The right hand of the Lord is the warrior side, the battle side,*
*the winning side.*

*Trust in the Lord, your right-hand man, the battle is His and you can only win when He is at your side.*

# June 14

## Psalm 137
### Keep Looking Up

*Christians and Christianity are the only things in our society that can be attacked with impunity.*

*The world will allow other religions, ideologies, and philosophies to kill, maim, enslave and restrict, and their teachings can be as hateful and prejudiced without constraint. But those that follow the Lord Jesus Christ are constantly bombarded with the scorn and attacks of evil men with evil intentions.*

*Despite all of this, our God knows and reminds us that the day of His wrath and the hour of our deliverance are not far away.*

*Take heart, for whether on your job, in your neighborhood or even with your family, God sees it all and His eternal plan will not be hindered or defeated.*

*Keep your hand on the plow, don't look back, and keep your heart looking toward home.*

*God is going to get the glory and you'll get the blessing.*

*Don't faint, look up!*

*Your redemption draws nigh.*

*Getting it Done*

*Implementation*

## *Week Twenty-Five*

*You know that memorizing scripture is essential to your growth; each day this week memorize and retain two verses.*

# June 15

## Psalm 138
### *"I'll Stop Being God"*

**"I will worship toward thy holy temple, and praise thy name for thy lovingkindness and for thy truth: for thou hast magnified thy word above all thy name."**

**vs.2**

*That's what that little phrase means at the end of verse 2. God places His entire honor in the truth and certainty of His word.*

*His name means nothing if His word cannot be trusted.*

*His word throughout the ages has been tested, tried, attacked, manipulated, misinterpreted and even twisted yet despite all of these things, His word, His true word had never failed, been defeated or compromised.*

*Our great and wonderful Savior has never lied, and never will. That's why His name is so great!*

*He can be relied on to do what only He can do, because He has all power and because He has this long breath of history, all of which He has done as promised. He has every right to hold sacred His name, despite our feelings, by faith allowing Him in His own time and way to do the miraculous and the wonderful.*

# *June 16*

*Proverbs 17*

### Evil Becomes Good, Good Becomes Evil

**"He that justifieth the wicked, and he that condemneth the just, even they both are abomination to the LORD."**
**vs.15**

*It is the ultimate perversion, to declare what is truly evil, good and right; and to determine what is good and holy, evil.*
*If nothing else, this pattern of the subverting of that which is holy and right for all that is evil and sinful, proves that man is a moral creature whose pursuit of the fulfillment of his sinful nature will only increase toward more evil and decadence.*
*The teachings of King Solomon bear out in this verse, that it is more than just choosing evil over good, it shows that the desire of sin is to justify itself for its wickedness.*
*To keep oneself away from the tide of destruction, the believer must stay close to the Lord and constantly in His word. Jesus said "the words I speak unto you, they are spirit and they are life." Know His word and live the righteous life.*

# June 17

*Proverbs 18*

## *Benefits of Believing*

*What a wealth of wisdom is found in this chapter.*
*The Lord reveals so much for hearts to ponder,*
*so many axioms of truth that if applied sincerely, correctly,*
*and diligently will yield divine favor.*
*Verse 10 tells us that the name of the Lord*
*provides safety for the righteous.*
*Verse 22 tells us that a man who has searched for and found a*
*wife has found a precious thing indeed and has gained favor for*
*himself from God Himself.*
*Verse 24 discovers the value of true friendship*
*over and above the conventional.*
*In fact, it tells us that a true friend will*
*surpass even a blood brother in loyalty.*
*The character in the wisdom found here is in stark*
*contrast to the world's wisdom.*
*The bible is real time application in the lives of people that trust*
*Him. Trust Him with all you have and reap the benefits.*

# June 18

*Psalm 19*

### *What More Could You Ask For?*

**"The law of the LORD is perfect, converting the soul: the testimony of the LORD is sure, making wise the simple."**

**vs.7**

We all have stains and sores on our souls from our sins and
choices that have scarred and twisted us.
We have done things contrary to God's word
and have reaped what we have sown.
There are so many warnings in the past that
we haven't listened to and heeded.
Without exception, we cannot fix ourselves;
the holes we've dug are too deep for us to repair. We need help
that is beyond ourselves, we need a divine plan that will take pity
on us and heal our souls.
**"The law of the Lord is perfect", "converting the soul."** The
word for converting is the same word we find in God's name
"Jehovah Rapha."
Rapha means to heal, to restore back to the original condition.
The word of God corrects us completely.

*Only God's word can change us completely and correctly. Trust in His word, stay in His word, and let it change your life and restore your soul.*

# June 19

## Psalm 49
### *Wrong Priorities*

*It is dangerous to be so driven by things and wealth that to see*

*only greed and possessions are the only things that matter.*

*The self-serving mindset of man has caused him to value wealth*

*and things over people.*

*The needs of the soul remain unchecked and the results are*

*people who are prosperous on the outside and desperately poor*

*on the inside.*

*Mankind sees itself as successful only because we have been*

*duped to believe that avarice means happiness.*

*Not so.*

*The life that Christ offers fulfills and satisfies;*

*but from the inside out.*

*He works in us and through us, and when that process is in*

*motion the outworking of His life is evident around us.*

*Don't lose sight of the big picture.*

*Cultivate your dependence on the life of God.*

*Resolve to live your life being fulfilled from the inside out.*

# June 20

*Psalm 79*

### *How Long?*

**"How long, LORD? wilt thou be angry forever?**
**Shall thy jealousy burn like fire?"**
**vs.5**

*It does seem like the rule and reign*
*of the unrighteous is permanent.*
*Sometimes it appears as though there is no chance for the righ-*
*teous to have a say or even know true justice.*
*In times of calamity it is easy to ask if God has forgotten us.*
*The days of affliction seem long and unending and the voices of*
*oppression mouthed by the ungodly seem relentless. But take*
*heart pilgrim, God has not forgotten us.*
*His ways and His timing are always perfect.*
*Even when deliverance is for the generation and not immediately*
*for the individual, our trust must go beyond our senses and trust*
*in the care we know.*
*God often places us, His people, before the world as sheep to the*
*slaughter, this is neither welcomed nor enjoyed.*
*But His desire from us is that we trust Him, and that we live day*
*by day knowing that our lives are based not on time, but eternity.*

# June 21

## Psalm 109
### Let God Do the Work

*It's part of this life, to be ridiculed maligned and insulted. The insolent find pleasure in slandering the right.*
*Even members of the family of God take personal pleasure in hurting the souls of others.*
*They relieve their own pain by causing it in other saints of God.*
*While this is wrong and certainly disheartening, it should not overtake us.*
*We were told by Christ that we should not be discouraged or offended (John 16:1).*
*The obstacles that we encounter will be used by the Holy Spirit to develop us and change us into His likeness.*
*We are given the power of God to endure and survive. Will it ever get better?*
*Probably not; for this side of glory offers very little in terms of comfort and relief.*
*All that the world offers for temporary good, it offers to those who will fit into its mold.*
*Rebel against it, our affirmation is found in Him alone.*

*Getting it Done*

*Implementation*

*Week Twenty-Six*

> *There is a bible project that you should devise and implement. If you need help creating one ask your pastor or Sunday school teacher for help.*

# June 22

*Psalm 139*

### Always There

**"Whither shall I go from thy spirit? or whither shall I flee from thy presence? If I ascend up into heaven, thou art there: if I make my bed in hell, behold, thou art there."**
**vs. 7-8**

He loves me, looks after me, and longs for me to be with Him.
This is the Savior we serve. He can guide us so well because He
goes with us everywhere.
He has no limits of time and space;
He knows no barriers to His great power.
One of His many character describing names is "Jehovah
Shammah" – The Lord is there!
How awesome it is that He identifies Himself
as one of His many perfect promises.
He's there!
Whatever, whenever, wherever, He's there, all the time, and in
every situation. He sees before (Genesis 22:14), He has prepared
for every contingency.
His great love refused to leave His children.
He is the Father/Friend that has no equal.

*He never abandons us; He is there because His attachment is based on incredible love, love that can never be broken; love that can only grow stronger.*

# *June 23*

*Proverbs 19*

### *Let It Go*

**"The discretion of a man deferreth his anger; and it is his glory to pass over a transgression."**

**vs. 11**

*Being wronged and mistreated is very hard to forgive;*
*even harder to forget.*
*We often see offence as a thing to revenge.*
*But true maturity sees that to hold bitterness*
*and anger against someone for what they may have done only*
*causes us the pain and suffering.*
*The need to hold the grudge and the desire*
*to seek vengeance only reflects immaturity and lack of trust*
*in God to make things right.*
*No one will ever yield to the idea that someone*
*not be challenged or held accountable for their actions,*
*especially when it comes to others hurt.*
*But the growth in our lives as we get closer to Jesus allows us to*
*forgive as He did (I Peter 2:21-23).*

*We can aid in the work of the Spirit in the lives*
*of those who have hurt or wronged us.*
*Be quick to forgive and let go of the things*
*that seek to destroy us.*

# June 24

## Psalm 20
### Some Trust in Chariots

**"Some trust in chariots, and some in horses: but we will remember the name of the LORD our God."**

**vs. 7**

*Power and might makes for false security,*
*when what we trust in is fallible.*
*At different times and ages the mechanisms of human conflict*
*change, but after a while they are replaced with even more pow-*
*erful and advanced instruments.*
*Each has its moment in the sun as the greatest in its class,*
*however, the fallacy in such situations is that soon something*
*greater will come along.*
*When we put our trust in the one who never changes,*
*when we see ourselves in the care of the one who has no equal,*
*we can rest totally secure.*
*He is the King that David places his trust. King Saul had all the*
*might and secular authority, but David had his trust in the only*
*power that had a perfect record.*
*God alone is the source of true security. Put your trust only in*
*Him and rest secure in His promise to fight your battles.*

# June 25

*Psalm 50*

### *The Gathering*

**"Gather my saints together unto me;**
**those that have made a covenant with me by sacrifice."**
**vs.5**

*He has set each moment since His ascension*
*to preparing a place for us.*
*He has adorned the splendor of His Kingdom*
*with the majesty of the New Jerusalem.*
*He has for His bride, the blood bought Church.*
*He will gather His saints in the air and the reunion that has been*
*the most anticipated event in the universe will take place. The*
*Lord is coming to take His Church home.*
*The requirement is that these have made*
*a covenant with Him by scripture, His blood paid*
*the price and the saints have made the choice.*
*Only those who have chosen to walk with Him*
*in covenant will spend eternity with Him.*

*Therefore, with great joy, the saints*
*look forward to His great promise.*
*Live the life, expect and live for His coming,*
*trust in the truth: He is coming back again.*

# June 26

*Psalm 80*

## Such Wonderful Love

*There is hope of the mercy of God when we sin.*
*He is the glorious God who is great in mercy and compassion.*
*He looks down at every man and knows his limitations*
*and weaknesses.*
*He knows what we are capable of and what lures us*
*away from Him.*
*He has been betrayed and abandoned by those whom*
*He has saved from hell, and has never, ever taken away*
*His love and forgiveness.*
*When the psalmist takes on the ministry of addressing the failure*
*of the saints to stay faithful, he calls upon the God he knows to do*
*what only He can do, forgive and repair.*
*All that saints need to do is call upon Him*
*and tell Him what He already knows.*
*If you have fallen, if you have strayed, go to Him in prayer,*
*confess your sin and bask in the light of His mercy.*
*He will abundantly pardon!*

# June 27

### Psalm 110

### **The Coronation**

*This is one of the greatest moments in scripture.*
*We see past the veil of the flesh and for a brief moment are*
*allowed to see into the throne room of heaven.*
*Here the Godhead places the control of the created*
*order into the hands of Christ.*
*He is given the throne; He is given the rule of the nations;*
*He is given the high rank of Great High Priest. All of the universe*
*will give Him worship and praise.*
*The rod of righteousness, the scepter of power,*
*and the throne of grace, are just a few of the honors*
*given to the Lord on the throne.*
*The thrice holy Lord of glory is lifted up and magnified. He is the*
*true King and everyone will worship Him.*
*When all of time is over and the kingdoms of this world are*
*become the kingdoms of our Lord and of His Christ, the world*
*will own Him as the great God; holy, just and true.*

# June 28

### Psalm 140
### Live the Life

All it takes to halt wicked men with ungodly intentions to rise
and do their evil is for the just to stand upon the principles of
holy living that the Lord has ordained.
The life and lifestyle of the believer lived out
before the world, excites and ignites.
It excites many of the lost to answer the call of the Holy Spirit
and give their lives to Him.
It causes the hurting and needy to turn to the Savior
for His great compassion.
But also, it ignites the ungodly to become fired up
to attack the saints.
The all impossible lifestyle of the Christian lived out before the
world, will also cause the unsaved to become angry with the
cause of Christ and desperate to destroy all those who dare live it.
Keep your focus and dare to live for Him. Some will be drawn to
Him for salvation; many others will rebel and reject Him.
Either way, He will be seen and ultimately glorified.

# June 29

*Proverbs 20*

**Protect Your Soul**

**"The fear of a king is as the roaring of a lion: whoso provo-
keth him to anger sinneth against his own soul"
vs.2**

*We are tripartite beings; three parts make us each one person.*
*We are not a trinity, where the three parts are*
*completely equal and in total unity.*
*God gave us a spirit to be God-aware, a soul to be self-aware,*
*and a body to be world-aware.*
*Who we are and how we identify ourselves would be*
*the matter and purpose of the soul.*
*We receive info and function day by day as souls,*
*but when we are in need or trouble, our soul looks to either*
*the flesh or the spirit for answers.*
*Throughout the bible, God warns us of the things*
*that will destroy our souls.*
*Fornication, adultery, dishonoring those in authority,*
*lying, those all war against our person and cause us to become*
*damaged within.*

*Take the advice of the spirit; avoid those things*
*that war against your soul.*
*Keep it clean and pure by following His word.*

# *June 30*

*Psalm 21*

### *King of the Universe*

**"For they intended evil against thee: they imagined a mischievous device, which they are not able to perform."**
**vs.11**

*God is Lord of all that is.*
*Every atom of every molecule of every cell*
*of everything must obey His will.*
*His Lordship is never in question, His rule can never be challenged, and His might and power can never be matched.*
*All evil intentions, all wicked plans and all the devices of evil are folly to Him, because He is God.*
*All that is, owes its existence to His permission.*
*At no time is that in question.*
*He commands all that is by the words of His mouth and never once has His authority been surrendered.*
*Mankind may stand in opposition to the will of God and against His people, but such opposition is merely words.*
*God will never permit His creation license to alter His will.*
*David rightly understood all of this and ends this psalm with this declaration: "Be thou exalted... praise thy power."*

# July

## A Time for Adjustments

*Lesson:* The Father of Mercies

**"Blessed be God, even the Father of our Lord Jesus Christ, the Father of mercies, and the God of all comfort"** II Corinthians 1:3

What a glory!

O ur God can be counted on *and* referred to as the "Father of Mercies"!

He is the originator of mercy, the provider of mercy, the source of mercy and the sustainer of mercy. He gives the sinner a chance at forgiveness; the broken a compassionate ear to cry to, and the lost a compass for their way. He knows our need and our weaknesses. He loves us in a manner that anticipates and accommodates our every situation. He, with God-only accuracy has the ability to know every action that will eventually require His love and care. And yet with all of His infinite greatness, He is able to know how very frail and fallen we are, and never ever alter His everlasting love for us.

You see, He sees after the needs of His family, just as a Father should. He perfectly supplies exactly what His children need in every aspect of their humanity, and lovingly showers His blessing of kindness in a way that only He can.

For mercy sees on the need and the needy; it seeks only to relieve and restore. It finds no solace in revenge or malice. It cares only about healing the hurting and the oppressed. God does this out of His nature. His acts of mercy are always enough and His deeds of compassion are never missed placed, because His loving-kindness flows from the essence of His deity and therefore can never be in error or misplaced.

Our God is so willing to grant this amazing gift because it is just another expression of His infinite love.

The Lord we know and love proves again and again that He alone is worthy of all our adoration. His merciful heart endears His children away from the cravings of their flesh and the strong offers of the world and Satan.

By the acts of His mercy it isn't very hard to understand the hymn writers' theme, "those who wholly know Him, know Him wholly true". We know Him wholly true because we have known His mercies, morning by morning.

### Outline of the Passage

Verse 3 explains for us the merciful heart of our Father

    A.  His mercy shows His loyalty to us

    B.  His mercy shows His love for us

    C.  His mercy shows His life for us

*Facts:* **The month of July, seventh month of the Gregorian calendar.**

It corresponds to the month of Tammuz; the fourth month of the Hebrew calendar. Taken by the Babylonian king, Nebuchadnezzar.

*Focus:* **Prayer and honesty.**

Work on becoming known as a person of true honesty. Become a person who can be counted on as trustworthy.

*Assignment:* **Research**

List the pilgrim journeys and their meanings.

**Memory Work:**

**Exaltation:** I Timothy 1:17

**Excellence:** II Corinthians 4:7

**Edification:** Jude 20

**Evangelical:** Isaiah 1:18

**Exhortive:** Psalm 23

**Educational:** I Thessalonians 5:18

## Making Changes

## Adjustments

# Week Twenty-Seven

> This week study the verses in
> Romans that discuss the plan
> of salvation; then become more
> acquainted with all that Christ
> in this book provides for us to
> live righteously.

# *July 1*

*Psalm 51*

**Mercy Lord, Please, Have Mercy**

*David uses three different words for mercy in this psalm. Here he gives full confession for the awful crimes he has committed. He uses the word "chanan" to first open his prayer to God.*
*It is the word that means pity.*
*It is the plea of one who is lesser to one who is greater. Then he uses the word "chesed", which means "lovingkindness".*
*As a noun David's use of the word implores God to act this way because this is what He does as God to those who would come to Him sincerely, begging for help.*
*Then he uses the word "tacham".*
*This word simply states that God can act mercifully because He is merciful.*
*Being merciful is not just what He does, it's who He is. We all mess up, we all knowingly sin.*
*When circumstances, consequences or conviction finally cause us to regain our sanity, God is there, He's there to show mercy if we come to Him in true contrition.*

# July 2

## Psalm 51

### *I Have Sinned*

*David uses three words to beg God for mercy; equally he uses three words to describe his crimes.*

*The first word "pasha" talks of the type of sin he committed.*

*A transgression is a knowingly, calculated act that was indifferent about the consequences.*

*Then his next word is "avon".*

*It means the motive of his sin. It takes on the meaning of a depraved act that can never be justified.*

*Lastly, he uses the word "chattah". He confesses the reason he acted this way; because he simply, is a sinner. Every sin ultimately is committed because of that one fact. We are sinners. We are sinners down to our genes and chromosomes, in our DNA and cell structure. We sin because we're sinners. With all that said, that is still no reason to sin.*

*God has given us His Son, His Scriptures and His Spirit.*

*There is no excuse for falling out of fellowship. If you've fallen, go to Him now.*

*Get the issue resolved; confess your sin and be whole again.*

# July 3

*Psalm 81*

### *Pilgrimage*

*Three times a year the men of Israel were to leave their home, from wherever they were and return to the holy city. Three times they were to leave everything they had behind and go up to Jerusalem and worship; once for Passover, once for the Feast of Pentecost, and once for the Feast of Booths. Each of their journeys was to remind them that they were pilgrims that they were in the land because the great God has given them this possession: because of His promise to Abraham, Isaac, and Jacob.*

*For the entire journey they were to sing praises to Him and recall the things He had done for them.*

*If they obeyed Him, His promise was that He would protect what they left behind and would secure the way before them, i.e., there was never a reason to fear or worry. He would maintain what was theirs if they honored what was His. Do God's business God's way. He has promised to keep us all along life's way.*

# July 4

## Psalm 111
### The Work of the Lord

*The prophet obviously is in awe of God's work!*
*Once while vacationing in Arizona,*
*I decided to visit the Grand Canyon.*
*At the welcome center there is a Native Indian tower and a*
*stone wall bracing against the deep gorge. On the wall there is a*
*plaque that reads: "All thy works shall praise thee, O Lord".*
*It amazed me that not only a plaque was there, praising God, but*
*more importantly, people were taking pictures of the plaque and*
*what it said as much as they were the views of the Canyon!*
*God's work should cause us to praise Him.*
*He has done nothing in error.*
*His love and mercy can never be depleted.*
*Stars and planets, woodlands, sunflowers, and yes,*
*deep gorges and lush meadows; all His works shall praise,*
*worship, and adore the King of Creation.*
*His works are great!*

# *July 5*

*Psalm 141*

### *The Prayer of God's Child*

*What an important prayer.*
*To ask God to help us in areas that we know we are weak.*
*Man, at his heart is fragile.*
*Every area of our world is vulnerable and exposed. Even in those*
*times when we feel most secure, a simple ill wind of life might*
*blow and all that we've done to be comfortable can be destroyed;*
*taken away in an instant.*
*To be aware that we are weak and helpless*
*is the first step in becoming strong.*
*When we are quick to hand over to Him*
*all of our concerns and let Him have all of our fears,*
*is the only way to survive in a totally hostile world.*
*David speaks for all of us.*
*The first place we need to master is the tongue.*
*We set in motion the most awful calamities*
*just by the words we say.*
*But the source of our words is our heart; there the real matters*
*of life are decided. Ask God to help where you're weak, depend on*
*Him to control your world, you'll find Him to be your best friend.*

# July 6

*Proverbs 21*

**Remember the Poor**

**"Whoso stoppeth his ears at the cry of the poor,**
**he also shall cry himself, but shall not be heard."**
**vs.13**

*"How dwelleth the love of God in Him?"*
*so ends the 17th verse of I John 3.*
*It is impossible to have the love of God in you and still not be*
*moved with compassion for the poor.*
*Over and over the Bible directs us*
*on how we are to treat the poor.*
*The prophet here warns that there are dire consequences for*
*those who would ignore the poor and they're cry for help. God*
*gives us a moral and spiritual measure for how we are to treat*
*them (Isaiah 1:17).*
*He expects us to show not pity but compassion and mercy.*
*Why?*
*Because truth be told, we're all poor; yes,*
*in some form or fashion we all are poor.*
*We all are deficient in ways that are impossible*
*for us to correct alone.*

*God wants us to consider the poor and needy as though it were we ourselves in pain.*

*Remember the poor today.*

*See them as agents of God's love for you to minister to. Put yourself in their world and show them love.*

# July 7

## Psalm 22
### *The Messiah's Cry*

*The most prophetic psalm in scripture,*
*four direct quotes from the cross, several more allusions,*
*and most stark is the very first verse.*
*Like no other words, they speak*
*to the awesome power of prophecy.*
*David had no way of knowing that the words he would be*
*speaking would speak the future life of the coming Christ. Only*
*the providence of God could articulate with absolute accuracy*
*the scenes around the cross over a thousand years before the*
*Lord's birth.*
*It puts to rest all the skeptics and critics;*
*the errors all those who look at the cross as just*
*a historic and not prophetic event are exposed.*
*All who turn away in disbelief must answer*
*to the reality of the power of God.*
*Look to your bible, find in it the infallible source of God's eternal*
*plan; find in it the eternal truth.*

*Making Changes*

*Adjustments*

## *Week Twenty-Eight*

*In Psalm 27:4, David reveals the one thing his heart desires. What is the one thing you desire above all else?*

# *July 8*

*Psalm 22*

**Lament from the Cross**

**"My God, my God, why hast thou forsaken me? why art thou so far from helping me, and from the words of my roaring?"**

**vs. 1**

*My God, my God, why?*
*It is the only question from the cross; the question asked to the*
*Father from the Son.*
*It is the most lamentable question ever spoken in the universe.*
*It is the sum total of what sin had cost.*
*For it shows that sin is so pervasive that God had to provide the*
*ultimate price: the life of His Son and for the briefest of moments,*
*broken fellowship with the Father. Why?*
*Verse 3 makes it clear: because "thou art holy". God had to turn*
*His back on the sin offering, even though the sin offering was His*
*Son (Habakkuk 1:13).*
*All of our sin past had to be paid by the blood of the innocent,*
*and as man's sin was so terrible, God's demand for an offering*
*had to be flawless, sinless... perfect.*
*Thus the Lord Jesus had to pay the full price.*

*When we look at the Christ we see all that is wonderful about the Kingdom. We see a God whose love for the world caused Him to give all He could to save it.*

# *July 9*

### *Psalm 52*
### *Thou Hast Done It*

**"I will praise thee forever, because thou hast done it: and I will wait on thy name; for it is good before thy saints."**
**vs. 9**

*As I have often said: "God has never written me a bad check."*
*Every promise He's made, He has fulfilled.*
*At no time has He ever been anything but amazing.*
*The imperative for our worship and praise is that rightly He is worthy of our adoration.*
*His love towards the saints and His care for their needs evokes exaltation and honor.*
*He has done it; He has redeemed us, He has filled us with His Spirit, He has justified us, He has sanctified and secured us, He has placed us into His family and provided a home in heaven.*
*He has done it!*
*Everything He has provided for the whole world; a Savior, and all that we have needed, He has abundantly given. Praise the Lord, He has done it!*

# July 10

### Psalm 82
### Love like Me

*The best of human action is at best human.*

*In other words, even when man tries to do well, because he was born in sin, his best could still be wrong.*

*To get the favor of God we must ask for His wisdom and discernment so that in all matters we can assess them righteously. God demands that those who seek to honor Him and appropriate His favor must have compassion on the weak and needy.*

*Remembering to regard, protect, and care for those less fortunate, but most importantly those whom God loves and takes pity on.*

*It is as much a character of godliness to help the hurting as it is to give your tithes and offerings.*

*God wants us to employ the love and mercy He has given to us in the service of helping others.*

*Love as He loves and you'll find it will make living as He lives so much easier.*

# *July 11*

## *Psalm 112*

### *A Good Man*

**"A good man sheweth favour, and lendeth:**
**he will guide his affairs with discretion."**
**vs.5**

*A universal opinion: "He is a good man."*
*The statement is rare and often times never spoken before the*
*person deserving of it, but it is the highest distinction that can be*
*said about a Christian man.*
*He knows his affairs and he righteously and justly conducts them.*
*He is honest to all and never places profit*
*above truth and integrity.*
*He has enough to lend but when he does, it is with wisdom.*
*He knows his business well and knows that discretion is as much*
*a wise business practice as investing.*
*This man is good not because he is flawless, but he is good*
*because he always seeks to please the Lord. All of his life is in the*
*pursuit of obeying his Lord.*
*This is the man God honors and rewards.*
*Simple question, are you a good man?*

# *July 12*

*Psalm 142*

### *Turn to Him and Don't Give Up*

*Life can often be overwhelming;*
*so many times we have nowhere else to turn.*
*So many waves sweep over the surface of our souls that it*
*becomes very hard to hold on.*
*It is then we cry out to Him.*
*When we have exhausted every earthly resource and put every*
*bit of effort to doing His work, when we have tried with all*
*our means to show love to our neighbors and give love to our*
*enemies with no sign of change in their heart; then we cry out to*
*Him and plea for relief.*
*We beg Him to measure the distance from failure and success,*
*we ask Him to cross the gap and do what we cannot; to give love*
*when we have expended it.*
*We have no other solace but Him, but there we can rest in peace.*
*He hears our cry and helps our cause.*
*He is our refuge and our needs are found met only in Him.*

# *July 13*

*Proverbs 22*

### *A Good Name*

**"A good name is rather to be chosen than great riches, and loving favour rather than silver and gold."**

**vs.1**

*A good name means a good reputation.*
*A good name is the product of someone that*
*understands what true integrity is.*
*A man with a good name has encountered others*
*and lived a life under close scrutiny and has said to the world: "I*
*do what I promise, I keep my word, I make promises that I can*
*keep and I keep them."*
*This man deserves the respect of those around him*
*and seeks to protect the respect his deeds have garnered and uses*
*his influence righteously.*
*His word and his good name are synonymous*
*with truth and honesty; God loves this man.*
*And his family is taught to preserve the wealth of having it.*
*A good name is worth far more than money and*
*much more than fame.*

*Work on having a good name, a good reputation.*

*Of course you'll have enemies, but have such a good name, that*

*when your enemies go to speak ill of you, no one will listen.*

# July 14

## Psalm 23
### The Great Shepherd

*Without a doubt the most well-known psalm written and argu-ably the most beloved. In its six short verses we see so much wonderful truth about ourselves and frailty, our Shepherd and His faithfulness, and our Father and His love. Like nowhere else in all of human literature is the full picture of man and his sad situation most aptly communicated. The genius of the Holy Spirit reveals to us our fears in the glen in verses 1-3, then He takes us to the gorge to deal with our foes in verses 4 and 5, and finally He peels back the veil of the finite to transport us into the future to show us His glory, in verse 6. The ever present great shepherd who is vigilant to know the state of His flock is our great shep-herd, and to know Him is to rest secure.*

*Making Changes*

*Adjustments*

## *Week Twenty-Nine*

*The Lord Jesus asked His disciples, "Whom say ye that I am?" What is your answer to the world that has different views of Him?*

# *July 15*

*Psalm 23*
## *The Gentle Shepherd*

*The tender heart of the shepherd to sheep*
*is never more evident than here.*
*The deliberate and personal attention the Great Shepherd*
*shows to His little ones is amazing. In each verse the bond*
*between the two is quite evident.*
*Here only do we see both the sheep and the Shepherd mentioned*
*together in every verse at least once.*
*In verses 1-3 he speaks of the Shepherd, in verses 4 and 5 he*
*speaks to the Shepherd.*
*In the last verse he speaks for the Shepherd;*
*the great love relationship of tender care and compassion*
*is conveyed so wonderfully here.*
*The knowledge that our great God gives Himself in such a com-*
*mitted way to His creation is a love story that could never be con-*
*ceived of in the heart of lost humanity; only God can construct*
*such a love story.*
*Rely on your Shepherd; trust in His loving care always.*

# July 16

## Psalm 23
### The Good Shepherd

*From the 23rd psalm we can see the person and character of each one of His covenant names. In verse 1 we see that He is Jehovah Rohi (our **pastor**) and as Jehovah Jireh (our **provider**).*
*In verse 2 He is Jehovah Shalom (our **peace**). In verse 3 He is both my healer: Jehovah Rapha (our **physician**), and my righteousness (our **propitiation**): Jehovah Tsidkenu.*
*In verse 4 He is Jehovah Shammah always there (our **present help**).*
*In verse 5 He is our **protector**, for He is Jehovah Sabboath, the Lord of Hosts, and my sanctifier as Jehovah Mekaddishkem (our **purifier**). His rod and His staff comfort us, He is the "called alongside one", the comforter (our **parakletos**).*
*Lastly in verse 6 we see Him wrapping us up in His abundance. El Shaddai, the All Mighty Breasty One, the God who is more than enough; the one who nourishes us with His great love and mercy, there is no one like Him, no other one is able to so completely care for the whole person meeting every need (our **portion**).*
*This is our Shepherd and this is how He loves.*

# *July 17*

### Psalm 53
### **They Know There is a God**

**"The fool hath said in his heart, There is no God.**
**Corrupt are they, and have done abominable iniquity:**
**there is none that doeth good."**
**vs.1**

*You'll notice that the words "there is" are not found*
*in the original text.*
*The verse should read: "The fool hath said in his heart, no God."*
*David knows that in all truth there*
*is no human heart once exposed to the truth of God's existence,*
*which could ever conclude that God does not exist.*
*God placed in everyone both the knowledge of Him*
*as well as the need for Him.*
*Only the pure folly of man constructs in his mind that God does*
*not exist, because his heart has been given all that is necessary to*
*seek God and to worship Him.*
*In every venture of men, God has revealed Himself to reinforce*
*His presence (see Psalm 19).*
*Our concerns should be to trust Him by faith and then watch as*
*we grow to know Him more.*

# July 18

Psalm 83

## Jehovah!!!

**"That men may know that thou, whose name alone is JEHOVAH, art the most high over all the earth."**
**vs.18**

His name is Jehovah. The great covenant making, promise
keeping, relational God, the lover of man's soul.
He only has the right to be given all the worship.
The name Jehovah is a miracle in itself.
It is the three tenses of language's verb usage.
When we speak of ourselves, we do so using three verbs,
reflecting three different periods of time and action;
"I am", "I will", and "I was"; each communicating
to the listener our place in the present, the past and the future.
Three distinctly different occasions; the three could never happen
at exactly the same time and/or space.
Not so with God. "Yehi" means "I will",
"Hov" means "I am", and "Yavah" means "I was".

*God declares, no matter what time of life you need Him,*

*He is that very present help any and every time you need Him.*

*He is Jehovah!*

*And there is no one else like Him.*

# *July 19*

*Psalm 113*

**How to Love**

**"Who humbleth himself to behold
the things that are in heaven, and in the earth!"**

**vs.6**

He must always do it;
He must always humble Himself for our sakes.
He will always do whatever is necessary
to express His love for you and I.
It doesn't matter how evil we've acted,
or how much we have sinned in His sight.
He'll do whatever it takes to redeem us,
to rescue us, to bring us out of the slave market.
Even go there Himself to be treated like a slave or even a criminal, and in so doing, He shows us what love really looks like.
He could show us only His wrath, vengeance,
and jealousy, but no, He leads with love.
He shows us how to love the unlovely.
He actively and personally displays His life of love and humility
before us so that we might in turn humble ourselves and love
others, after all, isn't that how He said people recognize us?

*By the way we love.*

*"Greater love has no man than this..." (John 15:13).*

# *July 20*

*Psalm 143*

### *He is Faithful*

**"Hear my prayer, O LORD, give ear to my supplications: in thy faithfulness answer me, and in thy righteousness."**
**vs.1**

*Lamentations 3:21-22; I John 1:9; I Corinthians 10:13,*
*whether it is new mercies in the mornings, forgiveness for our*
*foolishness or giving us an escape from an enemy; God is faithful.*
*II Timothy 2:13 takes it even further.*
*In those moments that many believers have found themselves;*
*those moments when the circumstances of living in a cloud, out*
*the light of God's continuing love for us, and all our emotions will*
*let us see are the weak, hollow, temporary victories it offers; and*
*in foolishness we have challenged and questioned God over His*
*right to be sovereign.*
*Many have walked away, choosing not to believe anymore.*
*High treason against the cross and blood that was shed there!*
*But even in that He remains faithful,*
*He can never, ever deny Himself.*
*He swore that He would be faithful, and thank God, He is!*

# *July 21*

*Proverbs 23*

### **Pursue True Riches**

**"Labour not to be rich: cease from thine own wisdom."**

**vs.4**

Labor not to be rich.
Riches and the desire of the same is a cavernous, bottomless pit
that swallows whole any and every one that craves it.
The desires of the heart to have more and more is an endless
hunger that even the strongest saint can be tempted by.
What may start out as honorable,
honest dreams of giving and benevolence with compassion,
more often than not, will end with the dark human heart con-
torting to whatever guise it needs to have what it wants.
The ravenous hunger of greed will rob even the most committed
soul to do things they would have never dreamed of.
Be careful with possessions.
Money is to be a tool; never a weapon.
A tool to promote righteousness in others, and to advance the
kingdom of God.

*Making Changes*

*Adjustments*

*Week Thirty*

---

*Each day this week compare
yourself to the fruit of the Spirit
mentioned in Galatians 5.
Now analyze:
Is your life showing the fruit of
His presence?*

---

# July 22

*Psalm 24*

### *Beyond the Seen*

*The kind shepherd, the universes sovereign, master of everything,*
*the world and every part of creation is all His. All the fruit of the*
*earth and all the kingdoms of the earth, the planet upon which*
*we live is all His, but also "the fullness thereof".*
*This includes not just the natural world we know, but also the*
*unseen world, the world that is of the spirit. The thing unseen*
*are a world unto themselves; but are still intimately involved in*
*everything around us.*
*Despite what skeptics say, there is a spiritual part of our world's*
*existence that cannot be ignored.*
*This world we know is dramatically influenced by the forces*
*unseen around it.*
*The Bible reveals what those forces are in Ephesians 6:10-12.*
*What we see and know in this natural world has very little to*
*show of the Spirit, but regardless, it is there.*
*Angels and spirits all around us,*
*and of all that there is; He is Lord!*

# July 23

*Psalm 54*

### Behind Enemy Lines

*David in his desperate run from Saul found himself between a rock and a hard place;*

*With Saul breathing down his neck behind him and the land of his country's enemies before him, he was in the worst possible situation a man could be in.*

*A classic example of being sandwiched in the middle. There was no time for peace talks or negotiations.*

*Sending an emissary to discuss terms was out of the question.*

*David was the hated hero of the battle with Goliath as well as being the hated undeserved enemy of the king of his own country.*

*He found himself and his men had run out of places to go, he was forced to go to a land he should have found sanctuary in, the land of the Ziphites, people and a place that should have hid and embraced him, betrayed and alienated him.*

*At home he was behind enemy lines, surrounded and again outnumbered. Thank God that he knew how to pray. Despite the circumstances, take your refuge in Him.*

# *July 24*

*Psalm 84*

### *The Pilgrims Progress*

*A rebel is one that hates home, a vagabond is one that has no home, a fugitive is one that is running from home, a stranger is one who is away from home, but a pilgrim is one that is going home; we are strangers and pilgrims.*
*This pilgrim psalm is written to remind us that this world is to be abandoned by us.*
*Our feet should find no resting place here.*
*All of the glories of it should not attract us, and all of the temptations of it should not lure us.*
*We have a home; we have a place. We are passing through here with a goal in mind and a destination in view. It will take strength upon strength (vs.7) to forge ahead, it will require God's grace for grace (vs.11 and John 1:16) to endure it, the Lord's glory (vs.11 and I Corinthians 3:18) to achieve it and faith to faith (verse 12 and Romans 1:17) to see it. Come on weary pilgrim, set your eyes on the goal, the Lord of Hosts is your guide and companion, you can make it!*

# July 25

## Psalm 114

### His Guide and Protection

**"Judah was his sanctuary and Israel his dominion." vs.2**

What we see here is the union of praise (Judah)
and strength (Israel).
God sent His people forward from the land of their bondage and
oppression, into a 40 year wilderness experience with praise
leading and strength following.
He showed the greatness and majesty of His power by displaying
awesome control of the elements, using a pillar of cloud by day
and a pillar of fire by night.
An incredible contrast of the elements:
shade to protect them from the sun during the day, and warmth
provided by the fire at night.
These occurrences served not only elementally,
but also spiritually.
It taught the Jews to follow God only and to obey His Spirit, the
person of the Godhead that is always in charge of leading us.
They were to follow the pillar whenever they moved, and were to
wait on Him when He stopped.
So should it be in the life of the believer.

# *July 26*

*Ephesians 6:12*

### *With the Spirit, In the Spirit, By the Spirit*

**"For we wrestle not against flesh and blood..."** *vs.12*

*We are not human beings having a spiritual encounter; we are*
*spirit beings (I Thessalonians 5:23; Galatians 5:16)*
*having a human encounter.*
*The walk, the warfare, and the work of the spirit are never depen-*
*dent on the will or the conditions of the natural world around us.*
*The sphere of influence that determines our actions and our situa-*
*tions is the "heavenlies".*
*It is not only a place, but also it is the rule of authority by which*
*all of the events of life and eternity are determined. We cannot be*
*swayed or distracted by things that occur in the realm of the five*
*senses. Ours is the aspect of the eternal and if we truly desire to*
*both please the Lord and dynamically affect this physical world for*
*the kingdom, then here is where our principle focus must be.*
*We must rely only on the conditions that God has given us in His*
*word. All things that matter are found complete in*
*our obedience to Him.*
*Don't ever let the natural world order your life. Trust in those*
*things that are eternal; the unseen things. For the things that can*

*be perceived by the natural senses are temporary and will like all things temporal, fade away.*

# *July 27*

*Psalm 134*

### Clean Hands – Clean Heart

**"Lift up your hands in the sanctuary, and bless the LORD."**

**vs.2**

*The raising of hands in worship is not new, it is replete*

*throughout scripture.*

*It is God's way of saying to man:*

*"Prove to me that your outward expression of worship and your*

*inward evidence of worship match."*

*The raising of hands intimate that*

*there is no known sin in our lives.*

*The hands raised to God with palms high say:*

*"I have taken great detail and effort to keep my sins*

*confessed before you.*

*I have honored you with both my lips and my life Lord.*

*" The close attention to this detail, God delights in.*

*He loves to look in the heart of His people and see the mirror*

*reflection of a holy lifestyle written on them.*

*God welcomes all who qualify this way into His presence. In this*

*short psalm we see just this same event happening with saints who have gathered together in the evening to express their*

*deepest adoration to God.*

*Join them, lift up your hands and love the Lord,*

*worship Him, honor Him."*

# July 28

*Proverbs 24*

### It's Not over Yet

**"Be not thou envious against evil men,**

**neither desire to be with them."**

**vs.1**

*It is hard isn't it? To remain faithful to the promise*

*of God when it seems like everyone else who does not,*

*and will not trust God, has every advantage.*

*The righteous appear to be the underdogs, the laughing stock,*

*the butt of every insult, the punch line of every joke. And the truth*

*is that nowhere in the scripture is the promise that in this life we*

*can expect all of this to change. It most likely will not.*

*But that's the point of this verse,*

*don't envy what they have or even that they have it.*

*The whole record needs to be examined.*

*God is the true judge of all things, and He will weigh the deeds*

*according to His holy measure.*

*His admonishment to us is to never be discouraged*

*by what the lost have acquired. He will appoint a day*

*when all will be accounted for, and only those whose hearts are*

*right will be rewarded.*

# *July 29*

*Psalm 25*

### *Encouragement*

**"For thy name's sake, O LORD,**
**pardon mine iniquity; for it is great."**
**vs.11**

*A kind word at the right time delivered in the right way,*
*"Apples of gold in pictures of silver."*
*The object of ministry is "to meet the needs of the people,*
*regardless of the need, regardless of the people".*
*Few people have the gift of encouragement and those who do are*
*almost always gifted with the use of words.*
*They have found a way to enter into a situation and evaluate*
*what the appropriate time and manner of the words they have to*
*say will be most effective.*
*I have yet to find a person like this*
*who isn't also a prayer warrior.*
*For to aptly minister as God's love agent,*
*prayer must be a constant.*

*A heart that speaks and listens to God, does not merely sympathize with someone (that is – feel for them), they are able to empathize with them (feel with them).*

*How are you when it comes to encouragement?*

# *July 30*

*Psalm 25*

## *Teach Me*

*Five times the word is used in this chapter. Five times David voices the importance of being taught by the Lord. There are lessons to be learned by experience, hands on learning, and life can garner a great deal by simple observation, sight learning. Explanation is what most schools use to instruct with, but all of these pale in comparison to the way the Holy Spirit teaches. He takes the word of God and uses it to cause the saints to view a conflict, situation or dilemma and then tells us to obey. God wants us to know Him best through listening and then obeying.*

*This is the way God teaches;*

*He doesn't give us the explanation all the time.*

*Spiritual matters are not always accessible to our senses, and so, observation isn't the best way; experience is a cruel teacher, it gives the exam first and then the lesson.*

*To obey God with His infinite wisdom*

*is the surest way to grow in Him.*

# July 31

*Psalm 55*

**Betrayal**

**"For it was not an enemy that reproached me;**
**then I could have borne it: neither was it he that hated me**
**that did magnify himself against me; then I would have hid**
**myself from him: But it was thou, a man mine equal, my**
**guide, and mine acquaintance"**
**vs.12-13**

*Here is a Dwightism: "You can only be hurt*
*by those you allow yourself to love."*
*The bible says "faithful are the wounds of a friend"*
*(Proverbs 27:6).*
*Loving someone deeply and then to be deliberately hurt by them*
*hurts much worse than anything an enemy could ever do to you.*
*Knowing that someone whom you've grown close to*
*has weighed your friendship and love and then decided to strike*
*out at you for the sole purpose of wounding and/or destroying*
*you is pain that is almost unbearable.*
*This is the place King David is in.*
*The Lord does not tell us who betrayed him,*
*but we know that it was someone close, and the closer the*

*person, the deeper the love, the more committed the relationship,*

*the bigger the heartache.*

*When some hurts us in such a manner,*

*only God can heal the wound and ease the pain.*

*Our response is to pray for the strength to forgive them*

*as soon as possible just because you've been hurt,*

*learn to let it go quickly.*

# *August*

## *A Time for Maintenance*

***Lesson:*** The Father of Lights

> *"Every good gift and every perfect gift is from above, and cometh down from the Father of lights, with whom is no variableness, neither shadow of turning."* James 1:17

### *Lesson*

To say that He is the Father of Lights is not just giving Him divine honors, because He created the luminous glories of the heavenly host,; but He transcends that thought as He is greater than all the great lights, He is the pre-eminent, uncreated, creator. All that man receives from above; rain, wind, heat, snow, light, fire, or whatever, He and alone is the benefactor. He is above all of His creation and the absolute point of reference to all there is. The reason why light is bright is because God is the perfect point of reference. The reason for the beauty in every flower is simply because He is essence of beauty.

He is the First being, not first in a rank of occurrence. But rather being First in position and power. First, in privilege and might; He is the First of all things and Father of all things created. Every good and glorious thing finds its' purpose, origin and fulfillment in Him – the Father of Lights.

### Outline of the Passage

    A.  He is the substance of our benefits ~ He is the compassionate God

    B.  He is the source of our benefits ~ He is the Creator God

    C.  He is the surety of our benefits ~ He is the changeless God

*Facts:* **The month of August, eighth month of the Gregorian calendar.**

It corresponds to the month of Ab; the fifth month of the Hebrew calendar. The month that temple was destroyed.

*Focus:* **Prayer and faithfulness.**

Faithfulness is one of the most neglected aspects of the saints. Set two realistic goals and stick with them both until they are accomplished.

**Assignment:** **Research**

Outline Paul's 3 ½ missionary journeys and place in time and location the time and location of each book he wrote.

**Memory Work:**

**Exaltation:** John 4:24

**Excellence:** Philippians 4:6, 7

**Edification:** Psalm 91:1

**Evangelical:** I John 2:2

**Exhortive:** Romans 12:1, w

**Educational:** II Corinthians 5:21

# Staying Faithful

## Maintenance

# Week Thirty-One

*Arguably the most important verse in the Old Testament is Habakkuk 2:4b, "The just shall live by his faith", maintaining a life that honors God takes work. Keep the details of your life in the care of the Spirit. Live by faith!!*

# *August 1*

*Psalm 85*

### *Keep it Fresh*

**"Wilt thou not revive us again:**

**that thy people may rejoice in thee?"**

**vs.6**

*"Breathe life into" that's what the phrase is implying.*

*We really need the fresh wind of the Lord to survive,*

*to accomplish, to rejoice!*

*But the routine of life often causes you to become*

*so used to the mundane and the average that the walk*

*with the Lord gets dull and ordinary.*

*Then we begin to drift away from Him slowly,*

*after a short time it is amazing how far we've gone,*

*and how easy it is not to even care.*

*Ask the Lord to revive you again and again; don't become lazy*

*and lax in your relationship with Him.*

*When you assess yourself, look at the communication*

*you have with Christ first.*

*Is it fresh? Is it constant?*

*If not, stop what you're doing, pull over and park.*

*Be honest with Him in prayer and ask Him to revive with fire and passion your love for Him.*

## *August 2*

*Psalm 115*

### *Live Your Life Out Loud*

*The prophet ridicules, insults and belittles not only false gods, but also those that fear and worship them.*

*He understands that there is not a God except the Lord Jehovah.*

*He makes this audacious declaration because he has lived the life that has depended on God in the most adverse situations; he has placed his trust in the God of the impossible.*

*He then calls on every Jew, and every saint to place their whole trust in the Lord of the universe.*

*By living a holy lifestyle, consistent with prayer, we shut the mouths of any one and every one that does not know Him. Speak up; speak out, about your God and King.*

*He is the one who alone does wondrous things.*

*Exalt Him, glorify Him in all things and trust Him, let your life be the biggest, loudest proof of the only true God!*

# *August 3*

*Psalm 145*

### *Thy Kingdom Come*

**"They shall speak of the glory of thy kingdom, and talk of thy power; To make known to the sons of men his mighty acts, and the glorious majesty of his kingdom. Thy kingdom is an everlasting kingdom, and thy dominion endureth throughout all generations."**

**vs.11-13**

*The Kingdom, the Kingdom, the subject that Jesus spoke of more than anything is the Kingdom.*

*He spoke by comparison and contrast, He spoke in parables and prophecy, He spoke about it to the poor and the powerful, He spoke about it in the synagogue and through the streets; to the religiously wrong as well as the righteously willing.*

*Why? It's simple, because He knew the King! He could speak for verses and verses about the place He loved the best because it was ruled by the person He loved the best.*

*The Kingdom is not just a place way up there; the Kingdom is the sphere of influence over which God has declared His own, that means everywhere, and He's bringing it into Kingdom order.*

*So as the psalmist rejoices in such truth, so also should we.*

*This psalm is called: "David's Psalm of Praise".*

*You should do that for yourself; write to Him, the King, your own psalm of praise.*

# August 4

*Psalm 26*

### *What He Wants for Me*

**"Judge me, O LORD; for I have walked in mine integrity:
I have trusted also in the LORD; therefore I shall not slide."
vs.1**

*The two qualities that God wants: On my end,*
*to walk and live a lifestyle that has no baggage, no reproach, a*
*consistent holy walk that encourages others while honoring God*
*in all that I believe and do.*
*And to trust in the Lord; His word as my principle and His Spirit*
*as my guide, obeying His voice where He leads me and whenever*
*He leads, to whatever He leads.*
*Following theses two very important and necessary points,*
*I will be ready for His evaluation of me.*
*I'll have no fear of what an enemy may try to do to me.*
*I'll be innocent of any wrong, because as He leads me, He also*
*directs my path.*
*As He then leads, He also directs and protects.*
*As He ordains, He also guides and provides.*
*All of these things working in tandem in my life will result in His*
*perfect will for me and His glory.*

# *August 5*

### Psalm 56
### *Fears and Tears*

**"What time I am afraid, I will trust in thee.**
**In God I will praise his word, in God I have put my trust;**
**I will not fear what flesh can do unto me. Every day they**
**wrest my words: all their thoughts are against me for evil.**
**They gather themselves together, they hide themselves,**
**they mark my steps, when they wait for my soul. Shall they**
**escape by iniquity? in thine anger cast down the people, O**
**God. Thou tellest my wanderings: put thou my tears into thy**
**bottle: are they not in thy book?"**
**vs.3-8**

*I'm often asked: "Are you insecure about anything?"*
*"Of course, lots of things."*
*"Like what?" "None of your business."*
*Everyone has areas that cause them to be uncomfortable,*
*insecure, or even afraid.*
*To say otherwise is a lie.*
*We are at best frail, imperfect, and flawed, everyone knows that.*
*From the small to the great, each inhabitant of the earth knows*
*what it is to be afraid.*

*However, just because those are the facts, it does not mean it should be the place we live. Consistently, I set the pattern of my life to show to my family and friends **strong faith.***

*I live a declared life of faith and trust.*

*Consistent with the truth that my God, in whom I've placed my trust, is a good master and Lord. He is my greatest friend and happens also to be my blood Father, but of those previous statements, and they all are true, and all are part of my quiet time alone with Him. To Him in private I tremble and show my **simplest fears.***

*No Brava, no hype, no fanfare; I can whine and cry, and nestle in His arms and cry alone.*

*He understands and receives me there.*

*He holds me closes and handles me as though I were His only child.*

*To the world around me – **Strong Faith!!***

*To the Father who loves and knows me – **Simplest Fears.***

# *August 6*

## Psalm 86
### The Poor and the Needy

**"Bow down thine ear, O LORD,**
**hear me: for I am poor and needy."**
**vs.1**

*Ten times in the Psalms you'll find the phrase: "poor and needy".*
*Twice it's used by Asaph, but David used it directly eight times,*
*and indirectly, another six.*
*He gives the analogy of a man who had accurately considered his*
*place and has surveyed his station before God and can only con-*
*clude that he is "poor and needy."*
*These are the two traits in a man who when he presents himself*
*to God, draws direct attention.*
*At every use of the word, David and Asaph present their petition*
*before the high counsel of heaven.*
*God will always hear the cry of the poor and needy who come*
*humbly to Him.*
*He's the God of all compassion and mercy;*
*the one who loves always from His heart.*
*"Blessed are the poor in spirit." Come before Him broken, you'll*
*leave whole; come before Him humbly, He will lift your head.*

*Whatever the reason, come before Him with your life in your hands, ready to do business in your soul.*

*Watch Him take you into His embrace and meet your needs.*

# *August 7*

## *Psalm 116*
### *Keep Your Promise*

### *vs.14-18*

*I will pay my vows.*

*Promises, promises. We have all made promises to God
that we did not keep.*

*Oh, some were made sincerely, and some were made
in a desperate moment, when having God act on our behalf was
critical. Some promises were made purely from the flesh, no
matter how urgent the request.*

*There we see the absolute quality of human nature revealed.
"Give me what I want God, and I promise you
I'll serve you forever."*

*The bargain is never righteous, nor is it honest.*

*We want what we want and all else doesn't matter, but here in
this classically beautiful song we see a man who appreciates the
Lord and all that He has done.*

*How that God has kept His word and never failed him. Here this
man is determined to keep his vow and honor his King.*

*You've made promises to the Lord, are you going to keep them?*
*Go through the pages of your life; is there something you've*
*promised to Him that has yet to be fulfilled?*

*Staying Faithful*

*Maintenance*

## Week Thirty-Two

> *Assess your true needs and your extravagances. Determine what you can do without and sacrifice what you've been holding on to unnecessarily.*

# *August 8*

Psalm 146

### *A Bed-rocked Truth*

***"Happy is he that hath the God of Jacob for his help,***
***whose hope is in the LORD his God:"***
***vs.5***

*Hope.*
*The world really has no clue as to what*
*the biblical word "Hope" means.*
*They think that hope is wishful thinking.*
*Wishing that what is will change to what we want, and what*
*isn't will change to our favor.*
*This is vain thinking, not hope.*
*Not biblical hope anyway.*
*Bible hope is the truth of God's plan happening as He determined*
*and described it.*
*It is when the saint hears God's voice and waits for it to happen.*
*This hope in a bed-rocked, unchangeable absolute fact*
*worked and willed out in eternity and wrought out*
*and witnessed in time.*
*Of this hope there is no way of stopping it.*

*This is not wishful desire, this is a fact based*

*on one immutable truth: God cannot lie.*

*This hope is not secured because someone nice said it.*

*No!*

*This hope is straight from God's word.*

*It is the only authority that cannot fail. Put your faith and trust*

*in the hope of His word.*

# *August 9*

*Proverbs 26*

### *The Cause of a Curse*

**"As the bird by wandering, as the swallow by flying,**
**so the curse causeless shall not come."**
**vs.2**

*I can think of two places that speak plainly about why calamity,*
*suffering and misery will come on a person: Hebrews 12:15 and I*
*Corinthians 11:29-30 (there are probably more).*
*Two reasons why a curse has followed you, a curse comes for a*
*purpose, Solomon says, and the cause of the curse is never unjust.*
*As we live day by day, the ease of slipping into ungodly habits and*
*un-Christian like character is amazing.*
*Only someone who keeps their attention focused on the intensity*
*of battle will catch the traps and defuse them before it's too late.*
*More often than we would like to believe,*
*Christians find that they are no longer joyful, no longer on fire*
*with a passion to grow.*
*The things around them seem to always end up being problems,*
*and problems seem to be insolvable.*

*If these things are true in your life, pause; do a good self-evaluation; check to see if you are remembering the Lord with clean hands and heart, see if you are harboring bitterness at all.*

# *August 10*

*Psalm 27*

### *One Thing*

**"One thing have I desired of the LORD,
that will I seek after; that I may dwell in the house of the
LORD all the days of my life, to behold the beauty of the
LORD, and to enquire in his temple."**

**vs.4**

*It's really quite simple; life is about one thing.*
*What do you want?*
*Your passions will define you.*
*What you really desire will be the path your life will take.*
*You have no other drive than to follow with*
*great fervor what you truly want.*
*It maybe money, power, possessions, it maybe noble,*
*honorable, even godly, but regardless, wherever and whatever*
*your passion is, what you desire; that one thing will be the aim*
*and the direction of your life.*
*No one will ever be able to do any other thing*
*than that which their hearts desire.*
*We may try to tame it, avoid it, manage it*
*and control it, but it's a fact.*

*What we want will define our world.*

*What do you want?*

*What drives you?*

*I pray that it is Jesus.*

*One thing should be your reason for being.*

*One pursuit should determine your life: Jesus and Him alone.*

# *August 11*

*Psalm 57*

### **Love Your Enemies**

*Let's face it; there will always be those who don't like us.*
*There will be people who find everything we do to be*
*an affront to them, even when we show them kindness*
*they will always see it as evil.*
*Every kind word will sting them and sound like an insult and no*
*matter how much you may sincerely try to explain, console, or*
*seek to make things right, they will find something evil in it.*
*They have no interest in restoration, fellowship or brotherhood.*
*So what can you do?*
*Pray for them.*
*God is not so much concerned as to how you feel you've tried...*
*He wants you to be steadfast.*
*Keep it up, persevere through the pain.*
*It's amazing what God can do through you showing love*
*in the hour of adversity.*
*Giving great love, when none has been shown to you, shows the*
*true love and work of God in your life.*
*We're going to have enemies, there is no changing that, but*
*loving them despite everything is the true work of God.*

# *August 12*

*Psalm 87*

### *The Holy City of God*

**"Glorious things are spoken of thee, O city of God. Selah."**

**vs.3**

*Jerusalem - The city of the Great King.*
*God loves that city; it is the place where He decided to place His*
*temple, tabernacles, and the testimony.*
*He sets His name there.*
*Jerusalem means "city of peace". It is the earthly example of the*
*capital city of Heaven.*
*Like no other place on the planet, Jerusalem has always been the*
*place that garners God's attention.*
*Cultures and countries have tried everything to wipe it off the*
*face of the planet. From Sennecherib to Vespasian, someone*
*always thought this city had no right to be called, the Holy Land,*
*but it is and it still stands.*
*It has been the site for so many conflicts, weathered countless*
*attacks, but yet it stands.*

*God so loves this place,*

*He demands that everyone*

*everywhere pray for its peace.*

*Do so, and receive His blessing and favor.*

*Pray for the peace of Jerusalem.*

# *August 13*

## Psalm 117
### *Merciful Kindness*

*He is kind to the just and the unjust, the saved and the lost, to the lover of God and the critic; God is good.*

*The phrase that the psalmist uses here: "merciful kindness" is exclusive to this book, nowhere else is it used in scripture, here and in Psalm 119, the expression is reserved by the Holy Spirit to magnify the wonderful aspects of God's nature.*

*It is the Hebrew word "chesed".*

*It means kindness, beauty, favor, good deeds.*

*It's straight from the heart of God to the need of the hurting.*

*He loves as only He can and does so with unabashed favor.*

*This is the God that makes it to rain on the just and the unjust.*

*He has every right to stop man cold and show no blessing, but no, our Lord must act within the context of His nature. So in your walk, bless Him for His favors and His merciful kindness.*

# *August 14*

Psalm 147

**He Knows**

**"Great is our Lord, and of great power:**
**his understanding is infinite."**
**vs.5**

He is great, that is an aspect of His nature.
He is great in power, which is an aspect of His ability.
He is infinite in understanding,
which is an aspect of His attributes.
He knows everything.
He knows all about our troubles and our fears; He knows.
He knows all about our weakness and failures; He knows.
He knows all about our sins and desires; He knows.
He knows and He loves us anyway.
Never will He throw us away;
never will He abandon us because of our problems.
The wicked, the heathen has nowhere to run.
No one to turn to, but His parting words to His people
was the grandest assurance anyone could ever ask for:
"Lo, I am with you, even to the end of the world."

*He knows your heartache.*

*Talk to Him and get that reassurance again.*

*He knows.*

*Staying Faithful*

*Maintenance*

## *Week Thirty-Three*

*Read through the book of James
every day this week.*

# *August 15*

*Proverbs 27*

### *Risk Conflict in Love*

**"Iron sharpeneth iron; so a man sharpeneth**
**the countenance of his friend."**
**vs.17**

*When iron strikes iron, two things are sure to happen,*
*sparks will fly, and heat will rise.*
*Guarded, tender-footed friendship is no friendship at all really.*
*If as friends we are not willing to put ourselves at risk for the one*
*we love, we really don't love them at all.*
*When we allow someone into our world, we are saying to them:*
*"You have the right to see me clearly; you have the right to know*
*my deepest most intimate thoughts and fears". When we expose*
*ourselves in this way, we are inviting others to see us with all of*
*our blemishes and warts.*
*To let others in is to let them examine critique*
*and yes, criticize us.*
*It won't feel good, it won't bring a smile, but it will sharpen the*
*blade of our souls, it will make keener our insight, it will expose*
*those "blind-spots" that on our own, we cannot see.*

*Avail yourself to the true love of being a friend.*

*Risk being vulnerable; do whatever is necessary to see the kingdom of God advance through giving all you are to a brother or sister in godly love.*

# *August 16*

*Psalm 28*

### *Tougher Times Ahead*

*There are tough times, there are the times when all seems des-
perate, things aren't going our way, it seems.*
*All our explanations are not in sync with the realities*
*of the moment, even the prayers that we pray seem*
*to be hollow and useless.*
*We look for encouragement everywhere,*
*in all the usual and unusual places, but it too is just not forth-
coming. So what do you do?*
*Is this going to be one of the times you hide your pain, disap-
pointment, and fears from everyone else so that the God you've
spoken to boldly about before, the God you have said repeatedly
would be always be there for you, always on time, never leave or
forsake you, this great God won't look like a failure?*
*Are you living proof that He doesn't keep His word, that*
*He cannot be relied upon?*
*So what will you do mighty Christian?*
*I'll tell you what to do: You bless the Lord, you magnify Him, do
what you've always done, and bless His name!*
*Brag on His greatness.*
*This is a moment of trial and testing.*

*Do you dare ever stop trusting in Him?*

*Do you ever let your hope perish from Him?*

*NO!!!!*

*Stand fast!*

*Prove the power of the Christ who lives within.*

*He keeps us in the storm and uncomfortable times of life.*

*Show the world the blessed grace that keeps us*

*despite adverse situations.*

# *August 17*

*Psalm 58*

### *Yield to the Greatest Power*

**"The righteous shall rejoice when he seeth the vengeance:**

**he shall wash his feet in the blood of the wicked."**

**vs.10**

*We are not a people who seek violence or vengeance.*

*Our Lord has in fact told us just the opposite.*

*We are to love our enemies, pray for those who out of pure spite*

*and hatred use us and hurt us.*

*We are to be God's witness of love, peace, and grace despite all*

*the evil that often will been done to us.*

*The world will be won to Christ by only one means; love. There is*

*no power greater than the power of love.*

*However, there is going to be violence, there will be vengeance,*

*retribution and judgment.*

*God is just and He does hold the record of everyone's deeds, espe-*

*cially those deeds done against the righteous.*

*God the righteous judge will mete out His decree against all and*

*upon all who have wickedly injured His people.*

*He knows and He will exact what is necessary*

*to avenge His people.*

*Don't hang your head, when the wicked seem to overtake the*

*righteous, God knows and His account will be balanced by and by.*

# *August 18*

*Psalm 88*

### *Tell Him What's on Your Heart*

*I love the book of Psalms.*
*I love it for a very practical and personal reason; it teaches me*
*how to talk to God.*
*The things that the psalmist (usually David) tells me that my*
*thoughts and my prayers, my songs and my praises need to be*
*completely honest, straight from my heart,*
*totally from my soul and only in truth.*
*The psalms show me that God wants to hear me*
*cry out when I am overwhelmed.*
*God wants my passion and my emotions. Sometimes that emotion*
*is fear; other times its anger, frustration, or confusion.*
*Regardless of the situation, He wants us to express ourselves*
*completely, but always reverently, never in my discussions with*
*God, not matter how passionate, should I be irreverent;*
*After all, He is God.*
*I am allowed to talk to Him, and that is amazing, but in my deal-*
*ings with Him I must never forget who He is.*
*Tell Him everything, He knows it anyway.*
*Give Him everything in your heart,*
*but never forget to whom you're speaking.*

# *August 19*

*Psalm 118*

### *This is the Day!*

**"This is the day which the LORD hath made;**
**we will rejoice and be glad in it."**
**vs.24**

*This is the day the Lord has made.*
*Technically, the true believer in Christ has*
*no right to ever claim to have a bad day.*
*The vantage point of the redeemed is not one of earthly posi-*
*tioning or fleshly observation.*
*We are seated with Him in heavenly places; we are secured in*
*Him in the fullness of eternity.*
*He has made us complete in Him with all power; our future is*
*secure, our salvation is set.*
*Yes, we'll have horrors and heartaches, of course we experience*
*the pain of the loss of a loved one, and no one would ever claim*
*that in Christ we are free from disappointment and fear.*
*But we are given a mandate from glory,*
*"This is the day the Lord has made".*
*Our Father made the day, which means that all things that may*
*happen are well known and orchestrated by Him.*

*He made the day with us in mind.*

*So despite how it looks, despite how it may feel;*

*we all have one response; because He made the day and*

*we know He loves us: Rejoice and be glad!*

## *August 20*

*Psalm 148*

### *Praise Him!! Praise Him!!*

*In just 14 short verses, all that is to be known about our natural*
*material world is mentioned; every aspect of creation is covered,*
*from the heavens above us to the ground beneath us.*
*Every animal class, every plant and planet, stars and moons, all*
*the heavenly host, everything that is, is mentioned.*
*And all are given the same command:*
*Praise Him! Praise Him! Praise Him!*
*The reason for such reckoning to order is very simple; it's given in*
*verse 13, "His name alone is excellent.*
*His glory is above the earth and heaven."*
*His name is His mighty reputation*
*of promises made and promises kept.*
*His glory is the inherent follower of His excellence.*
*This is why He is to be praised.*
*All of creation knows it; every tree that stretches out its arms in*
*worship, defying gravity in its adoration.*
*Every sweet song the birds sing to Him in worship.*
*They all are aware and are grateful for His Fatherly care of them.*
*We too are commanded to exalt Him and love and adore Him.*
*Come join in the worship of our great God and King.*

# *August 21*

*Proverbs 28*

### **Mercy: The Truth Act of Love**

**"He that covereth his sins shall not prosper: but whoso con-fesseth and forsaketh them shall have mercy."**

**vs.13**

Mercy: *The act of God suspending or dismissing His rightful sen-tence against sin and unrighteousness.*

Mercy: *The pity shown by a loved one, usually a parent, on one who has committed an act deserving of punishment.*

Mercy: *The art of caring for those who are in some way incapable of helping themselves because of disability, disadvantage, or misfortune.*

Mercy: *The love given to another regardless of the qualifications of the one receiving it.*

Mercy: *To rescue those who are in eminent danger.*

Mercy: *God's calling card of care. He is merciful, kind, thoughtful and gracious.*

*His love covers all of the above,*

*each of those situations and more.*

*He is merciful to those who will never know it and*

*to those who don't even know Him.*

*That great love that He has extended further*

*than anyone can really describe.*

*If you have done anything that you know is wrong, confess to*

*Him and receive the rich reward of His mercy.*

*Staying Faithful*

*Maintenance*

## *Week Thirty-Four*

> *Each day this week*
> *spend some time*
> *reviewing your giving.*
> *If it hasn't increased since*
> *last year, find out what other*
> *things may be taking income*
> *from your budget and pray*
> *about what you can give up for*
> *the kingdom.*

# *August 22*

Psalm 29

### *Worship for Eternity*

**"Give unto the LORD, O ye mighty, give unto the LORD glory**
**and strength. Give unto the LORD the glory due unto his**
**name; worship the LORD in the beauty of holiness."**
**vs. 1-2**

*I was asked once a while ago by a young adult,*
*"When we get to heaven, all we'll do is praise the Lord?*
*Is that it?*
*That sounds incredibly boring, don't you think?*
*Is that all that's going to go on for eternity?" I responded,*
*"Well you do have an alternative; go to hell."*
*As you might guess, they were slightly put off with my answer.*
*The answer to that question is both yes and no.*
*The psalmist David puts forth here,*
*that He is worthy of that type of attention.*
*The Lord deserves all of that worship, honor and praise.*
*He deserves glory and blessing.*
*These are accomplished by the process of us not only saying these*
*things, but also by matching our words with our works.*
*That's why I said the answer is yes and no.*

*The bible does imply that we will continually worship Him,*

*but in Revelation 22:3 is says, we'll serve Him.*

*That too is worship and praise, doing His will forever.*

# *August 23*

*Psalm 59*

### *Jehovah Sabboath*

**"Thou therefore, O LORD God of hosts, the God of Israel, awake to visit all the heathen: be not merciful to any wicked transgressors. Selah."**

**vs.5**

*The Lord God of Hosts; the Lord God of the armies of Heaven.*
*The Commanding General of the Military might of Glory.*
*Jesus, Lord over all.*
*David knows the nature and the strength*
*and the intentions of his adversaries.*
*He knows for sure that even with his mighty men,*
*the valiant force of his friends, that he is no match for them.*
*That's why he can so quickly call on the Lord Jehovah Sabboath;*
*the High Lord of Heaven.*
*This soldier knows no failure, He's never lost a battle,*
*every conflict is a victory for Him; there has never been*
*a match or an equal of Him.*
*Your enemies may be more in number*
*and relentless for your destruction.*

*Despite what they do or what they are,*
*you have the marshaled forces of the Lord God of Hosts.*
*Call on Him, give Him your sword, let Him fight for you and let*
*Him win the battle.*

# *August 24*

*Psalm 89*

**His Throne**

**"Justice and judgment are the habitation of thy throne:**
**mercy and truth shall go before thy face."**
**vs.14**

*The seat of His authority, the position of His might; it is founded*
*on the two principles of His divine holiness: Justice and Judgment.*
*He sits enthroned as the High Judge of the universe.*
*All that is good and righteous exists and flows from Him. He is*
*therefore the only one who can truly determine life or death.*
*He alone is the only one who says who is worthy of blessing.*
*He is the sole person that can actually be offended*
*by anything evil or wicked.*
*Because all laws and rules are the direct result of His holiness, He*
*is the only one who is wronged when we sin.*
*He is the only one who deserves our repentant prayer and He is*
*the only one who can truly forgive.*
*When you pray, look toward His throne with your heart.*
*See Him high and lifted up.*
*Confess your sins quickly and then thank Him for His mercy.*

# *August 25*

*Psalm 149*

### *Beautiful People*

**"For the LORD taketh pleasure in his people:**
**he will beautify the meek with salvation."**

**vs.4**

*Meekness and beauty; it takes one to get the other.*
*Strange, isn't it, that the Holy Spirit puts the two of those*
*together; meekness and beauty?*
*God's gift to the meek, I mean, the truly meek, is to make them*
*beautiful using the element of salvation.*
*Meekness means power under control; it means having the*
*power to retaliate and choosing not to.*
*To be meek means you have within your power*
*the opportunity to handle things your way;*
*to allow your resources to meet your needs and challenges,*
*yet you have decided to forgo your way and instead lay your*
*weapons at His feet and let Him take the heat.*
*He will honor you by transforming you into an object of His glory.*
*No one said it would be easy, no one said it would feel good,*
*but someone has said, He that hath begun*
*a good work in you will perform it.*

# *August 26*

*Proverbs 29*

### *Warning! God's Holiness will Prevail*

*"He, that being often reproved hardeneth his neck,
shall suddenly be destroyed, and that without remedy."*
*vs.1*

*Mercy will not last forever.*
*He loves, yes, and His is kind of course, but He is also just and
holy. He will never compromise one aspect of His nature for the
sake of another. His love is balanced by His righteousness, His
kindness by His discernment. All that He is, is in balance and is
never in disparity, the sure power of His person exists because He
can never be untrue to Himself.*
*If you have been resting easy in your sin without the fear of God's
chastisement and justice, you should know two things.*
*One, as the verse here says, if you have been convicted repeatedly
and have hardened yourself to remain in sin, you'll be suddenly
and swiftly dealt with.*
*On the other hand, if you have been involved in sinful activities
and have received no conviction, no guilt and no chastisement,
you may not be saved at all (Hebrews 12:8). Make sure now
before it's too late.*

# *August 27*

*Psalm 30*

### *"Troubles don't last always"*

**"For his anger endureth but a moment;**
**in his favour is life: weeping may endure for a night,**
**but joy cometh in the morning."**
**vs.5**

*An older sister at my church growing up used to always say that whenever someone was poor or hardship was heavy on their mind. "Troubles don't last always."*
*I'm not sure if that's good English, but it is good doctrine. Life is full of aches and pains, isn't it?*
*You could, if you looked hard enough,*
*find something new to complain about every day; from an attack of the evil one, a calamity somewhere in the world, a new body ache, trouble among family members and so on.*
*David however, knowing that wallowing in the self-pity and morbid introspection will only sink us deeper into the quagmire of depression, he shakes us and reminds us that weeping can be expected.*

*The story doesn't stop there; Joy is on its way!*

*No matter how bad it may seem, presently, Rejoice!*

*Troubles don't last always.*

# August 28

Psalm 60

## Dry Spots

Expect them when they come.
Those periods of life when we seem in a rut
and the things of holiness seem to take a backseat
to the affairs of the physical world around us.
Dry spots in our walk: when praise is low
and our joy tank is near empty.
Those moments happen to everyone, but listen,
don't you settle in there, God has more to offer than the world.
Don't you stake down your tent, that bad wilderness you're in is a
way point, not a destination.
Your struggle through is just that, a passing through place.
If you stop and settle in the dry place, you'll die. There are always
enough graves in the wilderness, don't let yours be one of them.
David said, "Through God we shall do valiantly".
Get up and move on, this place is not known for its scenery, it's
known for its sorrow.
Tread ahead, make headway, and go valiantly in Jesus name!

## *August 29*

*Psalm 90*

### *Live! Day by Day!*

**"So teach us to number our days,**
**that we may apply our hearts unto wisdom."**
**vs. 12**

*With solemn perspective, consider; look back over your days on*
*earth, as far back as you can remember.*
*Are you satisfied?*
*If you are, rejoice!*
*If you're not, resolve.*
*If you have done everything, accomplished with victory*
*all of your goals and fulfilled all of your desires, if you see nothing*
*but success, then dance, rejoice, give God the worship and praise*
*He truly deserves.*
*However, if you still see that there are worlds to conquer, sinners*
*to be witnessed to, lands to evangelize, songs to be written and/*
*or praise to be sung to the Lord; resolve.*
*Live each day hard.*
*Have something to show for each day from now on. Write it*
*down, big and bold, not what you're going to do, but what you*
*have done.*

*Apply your heart to wisdom. Do things better every day. By His Spirit, change your life and the world.*

# *August 30*

*Psalm 120*

### *Stiffen Your Back!*

*It really doesn't matter what your enemies think of you. Anyone who is looking for great approval from the citizens of earth is following a vain path.*

*What God has done for us may seem a bit strange, but He has ordained life so that not everyone will like you; there will be people who are only happy when your life is not going well.*

*There are people who will delight in your pain, no matter how kind you may be to them.*

*God uses such things as this to strengthen us; to sharpen the edges from our swords.*

*You will always be less than you should be to someone every moment of your sojourn.*

*These afflictions of life are just that; life!*

*Don't fight a useless battle. Live your days to please Jesus.*

*If you do, you'll have more joy than you can ever use and peace that will cause your enemies to wonder.*

# *August 31*

*Psalm 150*

### *Praise!*

*Only six verses in total, but more than*

*a dozen commands to praise the Lord.*

*Let's do it!*

*It's important if we do it to follow*

*the choir director's instructions.*

*Here they are:*

*1). Who should we praise? The Lord (vs.1).*

*2). Where should we praise Him? In His sanctuary (vs.1).*

*3). Why should we praise Him? For His mighty acts according to*

*His excellent greatness! (vs.2)*

*4). With what should we praise Him? With the trumpet, with the*

*psaltery, with the harp, with the timbrel, and strings, and organs,*

*and cymbals of all types (vs.3-5).*

*5). How should we praise Him? With the dance.*

*6). Who should praise Him? Everything that has breath!*

*All of creation, anyone, anything; all of heaven and earth. Join in*

*the celebration, Praise Him!*

# September

## A Time for Blessing

**Lesson:** The Father of Glory

*"That the God of our Lord Jesus Christ, the Father of glory, may give unto you the spirit of wisdom and revelation in the knowledge of him:"* Ephesians 1:17

**Lesson**

While the New Testament reveals *glory* to be "special honor, praise or worship", the Old Testament uses a definition that means, "weight". The wisdom of all that is, was and will be belongs to the Father. He is the only one who can rightfully manage the affairs of all without pause or error. The New Testament use of the word "glory" incorporates brightness, worth, brilliance and splendor. Thus as the Father, He is the singular source of all fulfillment. He is absolutely the only being that glory emanates from naturally. The Father is the reason for glory's' existence. Therefore any object, person, experience or feeling, is validated as true and authentic only if the Father deems it worthy.

The value of anything is not determined by its' price; it is determined by Gods' assessment of it.

It is no wonder that in Christ alone the Father has found the object of His complete approval and acceptance.

(Col. 1:19; Heb. 1:3).

### Outline of the Passage

The Godhead expresses itself in Glory

    A. The Source of Glory (The Father)

    B. The Son of Glory (Jesus Christ)

    C. The Spirit of Glory (The Holy Spirit)

**Facts: The month of September, ninth month of the Gregorian calendar.**

It corresponds to the month of Elul; the sixth month of the Hebrew calendar. It is the month in which the temple wall was built.

*Focus:* **Prayer and blessings.**

It is the indicator of His favor toward and on us. Divine favor is pour out is always more than we deserve and in most critical need of. But with what we have received we, should learn to bless others. Seek out one person a week to bless.

*Assignment:* **Research**

Prove Christ as prophet, priest and king in the New Testament. Prove Him to be a Prophet after Moses, Priest after Melchezadek, and a King after David.

*Memory Work:*

**Exaltation:** Psalm 8:1

**Excellence:** Psalm 37:37

**Edification:** II Corinthians 5:19

**Evangelical:** Ephesians 2:8, 9

**Exhortive:** I Corinthians 15:58

**Educational:** I Timothy 2:5

# *Remembering Gods' Goodness*

## *Blessings*

## *Week Thirty-Five*

*Write your Psalm of rejoicing*

*this week.*

# *September 1*

*Proverbs 30*

**The Knowledge of the Holy**

**"I neither learned wisdom,**
**nor have the knowledge of the holy."**
**vs.3**

*It must be the single most important and urgent desire of*
*everyone: To know God.*
*To know God is the chief end of every man.*
*Without the urgent, passionate, relentless desire to know Him,*
*every single pursuit of mankind is in vain.*
*You can never expect to be happy and satisfied without the*
*knowledge of the Holy.*
*Paul threw everything away, for Christ as a prize, to know Him.*
*He had been captured by the grace of the God he could not*
*explain and it drove him to love Him and love Him above and*
*beyond every other thing.*
*You must, if you truly desire to live, you must set your sail, chart*
*your course to know Him, all of His attributes, learn about His*
*nature, discover the wonders of His great character, bask in His*
*presence, know God, intimate with Him in the beauty of His holi-*
*ness, the temple of your heart.*

# *September 2*

Psalm 119

### **His Word**

*It's all about the word, all of this psalm;*

*it's all about the word. 176 verses and only four*

*do not mention the word of God in one form or another.*

*Magnificent isn't it.*

*God has dedicated the longest chapter in the Bible*

*to what else? His word!*

*Some of the most precious statements ever penned on planet*

*earth are found here.*

*Some scholars believe that what we are reading here is the 18*

*silent years of Jesus; that period between ages 12 and 30.*

*It was His formative years in the secret school of the Spirit, His*

*time with the Father when and where His most intense training*

*took place.*

*It is given to us to observe and to order ourselves to be like Him.*

*Take the time, you have 22 small sections (micro-chapters if you*

*would) to fall in love with the Lord and His law.*

*Do it and grow and may the prayer of verse 18 be yours eternally.*

# *September 3*

*Psalm 119*

### *Thy Word*

*In this most fascinating psalm,*

*we see the glorious wonder of God's word.*

*As we read it we discover many wonderful truths*

*that enrich us each day.*

*The first thing we see is it is broken down into 22 sections.*

*Each section has only 8 verses.*

*Each section is identified with a different letter*

*in the Hebrew alphabet.*

*The amazing thing is that for each section,*

*each verse starts with the letter of that section.*

*The next thing we see is that the word of God*

*in this chapter is in nearly every verse.*

*There are only 4 verses that do not directly mention God's word.*

*Find out where they are.*

*Next, the word is given several distinctions in this psalm, they*

*are: the word, the law, statutes, testimonies, ordinances, com-*

*mandments, precepts, judgments, and His ways.*

*Find all of them; highlight them in your Bible.*

*Then research why the Holy Spirit takes the time to address His*

*word that way.*

# *September 4*

## Psalm 119
### *Learning His Way*

*Our walk, the word, His ways.*

*So opens the first three verses of this psalm.*

*Amazing isn't it?*

*The sum total of all we need to live for Him,*

*summed up in 3 verses.*

*Our walk is to be ordered by the Lord, His teachings are the*

*means by which our purpose is defined.*

*Then fulfillment in Him is not executed by getting everything we*

*want, but instead by seeking Him in His word, God has given a*

*blessing for everyone who will honor His teachings.*

*Then our lifestyle is given holy perspective*

*by consistently maintaining a holy pursuit.*

*When we walk in the way He has designed,*

*sin is not a constant; Instead His word becomes the hallmark*

*(the identifying quality) of those who love Him.*

*Holiness is the aura that should most indicates that we are His.*

*These indicators, these simple principles to a lifestyle, are what*

*will please Him.*

# *September 5*

*Psalm 119*

### *Biblical Absolutes*

*Found in this section of the great psalm*
*are some very important life promises.*
*In particular, verses 9 and 11.*
*These are some of the most recognizable verses in this chapter.*
*Verse 9 promises that strict adherence to God's word will cleanse,*
*purify, wash thoroughly, a young man's way.*
*The word will become the cleansing agent, the detergent for the*
*life of the young person, so that their future is free of all the junk*
*and garbage that most others face.*
*What a great promise!*
*This is a biblical absolute like no other.*
*Then verse 11 gives a promise unparalleled in scripture. It guar-*
*antees that the heart that keeps the word of God in residence will*
*be least likely to sin against God.*
*Wow!*
*These are practical principles that give definite power to live a*
*life that will honor Him.*
*Absolutes you can count on. Trust in them;*
*claim them as your own!*

# *September 6*

*Proverbs 31*

### *What a Woman!*

*Like every young man, in the "single" season of my life,*
*I was looking for the "perfect woman".*
*(Forget the fact that I was not "the perfect man"!)*
*I was looking for the girl who would be a deeply spiritual, kind,*
*romantic, sexy female that was incredibly good looking and*
*wanted to have a houseful of sons and several dogs.*
*You can see how much work the Lord had to do in me.*
*Yet all the things that I desired really*
*were hollow, selfish and immature.*
*Solomon's mom pulls him aside and instructs him*
*on the things that really matter.*
*The principle she shows are life qualities; aspects of a person's*
*being not hanging tapestries that will fall away.*
*These endearing traits are the results of years of denial, personal*
*devotion and true maturity.*
*Well did he ever find this woman?*
*Probably not, because the scriptures show us he was looking*
*for the things that are not qualities but facades. Looking for the*

*beauty of the Holy Spirit in a wife or husband is one of the great adventures of the spirit walk.*

*Don't be discouraged, the right person is there for you.*

# September 7

Psalm 119

### Open My Eyes

### "Open thou mine eyes, that I may behold wondrous things out of thy law."
### vs.18

*Without the interaction of the Holy Spirit it is impossible to understand the word of God.*
*Not in part, but at all. God's word, being God breathed, takes the personal intervention of the Spirit to cause understanding to happen.*
*We are flawed, finite and fallen.*
*His word is pure, powerful and perfect.*
*The two will never merge without divine aid.*
*God must, at our request, open our eyes to see clearly what His word is teaching.*
*That is why when people who don't know Him try to understand it, or worse, explain it, they fall so far away from its meaning and truth, as to make it sound ridiculous. God's word is the only way we can be connected to Him.*
*He never separates Himself from His word.*
*Pray this prayer and let Him show you His matchless power.*

*Remembering Gods' Goodness*

*Blessings*

## *Week Thirty-Six*

---

*I Thessalonians 5:18, "In everything give thanks", are you able to do this? Having a heart of thanksgiving is a command. Are you able to give God thanks in every situation? This week review the things you are not happy with in your life, and then start the process of changing even the most uncomfortable situations to a time of worship to the Lord.*

---

## *September 8*

*Psalm 31*

### *God my Rock*

*What does it mean to have a rock in your life?*
*Well, let's examine the rock.*
*The rock is steadfast, it's there; it's not moving, it's permanent.*
*It's consistent; it remains the same, weather won't affect it,*
*storms, tornados, hurricanes, etc. It's not going anywhere. It has*
*nature on its side.*
*It is the paragon of strength.*
*Dauntless it remains the same; it does not alter itself*
*to conform to any agenda.*
*It's secure in that it has no down times,*
*no pressures, it has no enemies.*
*It's greater than all forces around it.*
*It's not seasonal. It doesn't change because*
*of the moods of the world around it.*
*God is our rock, dependable, secure, steadfast,*
*unmovable, and never changing.*
*He's always the same, always committed to keeping His promises.*
*He is never anyone but Himself.*
*God our rock, He is always there.*

# *September 9*

*Psalm 31*

### *Trusting Him*

**"But I trusted in thee, O LORD: I said, Thou art my God. My times are in thy hand: deliver me from the hand of mine enemies, and from them that persecute me."**
**vs.14-15**

*Why bother?*
*Why do we put our absolute trust in a God*
*that fails all of our senses?*
*Why do we give eternal allegiance to someone who chooses not*
*to conform to our senses so that we can relate better to Him?*
*These are viable questions, questions that the world has been*
*asking since the garden.*
*Why would we obligate ourselves to someone who will not at*
*least meet us half way?*
*It's a simple answer really; He doesn't need to meet us half way.*
*He put His only Son to bridge the entire gap between heaven and*
*earth, between time and eternity; between God and man.*
*He's already proven that it's not necessary for Him to conform to*
*mankind at any other level.*

*He's related to a lost people by loving them*

*beyond understanding.*

*That's why.*

*He is more than worthy of our trust.*

*He is worthy of our all.*

# September 10

*Psalm 31*

## The Lord: Our Truest Friend

*Father?*

*Of course!*

*Faithful?*

*Yes, absolutely!*

*But, Friend?*

*How?*

*How can God prove friendship?*

*How can He do the things necessary to maintain a friendship?*

*What qualities does He display to qualify His friendship-like com-mitment to us?*

*Well, apparently, David had no problem with this question.*

*He stated in verse 1 that God delivers,*

*He delivers in His righteousness.*

*He is correcting me as well as protecting me.*

*He holds onto the standard of His holy requirements.*

*Then he speaks of how God defends him in verse 2.*

*God not only sets us free, He talks to our enemy and*

*takes on the battle as though it was His own.*

*Then, most importantly, He shows David*

*how much He delights in him.*

*Verse 23, God loves oh, so much!*

*More than the imagination can conceive.*

*He is a Father, yes, and that is so wonderful,*

*He is even faithful, what a comfort!*

*But just as much, He is a friend, the perfect Friend,*

*and what a Friend He is!*

# September 11

*Psalm 61*

### God, My Life

**"So will I sing praise unto thy name for ever,**

**that I may daily perform my vows."**

**vs.8**

*What promise, I mean daily/lifelong commitments,*

*have you made to Christ?*

*How would you describe your daily walk with the Lord?*

*Are you one of those who try to fit Him in to your busy schedule?*

*Is He a passing thought from time to time each day? Stop it if any*

*of that is true.*

*Stop it now before you slide any further into the muck of religion.*

*Now it's your responsibility to restart, start over.*

*Put your life in do-over mode.*

*God has no desire whatsoever to be a part of your day!*

*He wants no inclusion in your world.*

*He certainly doesn't want to be first in your life,*

*He wants to be ONLY!*

*Don't include Him; give Him complete mastery,*

*give Him total sovereignty.*

*Bow before Him in reverence daily and recommit to Him.*

*Come to Him as a slave before His master.*

*Give to Him total commitment, total obedience, and total love.*

# *September 12*

*Psalm 61*

### *The Reason I Serve Him*

*I'll let this psalm of David give the reason why I have completely*
*surrendered to Christ.*
*It's totally self-serving I admit.*
*First, vs.1 – He hears me.*
*Whenever I cry to Him, He hears me.*
*He is never too busy, never distracted.*
*Vs.3 – He hides me.*
*It's proven whenever the gale force winds and storms of life bom-*
*bard, and I need a shelter, that's what He does.*
*Vs.6 – He honors me.*
*He rewards my meager, faithful days with His great goodness.*
*And finally, most importantly, vs.7 – He helps me.*
*He helps me not so much because I'm always in trouble (which I*
*am!), but because I am so helpless; I'm lost, I'm pitiful.*
*I have given myself completely to Christ because I have con-*
*fronted the truth about me.*
*Have you? Have you at least told yourself the truth*
*about who you are?*
*It is then and only then, you'll see that He is the only one worth*
*serving with all you have and are.*

# *September 13*

## *Psalm 91*

## *The Secret Place*

**"He that dwelleth in the secret place of the most High shall abide under the shadow of the Almighty."**

**vs.1**

*The place of removal; it's where God told Moses to go,*
*that place "by me" (Exodus 33:21).*
*It is the sequestered place that*
*the Lord assigned to Elijah (I Kings 17:3).*
*It was "there" He would care for him, nourish and refresh him.*
*The secret place, that quiet, God invited covert that*
*requires that everything else is dismissed and put away, as in the*
*story of Jacob (Genesis 32:24), when God has our full attention*
*and there are no interruptions.*
*The Secret Place of the Most High!*
*This is the Holy of Holies in the heart of you, where no earthly*
*concern can pierce through.*
*It is the quiet chamber of awe and splendor, where the conversa-*
*tion with the Lord God Jehovah is sanctified; in other words, the*
*daily prayer chamber of Jesus (Mark 1:35).*
*When (be honest now) was the last time you were there?*

# September 14

*Psalm 121*

### The Lord Which Made Heaven and Earth

*Simple question, strong answer.*
*It really is a question you know, "...*
*from whence cometh my help?"*
*That's the question the prophet is asked in this song.*
*Where does your great help come from.*
*It's not unlike the question Delilah plagued sex-craved Samson*
*with, "From where does your great strength lie?"*
*The intent of the question belies its motive.*
*Simply, there is nothing obvious with you that give reason for*
*your incredible advantages.*
*So the prophet explains correctly, the way Samson should have:*
*"My help cometh from the Lord."*
*The world should marvel and wonder at us.*
*They should be perplexed and confused as to why it seems we*
*have favor and advantage.*
*Such should be the case, so that when we give them the answer,*
*they must concede there is a God, and that God that is, loves them*
*too (Psalm 126:2; Matthew 5:16).*

# Remembering Gods' Goodness

## Blessings

# Week Thirty-Seven

*Each day this week read Isaiah 61:1-3, following the directions the prophet gives to those who are depressed.*

# September 15

## Psalm 1

### The Blessed Man

**"Blessed is the man that walketh not in the counsel
of the ungodly, nor standeth in the way of sinners,
nor sitteth in the seat of the scornful."**

**vs.1**

*The three words that stand out here are: counsel, way and seat.*
*Each word shows the components of a life style progression.*
*The "counsel" of the ungodly denotes –*
*the advice, opinion, direction or instruction.*
*The blessed man is he who finds the wisdom*
*of the world to be foolish and vain.*
*No matter how attractive it may seem, it is in its entirety,*
*ungodly, and it has no kingdom life or value to it.*
*The second word is the word "way";*
*it is the Hebrew word "derek".*
*An earth moving machine is often called a "derek".*
*It cuts a path.*
*The cut path of sinners is always constructed to lead to destruc-*
*tion; it has no other purpose or ultimate end.*
*The end of all sin is the same: destruction.*

*The final word "seat" denotes dwelling, the living or lifestyle.*

*The scoffers usually sit and criticize anything and everything*

*they can think of.*

*They're never happy and constantly complain.*

*Godly men avoid them.*

*Now, what is the path that you follow?*

*Is the counsel of Christ your constant guide and direction?*

*Are you following the path He has made for you from the foundation of the world?*

*Finally, how you livin'?*

# September 16

*Psalm 8*

**Excellent**

**"O LORD our Lord, how excellent is thy name in all the earth!**
**who hast set thy glory above the heavens."**

**vs.1**

*"God's inherent excellence", made by the absolute quality of His*
*own divine holiness."*
*That's what glory is, His inherent excellence.*
*He has set His glory, the "weight" of His majesty*
*above the heavens.*
*He is by His very nature above all that is or ever will be. Men in*
*their arrogance think that from their vantage point it is possible*
*to analyze and critique God;*
*How laughable.*
*The Lord sits above His creation and calls it into account.*
*He is the only excellent one there is!*
*His name, the accurate history of His deeds, is holy and pure.*
*Every deed of His hands is awesome and glorious.*
*His nature, character and holiness are displayed*
*in all of His creation.*

*Yet, with all the wonders of His might and majesty,*

*His glory and His beauty unmatched anywhere, He still chooses*

*to encounter sinful man;*

*He decides to love and forgive him.*

*He still sent His Son to die for him.*

*Oh Lord our Lord, how excellent is Thy name!*

# September 17

### Psalm 16

### *All I'll Ever Need*

### *"Preserve me, O God: for in thee do I put my trust."*
### *vs.1*

To be <u>preserved</u> means that whatever outside forces try to influ-
ence, taint or disrupt the way of my life, He will step in and dis-
miss it altogether.
The Lord my <u>portion</u> – vs.5, sets in motion the concept that, as He
promised, He's all I'll ever need.
He has assigned the care of my needs to the riches of His glory
(Philippians 4:19).
So I'm never spiritually bankrupt or my soul is never in need.
He has made the same <u>promise</u> (vs.7) to me that He gave to
Abraham (Genesis 15:1).
He is my shield and security, there is no greater <u>protection</u> avail-
able anywhere, for God cannot fail.
His <u>presence</u> – vs.11, is my comfort and my joy and His <u>pleasure</u>
keeps my life fulfilled and ever content.
He is my light and my day, my song and my dream come true.
This Father of mine allows me to be with Him for eternity.
I cannot help but want to be with Him forever.

## *September 18*

### *Psalm 37*

### *4 Keys to Contentment*

*1. (v.3) "__Trust in the Lord and do good__".*

*The word trust here implies the idea of handing over the weapons of war that one might have to defend himself and the things precious to him.*

*It is a sure-fire way to win battles; surrender to the Great King.*

*2. (v.4) "__Delight thyself also in the Lord__."*

*Find all of your soul's needs and desires in Him. In so doing you allow for the Holy Spirit to affect a change in your world that soon begins to look like His planned will for your life eternally.*

*3. (vs.4) "__Commit thy way unto the Lord__."*

*The word "way" here is the Hebrew word "derek", it means a deeply cut trench or path that exposes very little so that the enemy has a smaller target.*

*Let the Lord determine your way,*

*and your enemy will be confounded.*

*4. (vs.7) "__Rest in the Lord and wait__". Arguably resting in the Lord and waiting for Him to accomplish His will and plan for us is the most difficult task we face as believers.*

*Waiting patiently is not a desirable prospect, but it is the critical key to the walk of faith.*

*Our timing is not His timing, remember,*

*part of this walk is to be changed into His image.*

*Let Him do what only He can do.*

## *September 19*

*Psalm 67*

### *The Bounty of Heaven*

**"Let the people praise thee, O God;
let all the people praise thee. Then shall the earth yield her
increase; and God, even our own God, shall bless us"**
**vs. 5-6**

*It is a biblical absolute, a guarantee from heaven
with no small print attached.
When God is praised, magnified, and adored the earth
shall yield all of its beauty and we will be blessed of God.
Praise is what God deserves.
A life without praise is a dry desert of extremes,
parched and cracked.
To the one who will honor Him, God responds with fulfillment,
satisfaction, and protection.
He gives the increase of heaven and the benefits of glory.
When we Honor Him and say about Him the things He has
revealed to us about character and nature, He responds by
changing the tone and tenor of the world around us and meets
all our needs as only God can.*

## September 20

*Psalm 33*

### Raise the Praise

**"Rejoice in the LORD, O ye righteous: for praise is comely for the upright. Praise the LORD with harp: sing unto him with the psaltery and an instrument of ten strings. Sing unto him a new song; play skilfully with a loud noise."**

**vs.1 - 3**

*God is wonderful; He is truly and beyond compare.*
*His majesty and glory are the reason alone*
*to lift Him up and honor Him.*
*But much more than all these, on a personal level (vs. 20) "**Our***
*soul waiteth for the Lord, He is **our** help and **our** shield."*
*Many great things, infinite great things can be said about God,*
*but nothing can be more precious than to be allowed to take pos-*
*session of Him as our own.*
*The prophet waits until the last 3 verses to get to his point. After*
*mentioning everything he could about God and His awesomeness,*
*he moves from the 3rd person to the 1st and uses language of per-*
*sonal intimacy – "I am His – but He is mine".*

# September 21

*Ruth 2:15-16*

*Handfuls of Purpose*

### Deliberate Acts of Kindness

*The kindest evidence of God's love*
*and life within us is a quality called "mercy".*
*Mercy is when out of a heart of compassion,*
*someone seeks to meet the apparent needs of another; someone*
*who cannot help themselves and is not in a position to repay*
*the act. This is greatly illustrated here in the story of Ruth the*
*Moabite.*
*She has connected to Naomi, her mother-in-law*
*and by love, she has committed herself to be faithful to her family,*
*her heritage and her faith.*
*This catches the eyes of the kinsman redeemer.*
*Being an Old Testament type and picture of the Lord Jesus, he*
*shows her kindness and mercy by insuring that she is cared for*
*without embarrassing her or making her feel pitied.*
*This is from a person, who owes her nothing,*
*but shows her love regardless.*
*Here's a project: show the love and mercy of Jesus to someone*
*you don't know today.*

# Remembering Gods' Goodness

## Blessings

# Week Thirty-Eight

*Read Psalm 34 everyday this week.*

## *September 22*

*1 Samuel 1:12-19*

### *Honorable Heart/ Priceless Prayer*

*Does my life reflect that God, to whom I am praying, can see that I am sincere? When I call out to Him, begging for His hand to work on my behalf, do I produce evidence that shows that I am seeking His heart constantly when I am <u>not</u> in need?*

*Does my daily existence find me in His presence seeking His face more than His favors?*

*The wonder of having Jesus is not that as God, He can do anything, but because He is God, He is **my** everything.*

*Hannah was barren.*

*Her marital opponent had several children which in that society was a sign of God's favor.*

*But Hannah knew the God of Israel.*

*Her decision to entreat God was based on a relationship.*

*Calamity and hardships are present constantly in the fabric of human life.*

*Being a Christian does not exempt us from this.*

*But when time comes for us to call on Him in need, it should be out of a relationship with Him.*

*Such a relationship divinely entitles us to be intimate and personal.*

*Don't run from this encounter, here the deep discussions can take place and our God will engage us in levels of revelation beyond our wildest dreams.*

# *September 23*

*2 Samuel 1:25-26*

### *Friendship*

*It has been maligned by the repugnant*
*and vile thinking minds of our generation.*
*To promote sexual deviancy and the homosexual need for valida-*
*tion, wicked minds have condemned themselves by spouting erro-*
*neously that this passage implies a sexual relationship between*
*David and Jonathan.*
*These men were united as the scripture states as brothers.*
*Both of them were so committed to the bonds of friendship that*
*they made covenants with each other that even surpassed the*
*affection the man would expect from the opposite sex.*
*This is what true love for someone else means.*
*In 1 Samuel 18, Jonathan, the crown prince, the heir apparent to*
*the throne commits all that he has to his hero and new brother*
*David, his sword, his shield; even his crown and throne.*
*This is an example of true friendship,*
*of true surrender to someone greater.*
*What have you given to Jesus, does He sit on your throne?*

# *September 24*

*1 Kings 2:3*

### **Absolute Guarantee**

*Anyone who says that living the faith walk*
*of Christianity is easy, is either a new believer or not a believer;*
*and **I won't take that back.***
*That statement is simply untrue, but all throughout scripture,*
*God gives us instructions on how to get through the pain with joy.*
*He tells us how to endure the night with singing,*
*He examples the walk of faith with real people*
*in similar situations that we go through.*
*He makes sure that all along the way,*
*the difficulties of this life are survivable.*
*This passage is one of them.*
*David tells his son Solomon that if he would just obey the law of*
*God, he would prosper.*
*No one is flawless, faultless or infallible.*
*But the Holy Spirit of God is determined to make us like Christ.*
*Here is your assignment: keep God's word,*
*love the Lord with everything you are and have, rely on Him;*
*difficult, yes... but possible in Christ!*

# September 25

## 2 Kings 6:12-18
### Open Our Eyes Lord

*The truth is the enemy is always surrounding us.*

*We face enemies before us - this world's system.*

*We encounter enemies above us – Satan and the forces of wicked-*
*ness, and most of all an enemy among us - the flesh and its sinful*
*appetites and cravings.*

*These facts will never change,*

*as long as we are of this mortal coil.*

*But there is also another constant truth; "they that be with us are*
*more than they that be with them."*

*Surrounding these that would seek to surround you, are the*
*armies of the Lord God of Hosts; Jehovah Sabboath is His name.*

*Don't forget the truth of His promises.*

*Whenever it looks as though you are outnumbered, call to mind*
*these verses and claim them as promises that He has said He*
*would keep: Psalm 91:8; Psalm 31:15; Psalm 33:18; Psalm 34:19;*
*Psalm 37:25; Matthew 28:20.*

*Ask the Lord to open your eyes, not so much your physical eyes;*
*but your spiritual eyes, to see by faith, the truth of His promises.*

# September 26

*2 Kings 5:1*

### But...

He was a seasoned soldier, "Captain of the host". He was a steadfast servant, "a great man with his master".

He was a stalwart soul, "because by him the Lord had given deliverance unto Syria."

He was a successful strategist, "He was also a mighty man."

But he was sadly sick, "but he was a leper."

Everyone could list their virtues, accomplishments, successes and glories; it's easy to show the good, beautiful sides of our profile, but... we all have a fatal flaw.

We all are born with a sickness that is fatal.

Yes, I know that as believers we are free from the penalty of sin and the punishment of sin.

But until we are called home, we still must deal with our sinful flesh and thus the practice of sin is still a major problem.

Don't let your excuses dupe you into a false sense of security.

You must always remember without His strength, we may have successes and victories, but we are still going to face trouble.

But, whatever we face, we do not face it alone.

He is ever stalwart; He is ever vigilant;

He, our God never loses the battle.

# September 27

## 1 Chronicles 13:7-14
### The Right Thing, the Wrong Way

**Motive:** *To get the ark where it belongs... back in Israel.*

**Intent:** *To get it there as swiftly as possible.*

**Error:** *Moving the ark on a cart drawn by horses,*
*instead of the God ordained way of having men*
*(a specific group of men) carry it.*

**Result:** *Uzza touches the ark and is killed.*

*Now why all the fuss?*

*Why is God so upset?*

*Why is He willing to kill someone*
*who obviously was trying to help Him?*

*Well, that's the point; God does not need any help.*

*God wanted men to always feel the weight*
*of spiritual responsibility.*

*He wanted Israel to always regard His presence*
*as privilege and respect His presence as holy.*

*To do anything else was an act of man imposing himself on God,*
*thus acting as if he were wiser than God.*

*Despite your motives and intents, always do the right things, the*
*right way. Always follow God's plan.*

# September 28

## 2 Chronicles 14:2-3
### Do the Right Thing

*To get God's favor and to experience the abundant life He prom-ises, there must be a changing of perspective.*

*The path of life you've been taking regardless of how successful it has been for you, will never give lasting peace and true fellow-ship if it does not align with the will of the Lord.*

*You can try everything that reason and philosophy recommend, but they all will eventually fail and you'll be left dejected, hollow and unfulfilled.*

*So how do you do it?*

*How do you change perspectives on a life you've always known and become used to?*

*Simple: do what Asa's did.*

*1). Do the right thing that pleases God.*

*God is only about what will give Him glory. So, glorify Him.*

*2). Do away with religion. Remove and deny everything that seeks to make itself bigger than the Lord in your life.*

*3). Develop a relationship with Christ.*

*Spend much time in prayer and solitary communication with Him.*

*Make your time with Him an imperative;*
*allow nothing to disturb or come before it.*
*Do the right thing.*

# *September 29*

## *Ezra 8:21-23*

### *With Our Backs Against the Wall*

*What is the reason most people*
*who are unbelievers reject Christ?*
*The answer is both surprising*
*and surprisingly simple: Christians.*
*Because believers have decided more to live*
*a life not consistent with the scriptures, but find validation with*
*worldly and fleshly endeavors; each day it becomes much more*
*difficult to win the lost to Christ.*
*Here Ezra confronts the issue head on.*
*He had no problem confiding in his God*
*before the king of a heathen nation.*
*He made his boast in the power of his God who would not only*
*provide for his people, but who would protect them.*
*He had made very powerful claims about the God of the Jews.*
*Now he must put his own faith into action.*
*To testify about a God who can perform*
*the impossible on our behalf is one thing.*

*To testify to the facts of a God who*
*had and does the impossible consistently in the*
*most impossible situations is quite something else.*
*Put your belief into action!*

## *September 30*

*Nehemiah 8:8*

### **The Essence of Bible Study**

*The three ingredients to effective bible study*
*are found right here in these words;*

*1). **"So they read..."***
*Reading, reading, reading.*
*A support verse that emphasizes the exact same principle in the*
*New Testament is 1 Timothy 4:13, **"Give attention to reading"***
*consistent, attentive reading.*

*2). **"in the book of the Law of God distinctly..."***
*Research.*
*The word means "to separate" or divide. Sound familiar?*
***"Study to show thyself approved of God,***
***a workman that needeth not to be ashamed;***
***rightly dividing the word of truth".***
*Separate, breakdown into small parts; research, learn as much*
*about the verse, passage, word or thought as possible.*

*3). "**and gave the sense and caused them***

*to understand the reading"*

<u>*Reasoning.*</u>

*Working through the text and with the help*

*of the great teacher, the Holy Spirit, we come to understand what*

*God is saying through His holy word.*

*Three things are needed to learn His word, don't neglect them.*

# October

## A Time to Seek Wisdom

**Lesson:** The Father of All

**"One God and Father of all, who is above all,
and through all, and in you all."**

***Ephesians 4:6***

*Lesson*

He is the Lord high God of all that is: Past present and future all culminates in Him. He is the true Father of all creation – the First of all that is, the impetus of everything in creation.

Everything that is subsequent to His original order, plan and design is not of the Father but of this worlds' system.

God and only God is the origin of all that is right, wonderful, majestic and awesome.

His intent and purpose is right and true without flaw or exception.

It is mans' opportunity to know and enjoy this one and singular Heart as his Maker, Father and Friend.

All creation looks to Him in adoration.

Every bird sings a specific song praising His wonder.

Each blade of grass and limb of bush and tree defies gravity's downward pull to magnify Him will outstretched arms in praise.

The roar of the lion heralds His regal presence in the wilderness. And even the small butterfly reflects the splendor of His creative genius.

To know Him and His love is the most consuming rapture anyone could ever know.

He is all in all, the answer to ever longing and the true end of every desire.

### Outline of the Passage

Verse 6 displays the greatness of the One God

    A. God and His position (Above all)

    B. God and His power (Through all)

    C. God and His presence (In you all)

*Facts:* **The month of October, tenth month of the Gregorian calendar.**

It corresponds to the month of Ethanim; the seventh month of the Hebrew calendar. It is the month in which the Jubilee was proclaimed and that Solomon's' temple was dedicated.

*Focus:* **Prayer and wisdom.**

God is so insistent that we walk in wisdom, He promises to give it to all who ask. Saved and unsaved alike. Pray every day of your life for wisdom. Don't act in any situation without it.

*Assignment:* **Research**

There are 8 different types of Psalms. Go through the entire book and identify each one.

They are:

Repentance – Rescue – Rejoicing – Remembrance – Return – Revenge – Relief – Restoration.

*Memory Work:*

**Exaltation:** Psalm 47:1
**Excellence:** Mark 1:35
**Edification:** Psalm 91:8

**Evangelical:** Romans 10:13

**Exhortive:** II Thessalonians 2:17

**Educational:** Galatians 4:4, 5

*Doing His Will*

*Wisdom*

## *Week Thirty-Nine*

*Read the first seven chapters of Proverbs this week; one each day. Then read the life of Solomon in I Kings. What decisions did he make that were contrary to the advice his father gave to him in the first seven chapters of the book? Can you see yourself in any of his bad choices?*

# October 1

### Esther 3:1-2
### *Flesh vs. Spirit*

He was the great grandson of King Agag. You remember him from 1 Samuel 15:32, the great king of the Amalekites. They were the people who took advantage of Israel as they passed through the wilderness on their way to the promise land. They were direct descendents of Esau; a man of the flesh. Amalek is always a type of the unbridled, untamed, rebellious flesh. It will always rear its head at a time when you are most vulnerable. Other than the people of Sodom, they are the only nation the Lord called, **sinners**. Haman is a descendent of this nation. Because Saul did not deal with the Amalekites as God commanded him, the offspring of their king is set to destroy the entire race of Jews. Mordecai, a type of the Holy Spirit, will not bow to Haman. For the Spirit of God will never submit to the flesh. He will never allow the flesh to rule. King Herod was a direct descendant of Amalek, and when brought before him, Christ would not even acknowledge him *or speak to him; simply because God does not and will not give place, honor or even attention to the flesh.*

*My friend, never bring the deeds of the flesh before Him.*

*Never defile the Lords' person by asking Him to accept His enemy: your flesh.*

# *October 2*

### Job 1:13-20

### **Trouble Comes on an Ordinary Day**

*"And there was a day..."*
*No dark clouds forbidding the back drop, no foul wind swirling;*
*there was no indication at all that this day would be any different*
*than the rest.*
*That's true of any time troubles come.*
*Trouble does not announce itself like in the movies.*
*Trouble does not circle a place on your calendar.*
*Trouble comes, for everyone, at any time, for no <u>apparent</u> reason.*
*There is always a reason, but there isn't always an apparent one.*
*Behind the scenes; just beyond the veil of the natural, there is*
*great activity.*
*Events much more dynamic than the human eye can see or the*
*human heart can stand.*
*The events of the Spirit that are invisible to the senses we trust in*
*so much, play a much larger role than most of us are aware.*
*That's why Paul says, "walk in the Spirit" and again, "though we*
*walk in the flesh we do not war in the flesh".*
*Like Job, see beyond your circle of circumstances*
*and trust in Him.*

*He knows all the details of your troubles and will be with you through them.*

# *October 3*

*Ecclesiastes 1:16-17*

## *A Life Full of Regrets*

*When he was a young man, he wrote a book of **romance** called*
*Song of Songs or Song of Solomon.*
*When he was a middle-aged man,*
*he wrote a book of **rules** called Proverbs.*
*But because he failed to listen to his godly father David (Proverbs*
*4:23), he fell (1 Kings 11:1-9) and as a result, as an old man he*
*wrote a book of **regrets**; this one, called Ecclesiastes.*
*Repeatedly throughout it he says in several different ways: "I*
*wish I hadn't done that."*
*Over and over again he regales his accomplishments*
*and the result is always the same, "its foolishness"*
*or "It's vexation of spirit".*
*How sad!*
*My dear friend Dr. Kenneth Grant, called him,*
*"the wisest fool that ever lived."*
*I think that is very accurate.*
*He tried wine and women; foolishness.*
*He dabbled in wealth and work; folly.*
*He experimented in wisdom and wit; and it was all frivolous.*

*So at the end of his life, with barely a discernible, at best marginal relationship with God, he tells young people: Honor God now (Ecclesiastes 12:1), don't regret your life as I do.*

*The whole duty of man is to fear God,*

*and keep His commandments.*

*Take his advice: Live for Christ Now!!!*

# *October 4*

*Song of Solomon 5:16*

### *Altogether Lovely*

*There's not enough space.*

*John the apostle said, the world could never hold all the books, if*
*someone could write everything that should be said about Him.*
*In this tome of romance, He is given so many terms of endear-*
*ment, so many comparisons to things beautiful and wondrous:*
*Rose of Sharon; Lily of the Valley.*
*Every description of Him is all at once both fantastic, yet frus-*
*trating, for while each is accurate, none is adequate.*
*We can speak of Him in flowing terms, about His greatness and*
*power; strong words about His character and compassion.*
*We could exhaust every word in every dictionary in every lan-*
*guage known; all would be phrased just right, but none would or*
*could be enough.*
*Even the writer limited by the bounds of language, metaphor and*
*simile just sums it up the best he could.*
*Four words that tell the tale: "He is altogether lovely."*

## *October 5*

*Isaiah 6:1*

### **High and Holy God**

*His position is high, His presence is holy.*
*He is the only one who is so high; He must look down into heaven.*
*His glory is high above the earth, His majesty is above all cre-*
*ation; He is other than all that is; never included, never equaled,*
*cannot be compared to.*
*He is high and lifted up!*
*He sits upon the throne of His own domain.*
*It is not an elected place; His is not opting*
*for popularity or social acceptance.*
*He is not one of many, He is only!*
*The response of all that draw near, are repelled by the abject*
*truth of His deity that rejects and dispels any and everything that*
*is not like Him.*
*In reverence, the sanctified, sinless sons of light*
*know of His inherent excellence and would not defile*
*the honor of His glory by looking upon Him.*
*This is God.*
*No other is like Him.*

*None other can approach Him.*

*This is the Lord God Almighty.*

*High and Holy!*

# *October 6*

*Jeremiah 15:16*

### *Thy Word*

*Not parts of His word, but deliberately the Spirit says, "Thy*
*words", every single word spoken by Him is divine.*
*There is not an error at all in any of His word.*
*Man is fallible, completely fallen and is guaranteed to fail.*
*His word is able, if obeyed, to bring joy and rejoicing to the*
*human heart, no matter how bad the condition of that heart.*
*Because the prophet uses the words of discovery, "**were found**",*
*we can trust that there is hope in His word.*
*They are the answers to our problems and needs.*
*But then he uses the phrase **"the joy***
*and rejoicing of mine heart."***
*This word is the help of the wounded heart.*
*His word is able to calm my storm in my weakest hour.*
*It gives me joy, it helps me!*
*And then it reveals to me the reality of my relationship to Him by*
*honoring me with His name.*
***"For I am called by thy name, oh Lord God of hosts."***
*His word does this!*

*His word identifies me as being more
to Him than just an element of His ability.
So saint, trust in His word!!!*

# *October 7*

*Lamentations 3:25*

### *Wait!!!*

*It is God's method of growth for the believer (Psalm 27:4; Psalm*
*62:5; Isaiah 40:31; Habakkuk 2:3).*
*It is the foundation for faith living.*
*It is the first word that the Spirit would say*
*to the expectant heart: "Wait".*
*It gives room for faith to work.*
*It does not need time to accomplish the work of God.*
*Time has nothing to add to the process that God uses to develop*
*and strengthen us.*
*God teaches us that patience is a quality of character that <u>every</u>*
*believer lacks (Hebrews 10:35-36).*
*<u>Wait on the Lord; He is doing a work in you</u>.*
*It is a fruit of the Spirit that will not work well*
*in the lives of clock watchers.*
*This little word has on its back, all of history.*
*It holds the story of untold victories and failures.*
*It is the telling evidence of immaturity or maturity.*
*It holds in its grasps the lessons of great works of God through*
*ordinary people.*

*The prophet Jeremiah knew this; he had been told of God, that*

*Israel because of her sin would be captives for 70 years.*

*But during that time God was going to change them.*

*They had to endure the purifying forge of patience*

*before they could be free.*

*Don't get discouraged when time seems to pass by while you wait*

*on God; you and I and every child of God, needs patience.*

*Doing His Will*

*Wisdom*

*Week Forty*

*The bible says that wisdom is the beginning of several things. Do an exhaustive research on that theme and discover all the verses that teach on this topic.*

# *October 8*

*Ezekiel 1:1-14*

### *Glimpses of Glory*

### *"I saw visions of God"*

*WOW! It is rare; but it happens.*

*From time to time, only for the purpose of His glory,*

*God will pull back the curtain of time, space,*

*dimension and the limits of the flesh, and reveal to the finite,*

*the glories of the infinite.*

*From time to time God will show an aspect*

*of His eternal plan to the eyes of sinful humans.*

*Here is one of the great instances in scripture where God*

*allows us to look into the face of heaven for a brief moment*

*experienced by His man Ezekiel.*

*The shining sons of glory, in this case the Cherubim, are shown in*

*their celestial splendor, moving at God speed to do His will.*

*The sight must have been awesome,*

*overwhelming and humbling.*

*All at once, Ezekiel is given perspective that no one before him*

*has been given.*

*But this need not be the reason to believe God.*

*The sights of the Spirit hold no greater weight than the day by day presence of God. You can see great wonders daily, always showing you God is working.*

*And the work He is doing is for your benefit and His glory.*

# *October 9*

*Hosea 8:7*

### *Sowing and Reaping*

*With heavy sighs we watch people make very bad decisions all the time.*

*It's not so much that they are poor choices that are sins against God, but also that the brief moments of pleasure will never equal the consequences of pain.*

*No amount of repentance can ever change the word of God.*

*All too often the pain and hardship one feels now is just the ful-filling result of bad decisions before.*

*"For they have sown the wind..." the Hebrew word for "wind" here means "breath", a puff of air, a small transaction.*

*"... they shall reap the whirlwind".*

*The word for "whirlwind" is the word "suphah"; or hurricane.*

*Your sin, my sin, absent from the mercy and compassion of God, may seem to be so small that it has hurt no one... foolish thinking.*

*The breath has become, or will become the hurricane.*

*However, if we sow righteousness, imagine the benefits!*

*Choose the good and not evil, the holy not the profane.*

*Let the laws of sowing and reaping work good in your life.*

# *October 10*

*Joel 2:21*

### *The Lord Will Do Great Things*

*He begins the chapter warning about certain judgment.*
*He shows how the armies of the Lord will*
*exact His wrath and vengeance.*
*The force of the heavenly onslaught will be like the world has*
*never seen or heard of before.*
*The Lord God of Hosts will prove His power and might and His*
*enemies will be powerless to stop Him.*
*This is long overdue, retribution for all the evil and wickedness*
*that God showed mercy for.*
*But that day of wrath will be one that history will never forget.*
*And as always with God's righteous indignation,*
*there is a chance for mercy and forgiveness.*
*"Fear not, O land; be glad and rejoice:*
*for the Lord will do great things."*
*That's just the way the Lord is; He has every right to be*
*scornful and merciless but instead, He chooses to show mercy to*
*those who would come to Him.*
*Give Him the opportunity to do great things for you.*
*Come to Him, His way and begin anew a sweet walk with the one*
*who loves you so.*

## *October 11*

*Amos 8:9-10*

### *Clues to Calvary*

*This prophecy has an approximate date of 784 B.C., yet with Holy Spirit exclusive accuracy, announces with very clear detail four indisputable clues to Calvary. Look at them:*

*1). "I will cause the sun to go down at noon"*

*– read Matthew 27:45.*

*Clearly this is no coincidence; God is informing the world as to what to expect in that day of redemption.*

*2). "I will turn your feasts into mourning", see Mark 14:1-2.*

*During the feasts of unleavened bread; Passover, it should be a time to remember, to reflect, to rejoice for the goodness of the Lord, but not this particular one.*

*This Passover will be the last that will ever be needed.*

*The reason is found in the 3rd clue.*

*3). "I will make it as the mourning of an only son".*

*How much clearer does it need to be? (Read Luke 23:27-32).*

*It's as if Amos was looking at the cross from his day.*

*4). "the end thereof as a bitter day".*

*Amos, eight hundred years before can see what many cannot see at all.*

*This is again proving the wonder of God and His word.*

# *October 12*

## *Obadiah 1:3-4*
### *God Will Have His Day*

*No one can hide from God's all Seeing Eye.*

*God knows everything about everyone.*

*Nothing escapes His view.*

*It is very tempting to ask God, "Do you see what is going on?",*

*"Why won't you do something about this?"*

*"Lord, how long must the saints suffer without Your aid?"*

*These unbelievers, the heathen are prospering at the expense of the saints, Lord... how long?*

*No matter where you are or whatever your position in life, you've witnessed some type of inequity.*

*You've been a part of some form of unrighteousness at the hand of the non-believer.*

*Take to heart what this passage teaches us; God is even more aware what the situation is and is actively involved.*

*He keeps better records than we ever could.*

*He will exact heavens vengeance, heavens way.*

*Trust in Him, both His plan and His timing are better than ours.*

*He knows when to act on our behalf.*

# *October 13*

*Jonah 2:8 (NIV)*

### *Worthless Idols*

*Wow!*

*What a powerful statement.*

*You know you can try to explain to someone that the conse-quences of their choices could be devastating, even life threat-ening, but sometimes the best way to ensure that they learn the lesson is just to leave them alone.*

*Often a person must follow the full course of their bad choices before they see the right.*

*When the decision to do what will eventually destroy them has been made, there is little else that can be done.*

*I have an axiom for such cases: "The only way to bounce back is to hit bottom first."*

*That's exactly what the prophet had to do.*

*He was clinging to the worthless idol,*

*the vain thought that He knew better than God,*

*and that God did not fully appreciate the situation.*

*As a result, he forfeited the grace that he should have received.*

*Let go of your idols, whatever they are, God always knows best.*

# *October 14*

*Micah 1:2; 3:1; 6:1*

### *Hear!*

*Listen!*
*How often in the ministry of the Lord did He say*
*"He that hath ear to hear"?*
*How many times did the Holy Spirit say to the Churches in Rev-*
*elation 2 and 3, those very same words?*
*How many times did the prophets of Israel yell,*
*"Hear the word of the Lord!"? How often has the evangelist*
*shouted from your pulpits and platforms, at the edge of river-*
*banks and on street corners to passersby; warning, exhorting,*
*and pleading that they should "hear"?*
*Micah begs the nation to hear the stern word of God.*
*He points out to them that God is not unreasonable, but rather a*
*loving, truly faithful God, that wants a relationship; an all loving*
*Father that gives clear direction. It's time to hear saint, what God*
*desires for you and your future.*
*Don't ignore the pleas of a very loving, patient God.*
*Don't be secure in your comfort.*
*God demands growth with consistency.*
*Hear what He has planned for you.*

*Doing His Will*

*Wisdom*

*Week Forty-One*

> *Read chapter nine of*
> *Proverbs and contrast the*
> *differences between the two*
> *women mentioned.*
> *Notice the dominant traits of*
> *both women.*

# *October 15*

*Nahum 1:3*

### *Like No Other*

*Throughout the Minor Prophets (and remember, they are only called minor because their books are significantly shorter than the major writing prophets) we see God meeting out judgment and great wrath.*

*After years of warning, patience, mercy and undeserved grace, God pours out His fury to a people who have become apostate.*

*Yet as we see here in the book of Nahum, God balances out His anger over and over again, showing that even though everything He has had to do to punish them was well deserved; He still sustains His amazing love for them.*

*Never once does God ever say to Israel "I hate you" or "I'll never take you back."*

*No, instead, He always keeps an open door; a clause ready for the truly repentant; a willing love for a wayward people.*

*In our stubbornness we often think that God is like us; never forgiving, not true... He stretches out His arms and His heart.*

# *October 16*

## Zephaniah 2:3
### **Strength in Meekness**

*Meekness; it actually means "power under control",*

*"having the power to retaliate, but choosing not to."*

*Not the definition you'll hear today is it?*

*Most people would say just the opposite;*

*a meek person is a weak person.*

*No a meek person is someone who understands*

*the great side of battle.*

*A man who has power but can't control himself is a danger to*

*everyone and should be stopped, for he will eventually do irrepa-*

*rable damage, usually to others.*

*But the meek are those who understand the strength and*

*strategy of trusting in someone greater than themselves.*

*Jesus was meek, as was Moses.*

*Meekness as is mentioned here will yield the attention and*

*blessing of God Almighty (Matthew 5:5).*

*Meekness does not come naturally, it's not a gift; it's a choice.*

*It must restrain its urge to fight its own battles.*

*My advice to you: Let go.*

*Give Him the right and opportunity to fight for you*

*and you'll inherit the earth.*

# *October 17*

*Haggai*

## *What about Me?*

*It's been 12 years since the perfect word of God*
*has been proven true, again.*
*Seventy years exactly after Israel was sacked,*
*looted and exiled; God's prophecy to Daniel and Jeremiah was*
*perfectly fulfilled; like always.*
*Israel is back in the land. God has given them a gentile king*
*that respects them and has allowed them to go back*
*to the land of their fathers.*
*They have rested in their own houses, began to reap*
*the fruits of their fields and flocks, but they have forgotten*
*the most important thing: to worship God, to worship God His*
*way, in His place; the temple.*
*It lies in ruins.*
*Each day they pass by it and give no regard to the Lord's house.*
*Rightfully, this covenant keeping, righteous God asks*
*"What about me?*
*When are you going to bring your hearts and minds back to me?"*

*In your busyness, enjoying the blessing of God,*

*seen and unseen, have you forgotten about Him?*

*Survey the temple of your heart.*

*What condition is it in?*

# *October 18*

## *Zechariah 6:12-13*
### *God's Man – The God-man*

*He must be all three: A priest after the order of Melchisedec*
*(Psalm 110:1-4), He must be a prophet like unto the prophet*
*Moses (Deuteronomy 18:18-19), and He must be a king after the*
*similitude of David, great David's greater Son*
*(2 Samuel 7:12-13).*
*He must be the prophet in that He will establish a new type of*
*worship in a new type of temple.*
*The worship will not in word only, but in spirit and in truth*
*(John 4:24).*
*A new type of temple because the dwelling place of God is found*
*in the redeemed hearts of men.*
*He must also be a king like David, for He must sit righteously on*
*the throne of the universe and bear the glory given Him from the*
*foundation of the world.*
*And lastly, the priest, for He will lead the worship, for He and He*
*alone brought peace through His blood.*
*This is the Branch, Prophet, Priest and King!*
*He is God's man – The God-man, the Lord Jesus Christ!*

# *October 19*

## *Malachi*

### *The Lord of Hosts*

*Twenty four times, God refers to Himself as "The Lord of Hosts",
Jehovah Sabboath. Twenty four times in this little book, He is
called by that name, more than all the other "Jehovah" distinctions put together.*

*He has always wanted us, and the unbelieving world to know
Him as the God who captains the holy armies of heaven.*

*He is the High General of the Angelic Host.*

*Never is He in retreat, never has He lost a battle;
never will He lose His own.*

*Your God is the only God there is.*

*Every other named deity is just a demon in a nice suit.*

*Despite the names men may give to them, all other gods are just
members of Satan's forces, sent out to deceive.*

*Let no one fool you, until they can conquer death, hell and the
grave; they are not worthy to be even mentioned.*

*Jesus is the Lord high God.*

*Jehovah Sabboath; the Lord God of Hosts!*

# *October 20*

*Matthew 16:1-4*

### *Weather Report*

*They asked of Him a sign from above.*

*Obligingly, Jesus gives them that and much more.*

*He points to the first heaven to show them how they have missed*

*the third. "Red skies at night, sailors delight.*

*Red skies at morning, sailors take warning."*

*That's what Jesus said and they understood completely, and then*

*He drops the bomb.*

*You can read the face of the sky, but not the signs of the times.*

*Application: It is easier to discern the signs that God*

*has given to even the mist unspiritual person than it is*

*to tell if it will rain or not.*

*God is screaming to the whole human race: "Wake up!"*

*"Look and see."*

*The signs of the times are ridiculously evident,*

*but the wicked one has blinded the minds of the sinners and in*

*most cases, the saints also.*

*Wake up dear pilgrim, can you read the face of the sky?*

*More importantly, can you read the signs of the times?*

# *October 21*

*Mark 1:23-26, 32-34; 2:1-5; 2:28; 4:35-41; 5:21-34; 7:1-13*
### **Lord!!!**

*Lord.*

*In Hebrew the word is "Adonai"; absolute ruler, highest authority.*

*In Greek the word is "Kurios"; master.*

*In all the passages listed we see Him, not as a mere man, walking*

*on and off the stage of history.*

*No, we see Him time and again as Lord!*

*The supreme one, master.*

*In the first chapter, He shows that*

*He is master over scriptures, then over spirits.*

*The demons trembled when He confronted them.*

*Later in that same chapter, He proves He is Lord over sickness.*

*In chapter 2, He is Lord over sin,*

*for who can forgive sins but God alone?*

*Again in verse 28, He proves that He is Lord over the Sabbath;*

*the weekly Jewish high holy day!*

*Over and over He proves that He and He alone is Lord.*

*The temporal or the eternal, the difficult or the mundane...*

*it matters not.*

*He is Lord; ruler of all; master supreme.*

*Doing His Will*

*Wisdom*

*Week Forty-Two*

> *Write a short essay on the
> difference between wisdom,
> knowledge and understanding;
> giving scripture to support
> your conclusions.*

# October 22

Luke 1:46-55

### God Has Done Great Things

It is called, "Mary's Magnificent",

the mother of our Lord takes time to praise Him.

She who has been chosen by God to be the Holy of Holies for Him

as an infant takes this time to write a psalm of honor.

Note, not as an equal, but as a servant, not as the mother of God,

but as a vessel for the Kingdom.

So many would love to deify her and bestow on her divine rank

and privilege, but she would have none of that!

She pauses in her excitement and awe to regale

the glories of her King.

She tells of her honor and her hope.

Her honor: "My soul <u>doth</u> magnify the Lord."

Her hope: "My spirit <u>hath</u>

(notice, this is in the past tense) rejoiced."

She calls Him her <u>God</u> and her <u>Savior.</u>

This is proof of how she saw herself. Honored – yes.

Faithful – truly!

But still a sinner needing a Savior.

While she upheld Him in her arms, He was upholding all things

by the word of His power.

# October 23

*John 13:1*

### Romance at its Best

*From chapters 1 to 12, the word "love"*
*"<u>agape</u>" was used 12 times.*
*As He walked among the confines of the earth, Jesus would show*
*the love of God as the world had never seen it before.*
*He gave to the lost, something to live for.*
*For once, man did not have to settle for just what was left among*
*the scraps of the finite.*
*Light shown in the dark and hope emerged.*
*This is narrative found in John's hand was the result of being so*
*very near to Him. But from chapters 13 to 21, the word is used 44*
*times, at a total of 56 times in just 21 chapters.*
*More than any other book; more than all the other three gospels*
*combined. It is a book of pure romance.*
*"God so loved", the truest depths of His love involvement can*
*never be measured or even fathomed.*
*He loves, He cares.*
*Show that love; if you are truly His.*
*Let that great power order your day, today and every day.*

# *October 24*

*Acts 2:1-12*

### *What Meaneth This?*

*What's going on here?*

*What does this mean?*

*Explain what's happening.*

*What are you doing?*

*Sound familiar?*

*These are the queries from the uninformed.*

*The sincere questions of those who are baffled*

*by what they are observing.*

*They are lost in the horrendous conflict of what they know should*

*be occurring and what is actually occurring.*

*This is the intersection of when their reason,*

*starts contradicting their reality!*

*It happened everyday of Jesus' earthly ministry.*

*Now it is happening again.*

*The collision of the finite and the infinite.*

*For when God acts because His people believe Him*

*and trust His word, all hope in the known and predictable*

*crumbles and fades away.*

*Heaven has troubled earth, and earth will*

*never again be the same.*

*"What meaneth this?"*

*The perfect set up for a successful sermon.*

*Live your life so that someone, everyone asks you that question.*

*Live your life at the intersection of faith and power!*

# *October 25*

*1 Corinthians 2:12-13*
### *The Holy Spirit Our Teacher*

**The classroom**: *life itself.*
**The chalkboard**: *the believer's heart.*
**The lesson**; *the just shall live by faith.*
**The Headmaster**: *God Himself.*
**The Teacher**: *The person of the Holy Spirit, the supremely self-*
*silent one, who only speaks for, and about the Lord Jesus.*
*His lessons are from the high hallowed halls*
*of heaven and ordained by God.*
*When He teaches, He uses the two holy immutable*
*elements still present on planet earth: God's word and God's will*
*(Matthew 6:10).*
*He does this because it is by those two*
*there can be no chance of error or heresy.*
*God's will; divine and immutable,*
*and God's word; exactly the same.*
*Both act as the immovable standard for excellence.*
*All truth is weighed, measured and determined here.*
*As God teaches, He will instruct His family*
*in all things spiritual using only these.*
*This is how we learn, in Holy Spirit University.*

*Every lesson is for our eternal benefit.*

*This is our Kingdom classroom… learn all you can!*

# *October 26*

*2 Corinthians 4:7*

### *Just a Toilet*

*There were several types of vessels used in the homes of people*
*from the near east at the time of the apostle Paul.*
*Vessels made of precious metals like gold and silver held things of*
*great value, such as myrrh or some other valuable item.*
*Vessels of brass kept the things of perishable worth, but*
*extremely important to the owner.*
*Metal like iron or tin, or scrap iron kept different oils; they were*
*usually for olive oil or oils for lamps.*
*Wooden vessels held water for drinking and washing.*
*But clay pots, i.e., earthen vessels,*
*held refuse, mostly used as toilets.*
*When Paul wrote this passage, he was putting emphasis on both*
*the vessel and what was in it.*
*The earthen vessel Paul mentions here, is the Christian; we the*
*believers, are not anything of great value on the outside.*
*These "clay pots" will die and decay, but the glory of the Lord*
*that resides within; it's an element most precious.*
*The glory of the Lord!*

# October 27

## Galatians 1:23
### When God Changes a Life

**"now preaches the faith he once destroyed".**
That's love.
All the evil Paul did: the saints were persecuted,
the sweet name he defied and denied, the families ruined;
utter chaos in the lives of so many.
But then the light of heaven captured his heart
and the Christ he denied became his master, and he would
never again be the same.
But what about the past?
What about all of the damaged lives from the relentless pursuits
of a man who seemed to have no compassion or conscience?
Yet despite all of his evil, despite all of his hatred, the saints were
able to not only forgive, but also embrace.
Once an enemy; now a brother beloved and accepted.
This more than anything proved the love of Christ to the world.
It takes no supernatural power to hate your enemies, but only the
power of God can cause a once compassionless opponent, to be
loved by the very people he destroyed.
The love of God, only it can truly change the hardened heart.

# *October 28*

## *Ephesians 2:10*
### *Christ's Good Work*

*The splendid product of a perfect plan, thought out in eternity,*
*wrought out in time.*
*The born again Christian; the handiwork of God!*
*The skilled craftsman of creation worked out the work and will of*
*His Father as only He could do.*
*So perfect was His work, that the Godhead said*
*it was "very good"!*
*Good is God's standard of excellence.*
*A flawless, faultless work of a wonderful God, but even though*
*the beauty of creation showed God's power, majesty and genius,*
*nothing could be greater than the saving work He did on Calvary.*
*It is unparalleled; for only He could take the lost*
*and rebellious and convert him into one who is*
*"the righteousness of God in Him."*
*Only He could do the work that causes the Father*
*to be well pleased.*
*This Christ is the Master builder,*
*the supreme designer of all eternity calls Him – His well-beloved,*
*and we are the proof of His labor.*

# Doing His Will

## Wisdom

### Week Forty-Three

*Solomon was the wisest fool that ever lived. This week do a character study on the major decisions he made that highlighted his wisdom, and then a contrasting study of the major decisions he made that showed his folly.*

# *October 29*

*Colossians 1:16*

### *He is Love!!!*

*"Created by Him and for Him"!*
*He does all things after the counsel of His own will.*
*"And for thy pleasure they are and were created."*
*The whole universe is His! Made by Him! Made for Him!*
*He is Lord! In this verse, we see that the*
*entire universe was made by Him.*
*How?*
*He just spoke it into existence, because in His words are the cre-*
*ative force of the Godhead.*
*All that will be is brought into being by the sheer force of His will.*
*He created the uniform specifications of His own satisfaction for*
*the sole purpose of giving Him glory and fulfilling His pleasure.*
*He created all things above the designs of secular powers; special*
*powers; spiritual powers and sensory powers.*
*All things were created by Him and for His glory, and let's not*
*forget; He created us for His glory, for His pleasure and therein*
*lays the secret to happiness.*

# October 30

## 1 Thessalonians 1:5-6

### The Principle, the Power and the Proof

Teachings and philosophies, reasons and
theories abound in the world.
People believe them or disbelieve in them.
To some of these ideas, people make religion from, going that
extra step to the point of entrusting their eternal fate to them.
They all may have flaws, inconsistencies that are overtly
apparent or so well constructed that the errors are not so easy to
see; on the surface.
But the real test of any idea or theory must go beyond what is
postulated, there must be power to carry out in reality what it
promises, and also corresponding proof that the promise made
has the power to do as it has been stated.
Paul the apostle says the same thing in these 2 verses.
The principle: God's word.
The power: God's Spirit.
The proof: assurance and joy, not vain assurance,
but assurance because He has never failed.
The principle: His word works!
Trust in it completely.

# *October 31*

2 *Thessalonians 2:1*

**Behold, He Comes!**

*Behold He comes!*

*Each one of the Apostle Paul's epistles takes up*

*the gauntlet of an excellent theology.*

*In other words, each book has a theme that highlights one of the*

*teachings that we hold as a doctrinal essential.*

*Romans is the book that teaches about Soteriology,*

*Ephesians – Ecclesiology, etc.*

*The joint epistles of 1 & 2 Thessalonians cover the teachings of*

*Eschatology – last things; more directly; the Lord's coming.*

*You'll find a statement about the Lord's coming in each chapter*

*of both books.*

*1 Thessalonians 1:10; 2:19; 3:13; 4:13-18; 5:1-4;*

*2 Thessalonians 1:7-10; 2:1-12; 3:5.*

*In each chapter the Lord's return is evident;*

*He is coming, no doubt about that.*

*In this, what Paul calls "the blessed hope",*

*we can be absolutely confident.*

*The premiere foundation of our lifestyle of holiness*

*rests on this fact.*

*He is coming for us who look for His appearing.*

*Don't put your hope and trust anywhere else.*

*Place it in the power of His promised return!*

*He is coming again!*

# November

## A Time for Evaluation

**Lesson:** The Father of Spirits

**"Furthermore we have had fathers of our flesh which corrected us, and we gave them reverence: shall we not much rather be in subjection unto the Father of spirits, and live?"**
**Hebrews 12:9**

*Lesson*

*H*e is the source of all life; the Father of all living, sustaining the reason for being of every creature. In His holy economy, the Lord has so ordain that there would be three types of life. Of all that exists when His created universe the types of understood existence are these: physical live, soul life, and spirit life.

The plants around us all have physical life; they do not have a soul or spirit. Animals have been given physical and soul being, but not a spirit. Humans have been given all three; a spirit, a soul and a body.

The body is given so that there can be contact with the world around us. The soul gives self-awareness. The spirit is given so that there can be contact with God.

Angels have a soul and a spirit. Lastly, God is Spirit.

Every single entity in existence answers to the Father. He is not only the source of all life; He is the reason of all life. There can be no fulfillment or true happiness without Him

### Outline of the Passage

Verse 12 examples for us the reason for reverence of God:
   A. Earthly Fathers
   B. Eternal Fellowship
   C. Excellent Focus

*Facts:* **The month of November, eleventh month of the Gregorian calendar.**

It corresponds to the month of Bul; the eighth month of the Hebrew calendar. It is the month the temple was completed.

*Focus:* **Prayer and discernment.**

Discernment is the one thing that is greater than under-standing and instruction. Pray for discernment so that the difference in the two worlds, the finite and infinite will not be mistaken.

*Assignment:* **Research**

All of the human character types are found in the book of Proverbs. Read the book over the course of the month and identify each type.

*Memory Work:*

**Exaltation:** Psalm 104:33

**Excellence:** John15:13

**Edification:** Romans 8:1

**Evangelical:** John 11:25, 26

**Exhortive:** Psalm 46:10

**Educational:** II Corinthians 10:3-5

*Integrity is the Goal*

*Evaluation*

## *Week Forty-Four*

> *Are all of your actions forthright and honest? If someone were to scrutinize your life would it stand the test of integrity?*

# November 1

*I Timothy 3:16*

**Jesus is God!**

*This verse is so important and so doctrinally powerful,*
*that the editors of the "New World Translation" of the Holy Scrip-*
*tures had to twist themselves into a theological pretzel to violate*
*it and change its meaning.*
*"God was manifest in the flesh"!*
*Nothing could be clearer; this can only be*
*referring to one person;*
*The Lord Jesus Christ.*
*This verse gives clear authority as to the proper way to identify*
*the person of Jesus as God, for He is the only one who meets all*
*aspects of this description: Only He was manifest in flesh (John*
*1:14), He and He only was justified in the Spirit (John 1:29-32;*
*3:31-34), He only was observed by the angels (Luke 2:13-14),*
*only He was preached about to the Gentiles (Acts 10:45; 11:1;*
*13:46; 14:27, etc.), only He has been believed on by the entire*
*world as the Son of God (John 20:31), only He ascended back into*
*the glory of His Father in heaven (Mark 16:19; Luke 24:51).*
*This verse like so many others, affirm that He is God!*

# *November 2*

*2 Timothy 2:11-13*

### *A Strange Promise*

*"He cannot deny Himself."*

*There is much controversy surrounding the security of the salvation of the saints.*

*It's really foolish and arrogant when one looks at it.*

*But this verse put to rest the discussion completely.*

*Here, the question raised so often,*

*is positing the loss of eternal life.*

*Question: How can you end <u>eternal</u> life?*

*Or hell?*

*"You mean I can sin as much as I want and still go to heaven?"*

*This question begs addressing.*

*The question is not "Can you sin as much as you want and still be a Christian?"*

*The better statement would be "if you sin constantly, without any chastening from God, you probably were <u>never</u> a Christian (Hebrews 12:8).*

*In the passage, Paul affirms clearly, that regardless of what a true Christian may encounter or do, if they are genuine members of the body of Christ, they are secure in Jesus, because Christ will never deny Himself as the purchaser of their salvation.*

*This fact is bed-rocked in scripture.*

*Nothing can change the eternal state of the Christian.*

# November 3

*Titus 3:5*

### *It's All Because Of Him*

*Nothing I could do, nothing you could do will ever be good*
*enough to warrant God's mercy, love and grace.*
*By His loving plan, He appeased the rightful requirements of His*
*own holiness by sending His only Son, His well-beloved to pay the*
*price for man's sin.*
*Nothing we could do would ever measure up to what was neces-*
*sary to pay the sin debt.*
*His work of regeneration was a solitary act of immense compas-*
*sion and mercy, bestowed on individuals who could do nothing*
*for Him, or the work He did on their behalf, or even for them-*
*selves and their eternal condition.*
*The plan and cost of redemption anticipated the fact*
*that the majority of mankind would reject His love*
*and refuse His salvation.*
*Even though this is true, His love and mercy abounded to all*
*mankind (John 3:16).*
*This is why we can serve Him and own Him as Lord.*
*His act of mercy, love and grace show that*
*only God can do all that was done.*
*Nothing else could appease His righteous demands of holiness.*

*And He did it all knowing that so few*
*would choose Him; yet He loved us anyway.*
*This is our God!*

# *November 4*

*Philemon 18-19*

### *For The sake of the Kingdom*

*If there was one word that stands out in the discussion of unity
and what it takes to make it work; my vote would be selflessness.
Simply, the only way there can be true God honoring unity within
the body of Christ, is for everyone to follow Paul's instruction in
Philippians 2:4-5.*

*When I take up the cause for the well-being of my brother
and sister, I can only do so effectively by putting
my personal interests aside.*

*Masterfully, Paul heeds his own instruction by doing so on the
behalf of two brothers, Philemon and Onesimus.*

*He gives opportunity for unity and fellowship to be restored by
taking the cost of restitution on himself.*

*He stands up and acts as the offender, thus paying the price for
reconciliation. WOW!*

*I wonder where he learned that technique!*

*Sounds like being Christ-like to me!*

*What are you willing to do to restore a situation back to where
Christ can be honored and pleased?*

# *November 5*

*Hebrews 2:14-15*

**Slave to My Sin**

*It's one of the most telling passages in the Bible.*

*It reveals the strategy and plan of Satan for the world, no matter how much a person or nation or group may pay homage to or serve Satan and his plan... he will still betray and destroy anyone that follows him.*

*These verses show that his evil, twisted plot is to offer to humankind an opportunity to know the pleasures of the self-life; a life that is void of God, His presence and influence, and be left with the slavery of an unfulfilled life; a dormant self and a hollow soul.*

*He does this by taking the very thing that man believes he cannot live without; enslaves him to the craving, and provides opportunities for him to do it.*

*He then uses, this very self-same practice and entices that man to slowly kill himself with it.*

*But thank God, Christ has come along to break that burden and give real authentic joy and peace with God!*

# *November 6*

*James 4:17*

### *More than the Expected*

*He has given us a higher standard.*
*God has raised the bar.*
*He wants more; He wants us to see the world system as a wicked*
*place ruled by a maniac, drunk with desires to be worshipped.*
*He therefore has given to us His Spirit, empowered us with His*
*holy word and given specific directions to reach a culture that*
*does not know Him and that does not realize the danger it's in.*
*To win them, we are not commanded to avoid evil*
*or to be passive.*
*We are not given "neutral" assignments or follow a moral path.*
*Instead, we are expected to do good: God's unique standard of*
*excellence and holiness.*
*We have the love of God, the word of God and now we are*
*required to do the work of God.*
*That's exactly what Jesus did.*
*He did good (Acts 10:38).*
*So pilgrim, don't get weary of doing what is right. You are*
*advancing the Kingdom by doing good.*

# November 7

*1 Peter 2:9*

### *Chosen*

*The Holy Spirit of God uses four different phrases in one verse to describe the body of Christ.*
*Four separate and distinct ways of painting*
*a picture of His Church:*
*1). Chosen generation – this speaks of our place in the Kingdom.*
*We are purposefully and specifically placed in this world at this*
*time to be the best and last voice to a lost culture.*
*2). A royal priesthood – This speaks to our position in the*
*Kingdom; repeatedly we are reminded that*
*we are a kingdom of priests.*
*That is a high and holy calling, showing that we are the ones*
*given to the spreading of His word.*
*3). A holy nation – this points to the purity of the Kingdom.*
*We are set aside to be holy and distinct from*
*everyone else on the planet.*
*4). A peculiar people – The unity of difficult people from every*
*corner of the globe, to show the purpose of the Kingdom; the*
*people who represent an infinite holy and righteous God.*
*And it is all for the same purpose: To show forth His praises.*

*Integrity is the Goal*

*Evaluation*

## *Week Forty-Five*

> *Does your Christianity reflect an accurate representation of Jesus Christ? Does the world know you are a Christian more because of what you do or what you are?*

# *November 8*

*2 Peter 1:16-21*

### *The Word Trumps Experience*

*It must have been wonderful.*
*To be there I mean, to be atop the mount of transfiguration,*
*where for the first time since He left the portals of glory, Jesus is*
*transformed; changed in form and image so that now, human*
*eyes can see Him in His splendor, majesty, honor, and glory!*
*It must have been absolutely the greatest thing their eyes would*
*ever see here on earth.*
*Then, add to that the occurrence to hear the voice of the Father*
*speaking directly to them!!!*
*It must have been amazing beyond words to describe.*
*But, despite all that they saw, true as it was*
*– there is one thing that trumps that grand, glorious experience:*
*the written word of God.*
*No, the word does not negate what they saw,*
*but instead it supports it!*
*Yet, Peter realizes what he saw, though it was true,*
*is only secondary to God's word.*
*Pilgrim, you'll have great experiences in your life, experiences*
*that are real and miraculous, but never raise any occurrence*
*above His word.*

# *November 9*

*1 John 3:3*

### *Special Help*

*John, the prolific writer of the New Testament, relates to us the
wonderful, glorious life awaiting us when Jesus comes.*

*We will be like Him!*

*We are the sons of God!*

*God loves us with an unimaginable love!*

*All of these things are ours now!*

*What a great promise of the future to see Jesus and to be just like
Him (Philippians 3:21)!*

*But this verse shows us something that I call a Biblical absolute.*

*If we just have this wonderful hope resident in us, if we keep
the longing of His soon return in the forefront of our hearts, we
receive heaven sent purity like no other.*

*God will add to our own acts of holiness and give special grace to
keep us holy and pure, just because we long and look to see Jesus.*

*Do not neglect this great promise, for with it also comes the
assurance of a crown (2 Timothy 4:8). Look up saints!*

*Keep your heart to the skies. He's coming again!*

# *November 10*

*2 John 1:1-3*

### *Battle for Truth*

*He is the only person of all the Bible writers to be given permission by the Holy Spirit to use the term "antichrist".*
*Paul calls him "that wicked".*
*We know him directly by the name that reveals that he is the "pseudo-christos" or fake christ; the imposter.*
*But John also reveals that he is not just a person, antichrist is also a spirit (1 John 4:3).*
*This is the foul spirit that has roamed the earth for two thousand years looking for the willing weak soul bent on perpetuating the source of wickedness.*
*Such are the individuals that fall for Satan's plan and pleasure, cults, false teachings and philosophies.*
*And yet there is another way the antichrist is manifested.*
*The Bible says that there are many antichrists gone out into the world.*
*This shows that it is not just a solitary soul, or a seducing spirit, but also a sinful system.*

*This world system is founded on the wicked*
*deceit of the antichrist.*
*Beware, be careful, be sober saint.*
*The antichrist is already here!*

# November 11

*3 John 9-11*

### *There Will Always Be One*

*Who would ever want to slander John, the beloved apostle?*

*He was the last man to see the glorified Christ.*

*His gospel, his epistles and his only book of prophecy in the New*

*Testament, have done more for the Church universal than anyone*

*could ever dreamed.*

*So why would this man Diotrephes dare push himself to be com-*

*pared to John, let alone say malicious things about him?*

*Well, to that I say; it's to be expected.*

*When we decide to honor God completely, it becomes the deter-*

*mined desire of Satan to slander and insult you.*

*Unfortunately, it comes usually from some misguided saint;*

*From someone for whom you appear to be evil; someone who is*

*jealous of you and covets your popularity or gift.*

*Whatever the reason, there will always be people who believe*

*that the Holy Spirit is over worked and needs their help.*

*Don't get upset, don't be discouraged, but most of all, don't ever*

*be distracted!!!*

*Continue to be obedient and do this will.*

# *November 12*

## Jude 4
### *Evil Men with Evil Intents*

*These are evil times; there is no doubt about that.*
*The world has been evil since the time in the garden.*
*This conflict we're engaged in will not cease*
*until the Lord returns.*
*What the church is going through at this present time is nothing*
*new, but what should take our attention is not the presence of*
*evil, but the practice of it.*
*Satan sets his sights on any*
*and everything that honors Christ.*
*Jude warns us to be vigilant and sober minded,*
*because there are individuals assigned by the evil one with the*
*intent of destroying anything godly.*
*These are <u>certain men</u> already in place, using <u>certain methods</u>;*
*the plans and schemes of darkness, on a <u>certain mission</u>; that is*
*to destroy the witness of Christ, preaching a <u>certain message</u>;*
*that is the heresy of hell; the message that denies*
*the Lordship of Jesus Christ.*
*Be watchful, be sober, and be ready!*

# *November 13*

*Revelation 22:4*

**Face to Face**

*It's been a long journey; a desperate fight;*
*a wearying battle, and it still goes on.*
*There will be more casualties and crisis; just wait and see.*
*The evil one has yet to believe that the battle is the Lord's,*
*but we know the truth.*
*We're assured in His word that there will only be one outcome:*
*Total victory with no souls lost.*
*The body of Christ will reign with Him.*
*There will be celebration like no other.*
*The entire heavenly host will gather around the throne, and*
*the most wonderful person, the most loving God will gather us*
*together to be closest to Him.*
*And this verse will be fulfilled.*
*We will see Him, face to face.*
*Up until that time it's been from faith to faith.*
*Constantly growing day by day, living each moment*
*expecting to see Him.*

*All of the scriptures pointed in one direction:*

*Jesus! Lord and master.*

*Soon faith <u>will</u> become sight.*

*Hallelujah we'll be home at last!*

# November 14

*Ephesians 1:3*

**In Heavenly Places**

*Our Promise*

*The Greek word for heaven is "ouranos",*
*the prefix "epi" expands the word to include the idea of the*
*spiritual dwelling of spirit beings – the "heavenlies", sometimes*
*referred to as the "high places".*
*It is that sphere of spiritual power and influence where the Lord*
*Himself rules and controls from.*
*It is the dwelling place of all beings spiritual.*
*The heavenlies incorporates the arena where all decisions of*
*eternal weight are made.*
*The eternal battle ground for all things*
*spiritual is accomplished here.*
*Paul's admonishment to "walk in the spirit"*
*assures the Christian to be discerning and mature enough to reg-*
*ulate their life in such a manner that the sensitivity of knowing*
*Him and being immersed in His word keeps them acutely aware*
*of those things available to us.*
*When we walk in the spirit, we engaged in battle of the Kingdom.*
*We engage is warfare that will win the souls of men.*
*Walk in the spirit.*

*Integrity is the Goal*

*Evaluation*

## *Week Forty-Six*

*Which words most
describe your personal life:
joy or happiness; faith or fear;
love or desire?*

# November 15

*Ephesians 1:3*

**In Heavenly Places**

*Our Provisions*

As we have stated before, the Greek word,

"epouranios", is our word "the heavenlies".

As we discussed before, "the heavenlies"

is that sphere of influence where all matters

of Kingdom and eternal weight are decided.

Here in this verse, we see that the Lord Jesus Christ had kept

again His promise to meet all our needs.

For here He supplied for us, all which can be given to us by

bestowing "all spiritual blessings in heavenly places".

Our God has given us all of our <u>provisions</u>.

These are the essentials in our lives that are oh so important to

maintain a holy and productive life.

"**All things that pertain to life and godliness**".

These provisions were specified in the subsequent

verses in this chapter.

These are the terms of our salvation contract.

*All that is required, both in principle and purpose, to please Him.*

*All you need pilgrim, is found in this chapter.*

*Dwell among the things of God, and reap*

*the benefits of God's provision for you.*

# November 16

Ephesians 1:3

### In the Heavenlies

Our Power

*Ephesians 1:19-21 – He is exalted! High and lifted up, sitting on the throne of His Father God; ruling from the throne of His father David; He is exalted above all the earth and all that is!*

*He is sitting in the heavenlies; He's displaying His mighty majestic greatness. It is here, because Christ is on the high, holy hill of heaven, we now have power in heavenly places.*

*We have been given the rightful privilege to sit in God's presence as servants of Christ. To be one whom Christ has appointed to accurately represent Him as King, Lord, and as the Almighty God.*

*This is a great and sacred calling given to the Church.*

*That, because of our salvation, we are allowed to operate in the name of Jesus for the Kingdom, you also have the power to bring about the work and will of Jesus Christ because He sits in control of the universe.*

*We find our power in Him to represent Him in heavenly places.*

# *November 17*

*Ephesians 1:3*

**In the Heavenlies**

*Our Position*

*Ephesians 2:4-6 – He is Lord!*

*When the Father wanted to please Himself, He did so by estab-*
*lishing that in Christ, all fullness in Him should dwell*
*(Colossians 1:19).*

*This being so, it would require that Christ was to be pre-eminent;*
*there is no one who will ever be above Him.*

*Nothing could exist without Him creating it.*

*There would be no one who could live independent of His way.*

*The entire universe would ultimately worship Him as Lord, and*
*that He would sit supreme on the throne of the universe high*
*above all things in the heavenlies.*

*Besides all this, He ordained that we are seated with Him,*
*"right now" in heavenly places.*

*This proves that we are positioned with Him;*
*it is our place to be with Him in glory!*

*We are involved with and in the events of eternity.*

*Our place is with Him... not soon to be, but right now!*

*Just as He promises we will rule and reign with Him!*

# *November 18*

*Ephesians 1:3*

**In the Heavenlies**

*Our Purpose*

*Ephesians 3:9-11 – The forces of darkness are referred to by*
*many names: Devils, evil spirits, evil angels, even demons.*
*But there is a way they are spoken of is more expressive,*
*unveiling more of their activities and intent.*
*It is the phrase, "principalities and powers", the word,*
*"principalities", refers to the graphical region of creation they*
*control or seek to control.*
*For an example of this, check out Daniel 9.*
*The word "powers" is the Greek word that means, "authority".*
*The wicked world of Satan has a plan for the entire universe and*
*he employs his minions to influence their area of control.*
*But, God has strategically given to the saints, the assignment of*
*living out His plan before the world, and by being a living witness*
*of His Kingdom; we thwart the evil of the devil and his plans.*
*The eternal purpose of the saints is to give the truth of the*
*unsearchable riches of Christ.*
*Live out your purpose.*
*Live for Him to His glory.*

# *November 19*

*Ephesians 1:3*

**In the Heavenlies**

*Our Problems*

*Ephesians 6:10-12 – Our promise, our provisions,*

*our power, our position.*

*These are all part of the innumerable spiritual blessings*

*found in the life of the believer.*

*We have been promised all things that pertain*

*to life and godliness.*

*Never should we find ourselves weak,*

*ill-prepared, destitute, or defeated.*

*In the heavenlies, God has equipped the saints to be victorious.*

*But with all that we have in Christ, we should not take up*

*a position of ease.*

*For not only will we find all of the promises of God in heavenly*

*places, Satan has positioned himself there too.*

*Our problems will manifest themselves because he has set his*

*forces at a place to wage war with the Christians.*

*He uses the fiery darts of doubt, deception and discouragement*

*to try to find a weak spot in our defenses.*

*Don't let him!*

*Stay in the word; be constant in prayer; be strong in the faith.*

# *November 20*

## Colossians 2:14
### **Not Guilty**

*He took all of the writing of offenses that were issued with my name on them; He grabbed every warrant for my arrest based on the innumerable crimes I had committed; He subpoenaed all of the files that held evidence proving my guilt for the millions of things I did; and upon receiving every bit of proof that I deserved the full just punishment from God, He spread His blood on each and every one, canceling out the power that they had over me.*

*Blotting out the accusations, eliminating the debt that I owed, and then He took every one of them and nailed them one by one to His cross.*

*He gave me pardon, not parole; but pardon, saying to all creation "He is not guilty!" Sins paid for, ok maybe; forgiveness, yes, without a doubt; but to be declared not guilty! That gives true testimony to the infinite grace of God.*

*Not guilty – never to be condemned... forever free.*

# *November 21*

*Romans 1:1*

**Separated**

*It is the Greek word, "Aphorizo",*
*the conjunction of two other words.*
*"Apo" – apart from, not connected with. "Horizo" – it's the word*
*that we get the English word "horizon" from.*
*It is the horizontal borders of sight, the point of reference that*
*divides the sky from the earth.*
*So we have a calling that is "apart from the horizon";*
*separated from the earthly and the heavenly; different from the*
*flesh and the spirit.*
*We are called of God to be separated from*
*all that is natural in this world.*
*He is assigning to us that we should live*
*"other than" the rest of existence.*
*We are given the directive to be the greatest*
*witness to the cross possible.*
*We do it by an existence of believers.*
*The believer given His Spirit, His word, His blessing,*
*His name and nature, can live different from everything*
*that is not like Him.*
*You and I can honor Him by living apart from the world.*

# *Integrity is the Goal*

## *Evaluation*

# *Week Forty-Seven*

> *If your co-workers were interviewed about your character; or your neighbors; or maybe your unsaved family members, would their assessment of you be a description that mirrored Christ?*

# November 22

## I Corinthians 16:8-9
### I Get a Chance to Fight!

*My mind reads these verses and is instantly reminded of a great*
*guy in the Old Testament.*
*He, like Joshua, wholly followed the Lord.*
*His name is Caleb.*
*When given a choice of land in the promise land, because God*
*had given him complete authority to choose any part of the*
*country he wanted; he didn't take the well watered land in the*
*valleys; he wasn't looking for good pasture land.*
*No, he wanted the hill country where the giants were.*
*Why?*
*Because he wanted land he had to fight to conquer.*
*Well, here is the apostle Paul, spiritually in the*
*exact same place as Caleb.*
*He has orders from heaven to abide at Ephesus.*
*The opportunity to preach and teach will end up*
*being legendary; God has opened a door for ministry*
*that will change the entire world.*
*Paul's excited about the chance to combat the enemies*
*of the Kingdom, saying "it is a great door opened unto me,*
*and I get a chance to fight!"*

# *November 23*

*John 3:16*

### **The Greatest Story Ever Told**

*For – The Ultimate Purpose*

*God – The Ultimate Perfection*

*So Loved – The Ultimate Passion*

*The World – The Ultimate Problem*

*That He – The Ultimate Parent*

*Gave – The Ultimate Price*

*His Only – The Ultimate Person*

*Begotten Son – The Ultimate Progeny*

*That Whosoever – The Ultimate Privilege*

*Believeth On Him – The Ultimate Proof*

*Should Not Perish – The Ultimate Promise*

*But Have – The Ultimate Possession*

*Everlasting – The Ultimate Period*

*Life – The Ultimate Prize*

*"Love so amazing, so divine, demands*

*my life, my strength, my all."*

*God could do no better than what He did on the cross.*

*Not that there were no other ways.*

*But this was only one way to satisfy the claims of His holiness,*

*and righteousness.*

*If God had chosen another means of salvation, He wouldn't be able to live with Himself.*

*We should glory, my friend, in the cross.*

*It's the greatest truth, and the greatest story ever told!*

# November 24

## Hebrews 8:6
### The Present Day Ministry of Jesus

*Is He just sitting on His throne doing nothing?*
*Does He just watch from the portals*
*of heaven the events as they unfold on earth?*
*Has He given up on everything until things*
*get so bad He must come back?*
*Is He just basking in the well-deserved praises of the angels and*
*the saints in glory gathered around the glassy sea?*
*What takes up the agenda of our Lord now that He has ascended*
*on High, far above all powers and principalities?*
*Where does He place His attention now that*
*He has all power in His hands?*
*These all are very important relevant questions.*
*Jesus has obtained a more excellent ministry now that the work*
*of Calvary is complete.*
*He has assignments from His Father and He has been attending*
*to each one very carefully, as astutely as only God can.*
*Be excited dear one, God is caring for every detail of your life, and*
*has given Jesus to die and now live for you.*

# *November 25*

## Jude 4
### **Wicked Men in Wicked Times**

*The cunning schemes of the forces of hell are shown for what*
*they truly are in this short book.*
*Using just 25 verses, the Holy Spirit both accurately and ade-*
*quately expose the devices of the devil in vivid color.*
*Employing the skill of a surgeon with a scalpel, Jude plainly*
*snatches the cover off the secret plans of the evil one.*
*He takes up the pen to warn us about 3 instruments that Satan*
*has chosen to stop the church of God:*
*Certain men, using a certain method with a certain message.*
*Juxtaposing the plot against the backdrop of the past, Jude gives*
*6 examples of the fate of those who for wicked purposes chose to*
*oppose the cause of righteousness.*
*These certain men were specifically ordained and trained to with*
*stealth and sinister schemes infiltrate the local body of believers*
*in every age and anywhere the gospel spreads.*
*Their method is a simple one: subvert the truth with a cunning,*
*clever and covert lie.*
*For the only thing that will stop the wickedness*
*of this world is the truth.*
*Now, the obvious question should be, "what is the lie?"*

*Here is their message: That Jesus Christ is **not** God come in the flesh.*

*Be wary my friend; be watchful: be warned.*

*Satan is a defeated foe, but yet an active adversary.*

# November 26

Hebrews 8:6; Philippians 2:9-11

### The Present Day Ministry of Jesus

Lord

There can be only one! The highest office

that our savior holds is "Lord".

It is the favorite rendering that

the Godhead has for the Son: Lord.

The Hebrew word, "Adonai", means supreme ruler, high master,

ruler over all. The New Testament word "Kurios" employs the

concept of "master", "first".

This is the distinction that all of creation

will know Him by. He is Lord.

The wicked one's most coveted desire is to be lord over all.

He wants all of the prestige and honor that comes with it.

For what comes with that high and holy role is praise, honor,

blessing, and worship.

The angels fall down at the glory of His presence.

They sing to Him around the throne, **"Thou art worthy oh Lord,**

**to receive glory, honor and power, for thou hast created all**

**things and for thy pleasure they are and were created."**

*He gains this title because He earned it, also because He deserves it, and finally because He demands it. He is the rightful owner, architect and sustainer of the universe.*

*He and only He is Lord.*

# *November 27*

*Hebrews 8:6; 7:35; Isaiah 59:16*

### *The Present Day Ministry of Jesus*

*Intercessor*

*He is the one appointed to represent the lesser to the Greater.*
*Jesus has taken on the role of standing between*
*heaven and earth and seeks to communicate for mankind,*
*the hurts, pains and needs of humanity to the ever listening and*
*ever compassionate Father.*
*Once He took on flesh, He was able to provide in the Spirit, every-*
*thing the world needs.*
*That's why we are blessed with all spiritual blessing in Christ.*
*He went to the Father in the garden and prayed to the Father*
*requesting all the things we could not see; He asked Him from*
*that which we would have never seen.*
*As our intercessor, He stands in the gap, faces the Holy Father,*
*and cries out for us, and because it comes from His well-beloved,*
*the Father hears Him and gives this Son of His all that He*
*requests. This is our intercessor, our man in the gap.*
*The "daysmen" that Job begged for (Job 9:33).*
*He loves us so completely that He saw in eternity-future, what we*
*would need, and interceded for us.*

# *November 28*

*Hebrews 8:6; 2 Timothy 2:5; Isaiah 59:16*

### **The Present Day Ministry of Jesus**

*Mediator*

*Someone must speak for God.*

*Yes, yes salvation is free; but wasn't cheap.*

*Yes, man is now able to access a righteous God whereas before he*

*would have no right to approach Him, let alone appropriate His*

*mercy, love and grace.*

*Yes, mankind can pray to the Father and the windows*

*of Heaven can release the glorious benefits of eternal blessing*

*and Heavenly favor.*

*These are all true, but just as much as we have need for an inter-*

*cessor, we also must have a mediator; one who speaks to the*

*lesser on behalf of the Greater.*

*Someone must stand as God to communicate to us that, while*

*God gives to us greatly - to the point of the cross, He is still holy.*

*He must still be revered and worshipped.*

*The standard of God's holiness has never fallen, even though*

*Jesus was the sin bearer, He never stopped being God.*

*He is our Lord; we must praise Him, He is our intercessor; thank*

*God, but also He represents God as our mediator;*

*let us worship Him!*

# *November 29*

*Hebrews 8:6; 1 John 2:1*

### *The Present Day Ministry of Jesus*

*Lord Advocate*

*He represents us in a matter of legality before the throne of God*
*and against all the slanderous accusations of our adversary.*
*He is the one who declares that the righteousness*
*that was once available to men by keeping the law can be*
*declared by faith in Him.*
*It was He who took all of the writs and warrants, all the proof of*
*crimes I committed and nailed each one to His cross.*
*He is the one who comes before the righteous Judge and has*
*never, ever lost a case.*
*This great attorney holds all the evidence of my salvation and*
*proves once and for all eternity that the verdict has been given,*
*the sentence has been pronounced; but the punishment has not*
*been commuted - all the charges have been dropped!*
*He is an expert in the law, because not only does*
*He know it, He wrote it!*
*And, not only did He write it, it's all about Him!*
*This attorney of ours is never too busy to listen;*
*He's never out of touch.*

*He does all of His work pro bono,*
*and He never turns away a client.*
*This Jesus pleads our case and stands*
*as our lawyer and always is in our defense.*

# *November 30*

*Hebrews 8:6; Luke 2:11*

### *The Present Day Ministry of Jesus*

*Savior*

*Hallelujah!*

*There is no office of Jesus that is*

*more precious than that of Savior.*

*The world can breathe a sigh of relief now, for He has conquered*

*death, hell, satan, the grave, and all of our enemies by His cross.*

*And to everyone who would come to Him by faith, He's estab-*

*lished the bridge first seen by Jacob in Genesis 28:12, spanning*

*the gap between heaven and earth, between eternity and time.*

*All of humankind has been liberated by the work of redemption.*

*You and I are no longer, helpless, hopeless or homeless because*

*He has saved us from our sins.*

*This is the position He loves above all else; Savior of man.*

*He took on the role of scapegoat, sin offering, Passover lamb,*

*trespass offering and peace offering. Whatever was needful for*

*man to be free, He accomplished.*

*"Guilty, vile and helpless we, spotless Lamb of God was He.*

*Full atonement, can it be?*

*Hallelujah, what a Savior!!!"*

# *December*

## *A Time for Purging*

**Lesson:** The Word of Truth

"**Of his own will begat he us with the word of truth, that we**

**should be a kind of first fruits of his creatures.**"

*James 1:18*

*Lesson*

*B*egotten means sired or born from. The holy process that God employs and it is always for His glory is not through the means we know, that of natural birth through a mother; but rather the birth sequence by the Spirit. God brings us into His family using His word, His Spirit, the death of His Son, His will and our obedience. This is the only way someone can come into His family. Good intentions, good works, nice family, these all have no credibility or power to place a human into the family of the redeemed. God begets us by the **word of truth**. No other plan or process will suffice.

World religions will continue to offer to lost man, plans and schemes to give him the soul salvation he so desperately needs. However, anything process other than what God requires is futile at best.

### *Outline of the Passage*

This shows us at a glimpse what God requires:
  A. God will in salvation
  B. God word for salvation
  C. God way of salvation

*Facts:* **The month of December, twelfth month of the Gregorian calendar.**

It corresponds to the month of Chisleu; the ninth month of the Hebrew calendar.

*Focus:* **Prayer and sacrifice.**

It has been a whole year now. You've made some choices and some mistakes. Look back, consider the year and purge. Get rid of any and everything that hindered you or slowed your growth process. Ask yourself the hard questions: Have you read through the entire bible at least once? Has your prayer time increased and become more intense? Are you serving the kingdom more now than a year ago?

*Assignment:* **Research**

Write an essay discussing the difference in these four issues: The Tent, the tabernacle, the temple and the testimony.

*Memory Work:*

**Exaltation:** Psalm 100:1, 2

**Excellence:** Isaiah 40:31

**Edification:** Jeremiah 33:3

**Evangelical:** Acts 4:12

**Exhortive:** Romans 8:38, 39

**Educational:** Luke 19:10

# *Learning to Let Go*

## *Purging*

## *Week Forty-Nine*

*Give up trying to run your life. Let Him have the total control and trust Him to do only what He can do. Make your prayer this week, "Lord, I trust you with everything".*

# *December 1*

*Hebrews 8:6; John 5:22*

### *The Present Day Ministry of Jesus*

*Judge*

*Amazing isn't it?*

*We can't lose!*

*We just read that the Lord; the Lord Jesus, the Lord Jesus our*

*Savior, is also our Judge!*

*We just can't lose!*

*He is the Grand Magistrate of Eternity!*

*No one sits higher then He!*

*All laws were written by Him, they were written for Him, they are*

*all written about Him.*

*Paul calls Him, and rightly so, "the righteous Judge"*

*(2 Timothy 4:8).*

*He is righteous and holy, separate from sinners.*

*His high court has not superiors, and His verdict is final and true.*

*All must stand before Him and there is no appeal after He ren-*

*ders His verdict.*

*He holds in His hand, the final authority,*

*the scepter of righteousness.*

*His robes are the distinct flowing folds of His own glory and His*

*bench is high and lifted up.*

*His glory fills the temple and all the earth must*
*and will bow before Him.*
*This is the Judge of all the earth!*
*And the question still resounds: Will not the Judge*
*of all the earth do right!*

# December 2

*Hebrews 8:6; 4:14-16*

### **The Present Day Ministry of Jesus**

*Great High Priest*

The high priests of old were declared sanctified by the high edict
of heaven after a long and meticulous process (Malachi 3:3).
They would once a year bypass the holy place, trembling in their
approach to the Holy of Holies.
One error, one mistake or misdeed would find them disqualified
before God and would bring about the worst judgment.
But this man is not sanctified… He sanctifies.
He is not the instrument of God's righteousness; He is the righ-
teousness of God.
This great High Priest is the living example of majestic purity.
All other things are measured to His example and standard.
This great High Priest is the ever living One; there was no priest
before Him and there will be no one after Him.
He is all that Heaven is about.
Sin's claims and powers have been conquered by Him.
Death released its grips by His authority.
Salvation has come down to man; our great High Priest has
entered in and paid the price once and for all.

# December 3

## John 14:21

### *All I Ever Wanted*

*Jesus has given to us the greatest promise one could ever want.*

*He gives to the one who would dare to love Him, the greatest*

*advantage possible in all time and eternity.*

*He promises that if one would love Him, if <u>anyone</u> would just love*

*Him; He would guarantee that the Father, the most powerful and*

*precious person in the universe, would love them back and love*

*with a God-sized love; love unmatched in all creation.*

*He would not only love them back, but Jesus would add His love*

*and care that is unlike any in the world.*

*Then lastly, He says that He would add the marvelous aspect of*

*personal revelation, "... and will manifest Myself to him".*

*There is no other thing anyone could ever,*

*ever need or want that is not found in the promise of these*

*words; for no act of man, no personal achievement could ever*

*accomplish what is given in this verse.*

*If I would just invest my love in Him, I am instantly propelled into*

*such divine favor that it staggers the mind.*

*I love Him. Period; end of sentence.*

*Deliberately love Him and begin to enjoy*

*the greatest benefit ever known.*

# December 4

*John 14:23*

### The Best Just Got Better

*As we previously read, Jesus opens*
*the Heavenly Reserve Bank of the universe.*
*He gives full assurance and guarantee that if anyone would love*
*Him; everything that he could ever need would be lavished on*
*him with the added aspect of having the personal revelation of*
*Jesus.*
*Then in verse 23, He turns the divine favor up higher than before!*
*He then adds, that to the soul that truly loves Him,*
*He ensures that the Father and the Son would come and make*
*their abode with them.*
*They would live exclusively in those who would give over all of*
*their passions and desires.*
*But the price for this added blessing, the saint must prove that*
*they have given such love to Christ.*
*How?*
*Simply through obedience.*
*The Father loves those who love His Son; He cares for and is com-*
*mitted to anyone/everyone who loves His Son.*
*But to receive that added touch of grace, He demands proof*
*through obedience.*

*Live out His teaching saint.*

*Give to Him the love offering of your life's pursuits.*

*The results of such are overwhelming and worth it!*

# December 5

*1 Peter 1:15-16*

### Be Holy!

*"Take time to be holy - speak oft with thy Lord."*
*So states the first line of the hymn of the same title.*
*We have two distant yet equally*
*important aspects of our holiness.*
*The first is our practical holiness.*
*The other is our positional holiness.*
*Our practical holiness is the life we opt to live on earth because*
*Christ has abolished the power that sin had over us.*
*Now, we sin, not because we have to, but because we want to.*
*Before the cross, everything we did was an affront to God;*
*nothing was righteous in His eyes.*
*We were sinful in our every act;*
*wicked in the essence of our being.*
*But because Christ went to the cross and paid the sin debt,*
*we are able to live a life on earth, by the power of His Spirit,*
*under the instruction of His word.*
*So, saint beloved, live that life of personal practical holiness;*
*glorifying God in all you do.*

# *December 6*

*1 Peter 1:15-16; 2:9*

### *We Are Holy*

*Precious believer, Jesus went into the dungeon of death to secure your place, and mine, in glory. One of the things that He accomplished was to put us in right standing before God.*

*This means that at no time, am I to be seen as unholy or unworthy before the only true God.*

*I am forever made righteous by Christ's blood.*

*This is called positional holiness.*

*I am not holy before God on my own; I am not holy before Him because of my nature, I am made holy because when I accepted the Lord Jesus Christ into my heart, He covered me with His blood, thereby sanctifying me forever.*

*This wondrous transaction can never be altered or removed. I am His and He is mine.*

*Positional holiness is never affected by practical holiness.*

*Practical holiness may waver, but not positional holiness.*

*I am forever seen as holy before the Lord.*

# December 7

*Hebrews 11:24-27*

### *Moses, God's Man*

*His Refusal*

*He was born in poverty, but raised in privilege.*
*He came into the world the son of a slave, but was trained to one*
*day hold the scepter.*
*In all of His life, for forty years, he was taught to hold his head*
*above the masses as their master, yet at the end of his life he was*
*known for his meekness.*
*At the tender age of a babe, God selected him to be a deliverer;*
*his life was selected and ordained to be different. But even in all*
*of that, he had to choose.*
*Verse 24 tells us that because he matured, he refused.*
*He chose to be a man of God instead of the head of a government.*
*All the rank and prestige one could ever want was offered and*
*refused, all for the love of God and His approval.*
*Your turn... what will you refuse?*
*Will you refuse this world and live for Christ, or will you accept*
*the offer and follow the world?*
*"You may have all this world, but give me Jesus!!"*

*Learning to Let Go*

*Purging*

*Week Fifty*

*Jesus said, "He who seeks to save his life shall lose it". In other words "self defense equals self destruction." Don't drop your sword, just hand it over to Him. This week ask for the power to let go of your control.*

# December 8

*Hebrews 11:24-27*

### Moses, God's Man

*His Righteousness*

*By taking the Lord at His word on the backside of the desert,*

*Moses forever turned his back on the world and its pleasures.*

*He took the imputed righteousness of the faith life and said*

*goodbye forever to the world.*

*His choice did not seem to have immediate benefit,*

*as often those choices do not.*

*He could not see ahead, the challenges of confronting*

*Pharaoh and his armies.*

*There is no way he could have anticipated the complaining of the*

*children of Israel or the wandering for 40 years.*

*And there was no way he could have known that he would never*

*enter the promise land, but regardless of all these things, he took*

*all that could be his in just the offer of knowing God.*

*We never know where God will lead His people.*

*No one can be sure of the road ahead.*

*But we do know that He leads us safely and perfectly into His*

*care and home.*

# December 9

*Hebrews 11:24-27*

### Moses, God's Man

*His Riches*

*A Hebrew slave that left the pomp and glories of Egypt to be a deliverer of God's people, how is it that he has the right to say he has riches?*

*Because the riches that Moses, and anyone also who chooses to follow the Lord completely, will have, are the riches of eternity, born out of the rich account of the coffers of Christ, where there is no lack or want.*

*He instantly became the wealthiest man on earth the moment he gave over his soul to follow the invitation of God, riches forever, unchangeable and secure.*

*Dear beloved of God; like Moses, let go of the world and live for Him. As is has often been said, "God is no man's debtor." Submit your life to His Lordship.*

*You'll enjoy riches like you could have never realized; not what the world can offer, not what the world validates, but the riches of Heaven.*

# December 10

*Hebrews 11:24-27*

### Moses, God's Man

*His Respect*

*Having the accurate knowledge of God,*
*the most high, makes choosing Him simpler.*
*When we have enough information to make a genuine life deci-*
*sion to follow Him and then decide to do so, we then complete the*
*equation of Hebrews 11:3 - "Through faith we understand."*
*The power to know Him and the opportunity to know Him, finally*
*meet and the transaction of faith can happen.*
*Moses had the burning bush encounter with God after God,*
*through revelation, explained Himself to him.*
*A relationship was offered, then received and at that point*
*Moses could respect the opportunity and the relationship the*
*Lord was presenting.*
*Before you go any further, pause, reflect and get the clearest pic-*
*ture of what God is offering from His word.*
*You'll see that the love life He posits is one that is worth living.*
*You'll then respect Him, and His plan and want to live for Him.*

# *December 11*

Hebrews 11:24-27

### *Moses, God's Man*

His Reward

*All of the imperial might of Egypt was bearing down on them.*
*There was no visible relief at hand.*
*No other hope than that which God Himself had promised,*
*was on his side.*
*Yet, there was no fear, no apprehension,*
*because the God of the burning bush, the God who sent the*
*plagues, would be the God of the Red Sea.*
*The God of his fathers would prove*
*to be His God, over and over again.*
*Why, you ask?*
*Because of all of the previous verses;*
*because of his refusal; because of his faith in God, and as a result*
*he was declared righteous before Him; because he had eternal*
*riches of Christ, greater riches than that of the treasure of Egypt;*
*because he had respect unto the reward of faithfulness, the only*
*result that could be, would be the reward that comes from the*
*same God who loved him.*
*Listen believer, despite all that the world offers, you refuse it!*
*For in all the truth there is – it pays to serve Jesus.*

# December 12

## Isaiah 6

### Challenged by the Savior

*vs.1*

*King Uzziah was one of the great kings of Judah.*

*Through his leadership and reign he fortified Judah to a position*

*of strength and power not seen since the days of his father David.*

*With the aid of the Lord, Uzziah had made the people of the Lord*

*strong with pride in the kingdom, their future, and the Lord.*

*He was marvelously helped by the Lord.*

*The scriptures tell us that he brought technology into the world*

*of the Hebrews that they had never known before.*

*King Uzziah was given this great and precious privilege because*

*he wisely followed the Lord with all his heart, and as the scrip-*

*ture says, he removed all of the graven images and idols that had*

*plagued and polluted the land.*

*This man was the prophet Isaiah's uncle, and with understand-*

*able admiration, that young man thought the world of his uncle.*

*But as you'll see, God has a plan for this young man, a plan that*

*would require moving his uncle out of the way, so he could finally*

*see the Lord.*

# December 13

*Isaiah 6*

### Confronted by the Sovereign

*vs.1*

*Uzziah, the great King of Judah,*
*was helped "marvelously" by God.*
*Fueled by the fervor he showed in making*
*Judah return to a spiritual place honor.*
*But with all things, no matter how great or good a man may be*
*he is nothing without the God that made him.*
*Uzziah had done well in Judah, but he in his pride forgot to honor*
*God in the manner that God demanded.*
*He had become so confident in himself he forgot God and pre-*
*sumed to do what God warned him not to do.*
*The young man Isaiah was to be the greatest of the writing*
*prophets in history.*
*Yet in his admiration of his uncle,*
*he had to be challenged and confronted.*
*It took the shameful death of Uzziah by the judgment of God to*
*open the prophet's eyes.*

*For it wasn't until then, he could not only hear the word of the Lord; now he could see the Lord. Now he could see himself. This is the most important transaction of His life and our lives. Before we are allowed to serve Him fully, we must see Him only.*

# *December 14*

*Isaiah 6*

### *Convicted by His Sin*

*vs.5*

*Once the king was dead and Isaiah could see*
*the Lord on His throne high and lifted up above all of creation,*
*he could accurately see himself.*
*And upon seeing himself, he could then*
*assess his situation and his sin.*
*He was not exempt from sin and wickedness.*
*Israel was not any better than the other people in the world; they*
*were different and separate only because God chose them.*
*He could now understand that God was higher than all and He*
*was the only one who should sit on the throne.*
*Being convicted by his sin and the confession of his sin allows God*
*a chance to do in his heart and life that which will change him*
*and the world around him forever.*
*This is the place that God wants all of us to be;*
*confronted by Him.*
*This means that we continually see ourselves in need of Him.*
*How do you see Jesus?*

*Learning to Let Go*

*Purging*

## Week Fifty-One

> *Most people don't know the difference between what God wants and what we are willing to give Him. We want to commit; God wants surrender. Spend this week clarifying the difference between the two, then make sure you've committed yourself to surrendering your life to Him.*

# December 15

*Isaiah 6*

### *Changed to be a Servant*

*vs.6-7*

*No one is qualified to be used by God.*
*No one is worthy, no one is holy enough,*
*and no one is good enough.*
*Without the intervention of God,*
*there is no one in all of humanity that meets even the minimal*
*requirements to be His vessel.*
*Isaiah is confronted with the truth of all of this.*
*He now confesses his sin and his sinful nature.*
*He acknowledges that the people he lives*
*among are just as guilty as he is.*
*But the response from heaven is not judgment, but mercy.*
*It's not the wrath of God that one should expect, but rather he*
*receives grace from God that radically alters his life forever.*
*He is supernaturally purged from his sin.*
*God not only cleanses him, He changes him for His glory.*
*We can expect the same thing too;*
*if we would determine to give our heart and lives to Him,*
*He'll dispatch an angel to work on our behalf.*
*Be changed now into a saint of Jesus Christ.*

# *December 16*

*Isaiah 6*

### *Captivated With Significance*

*vs.8*

*His sin has been confessed and acknowledged.*
*The iniquity of his past had been purged.*
*God has sanctified him for His service*
*by stripping away every obstacle that would disqualify him.*
*When all these things were completed, then the prophet is ready*
*to speak on behalf of the Lord.*
*It is then that he can clearly hear the voice of God.*
*Now his theology has roots and the authenticity of ministry has*
*found full expression.*
*The Holy Spirit speaks and poses a question that has resounded*
*in the ears of the truly faithful for centuries.*
*The person of the Godhead asks the question, and the purpose for*
*which Isaiah's life is made clear.*
*To be sent by God, to do His work is the greatest pursuit of all.*
*God's man doing God's work, it is glorious indeed!*

# *December 17*

*Isaiah 6*

### *Controlled by the Spirit*

*Vs.9*

*"Go and tell this people"*

*Such begins the God ordained,*
*Spirit directed maturity of the prophet.*
*From this point forward, he would live to be the greatest of the*
*writing prophets in history.*
*He would be used by God's Spirit to reveal some of the most*
*important information of all time.*
*He would tell of the coming Messiah; his truth, his death,*
*his resurrection and ascension.*
*He would announce the coming king's name,*
*Immanuel, he would communicate the deep truths of the end*
*times and the millennium reign.*
*Yes, the powerful words of the future were entrusted to him.*
*This is what it means to be a man whom God could use.*
*The effects of his prophecy and ministry are still with us.*
*Isaiah is proof of what can happen to one*
*who wholly follows the Lord.*

# *December 18*

## Psalm 97

### *The Care of My Soul*

**"Ye that love the LORD, hate evil: he preserveth the souls of his saints; he delivereth them out of the hand of the wicked."**
**vs.10**

*Man is a tripartite being, not a trinity.*
*Trinity is when all parts are equal.*
*Man is spirit, soul, and body. His spirit is given to him to be God-conscious, the soul, to be self-aware or self-conscious, and a body to be world-conscious.*
*The soul is that part of us that individualizes most of all, our personhood, how we communicate to ourselves and assess our view of all things.*
*Here the prophet tells us that "the Lord preserves the souls of the saints", i.e. after the sins of life have worked their wreck, ruin and damage, the world's evil attacks and schemes to manipulate and conform us, then the awful wickedness of Satan's desire to destroy us, our souls need desperately to be restored and preserved, and God does just that.*
*Only He can make that which was damaged brand new.*

# *December 19*

*Psalm 38*

### *Sincere Repentance*

### *"I will be sorry for my sin"*
### *vs.18*

*The major problems that people face in their walk
with Christ is that sin has become so convenient and accessible,
that people have become more concerned about managing sin
rather than mastering sin.*

*The concept of individual flaws that declare "my sin won't hurt
anyone else" has made conviction by the Holy Spirit and any
accountable judgment by others passé.*

*David shows us that a true walk in holiness requires that we
know God and by knowing Him we become acutely aware of
what offends Him and breaks fellowship with Him. And for true
follower of God, that is the biggest concern.*

*Loss of communication with the Father is the most
horrifying prospect there is.*

*For this saint realizes that the walk with Him is the
greatest treasure of all.*

# December 20

## Psalm 19

### He Speaks

*All too often, people ask, "Why doesn't God just talk to us and*
*speak directly to us face to face?*
*Why is He so mysterious and out of touch?"*
*Wow, nothing could be further from the truth.*
*God is always talking, the question is,*
*"Are we always able to hear?"*
*In this beautiful song, David shows us the 3 ways God has deter-*
*mined to speak to man.*
*First He speaks to mankind through <u>creation</u> (vs.1-6).*
*God shows the world His personhood in the things He has cre-*
*ated, and the message of creation should be enough to "convince"*
*man that, He is.*
*Secondly, He uses the <u>commandments</u>, His word.*
*He has said everything in the sacred text that needs to be said.*
*His word is enough to "convert" mankind;*
*it is the only means that can correct sins damage and cause us to*
*follow Him completely.*
*Then finally, He speaks to man's <u>conscience</u>, the internal gov-*
*erning principle God has given to every person.*

*The human conscience is the place where God "convicts" the lost by the truth that he already knows in his heart.*

# December 21

## Isaiah 7:14
### Christ the Child

*God assigns to the prophet, the task of foretelling, the coming of the Messiah into the world.*

*He is given the details of His miraculous birth in two places: chapters 7:14 and 9:6-7.*

*In the earlier chapters, we see the Christ enamored as the peoples Savior; the promise from Heaven that He would not be austere or distant; He would be "God with us".*

*The sovereign God of creation would also be the personal God or the poor and the needy.*

*He would always be there, a very present help in the time of need.*

*This child that would be born would have no time for an earthly throne, although He definitely deserved it.*

*He would not seek to live in palace or castle; He wouldn't even have a home.*

*His time would not be wasted on campaigning or politics.*

*No, He was born to be among the people.*

*As you remember the reason for Christmas was to never lose sight of who this child was... Immanuel... God with us!*

*Learning to Let Go*

*Purging*

## *Week Fifty-Two*

*This year is nearly over, have you accomplished all of your dreams? If not, what stood in your way? Don't go into a new year with leftover baggage. Spend the next seven days taking inventory of unrighteous feelings and actions; then make ready for a clean start.*

# *December 22*

*Isaiah 9:14-15*

## **The Crib, the Cross and the Crown**

*In this portion of scripture the prophet again*
*speaks about the birth of Jesus.*
*Writing nearly 720 years before His birth, Isaiah perfectly*
*describes the three outstanding aspects of the life of God on*
*earth: The crib, the cross, and the crown; each showing the future*
*truth of His birth, His death and His coronation.*
*The Messiah will be easy to recognize by virtue of these 3 details.*
*He will be shown in the right of glory and praise from the heav-*
*enly host, and then be rejected and scorned by the wicked hands*
*of fallen man, only to be received by His Father in heaven, with*
*all power in His hands.*
*Jesus the King of all, will be born with no fortune, would be con-*
*demned to death without a just reason, but lifted high above all*
*at His ascension.*
*High and lifted up!*

# *December 23*

*Isaiah 9:6-7*

**The Crib, the Cross and the Crown**

*The Crib*

*The birth of Jesus is one of the most amazing facts
in the history of the world.
Isaiah's prophetic announcement, "unto us a child is born",
sounds as if it is the exact words the angels spoke to the shepherds in Luke 2, "For unto you is born this day in the City of David
a Savior, which is Christ the Lord."
It's as though the angel parroted the exact same words given to
Isaiah 700 years before, His heralding of the Lord's birth would
be covered by the prophet Daniel also.
For while Isaiah spoke of the coming birth, Daniel spoke of the
calendar of His birth.
Daniel tells us enough information,
and with such accuracy, wise men came expecting to find Him
as the prophet Daniel had foretold.
"Unto you is born this day a Savior!"
Foretold in times past, but still able to save today!*

# December 24

*Isaiah 9:6-7*

### The Crib, the Cross and the Crown

*The Cross*

*For unto us a Son is given.*
*We've just seen that the birth of Jesus was a miracle of prophetic*
*accuracy, but as the verse goes on to remark, "...a Son is given."*
*This phrase reveals that the same baby whose birth would*
*attract wise men and angels; would someday have to lay down*
*His life as an offering.*
*That simple statement, "a Son is given" foretells that someone*
*will offer their son as a sacrifice, and remember, a sacrifice is*
*always to appease the greater for the lesser.*
*The one who is doing the dying has to lay down*
*their life for another.*
*This is exactly what Christ is doing; He is laying down His life for*
*the whole world.*
*His voluntary gift of pain and suffering*
*liberates the sons of Adam.*
*This is what makes Christmas worth celebrating.*
*A Son is given!*

# *December 25*

*Isaiah 9:6-7*

### **The Crib, the Cross and the Crown**

*The Crown*

*If you want to see the full display of this prophecy,*
*you should read Revelation 4, "and the government*
*shall be upon his shoulder".*
*He will be crowned as King of Kings and Lord of Lords!*
*All government rule and authority will be given to Him!*
*He will have no equals, no rivals and no foes; all that He created*
*will once again bow to Him.*
*He is given the Diadem, the multi-faceted crown.*
*That's why we sing "Crown Him with many crowns".*
*Every crown from every other kingdom, from every age,*
*will be His alone.*
*"The government shall be upon his shoulder", this means also*
*that He is the only one who can bear the weight of the universe.*
*His is the day we are awaiting to see.*
*The crowning day is coming – by and by!*

# *December 26*

*Isaiah 9:6-7*

### **The Crib, the Cross and the Crown**

*Wonderful – It is the exact same Hebrew word found in Judges 13:18, the word is "pele". It means wonderful, secret, awesome. I can't think of a better way to describe the Lord Jesus. The universe will own Him as the wonderful One! The Lord supreme and master; one day the power of His name will be seen as legendary to the entire universe. The world will see and know Him, yet with all of this, it will still reject Him; the world refuses to see this wonderful One, the One of whom angels adore. Won't you worship this wonderful One today? Forget all of the holiday foolishness and come to know Christ as the wonderful One!*

# December 27

*Isaiah 9:6-7*

### The Crib, the Cross and the Crown

*Isaiah just fresh from writing about the qualities of the coming King, shows that the Lord's servant would be recognized by several factors, all found in chapter 11 of this book. He would be identifiable because the Spirit of the Lord would be upon Him, and one of the seven spirits would be that of the spirit of counsel. He would be the ultimate counselor, because the Lord would anoint Him for just that purpose. He would know what it takes to speak to the lost and the arrogant. He would have direct and clear sight into the minds and hearts of men. He is the mighty God, with the heart of great love and compassion. If you need someone to talk to you, someone to counsel you, I know of no greater counselor than Jesus.*

# December 28

Isaiah 9:6-7

### The Crib, the Cross and the Crown

*The Mighty God*

*There has been great debate*
*over the matter of the deity of Christ.*
*Because the Godhead seems too much for the human mind to*
*grasp, the mystery of the Godhead becomes reason for many to*
*deny the obvious.*
*I have often said during my lectures, "Just because you don't*
*understand the fact, doesn't mean it can't be true."*
*This is one of the clear statements to the deity of Christ. This*
*coming Messiah, foretold by Isaiah, will not only be a wonderful*
*counselor, but He will be God Himself!!*
*This precious one will accomplish the impossible because He only*
*does the impossible.*
*The Lord Jesus Christ, central figure of humanity, comes into the*
*environs of sinners to save.*
*The glory of heaven, the song of the angels of God, the theme*
*song of the redeemed, is God!!*
*The phrase the Hebrews used for Him is "El Elyon".*

*There can be no mistaking it, the child in the crib;*

*the man on the cross, the one who will wear the crown*

*– the Mighty God, is Jesus Himself!*

# December 29

*Isaiah 9:6-7*

### The Crib, the Cross and the Crown

*The Everlasting Father*

*"He that has seen Me, has seen the Father."*
*There is no marginal difference between*
*any person of the Godhead.*
*When the Godhead is presented*
*to mankind it is always in the person of the Son.*
*"For it pleased the Father that in Him should all fullness dwell."*
*"For in Him dwelleth all the fullness of the Godhead bodily."*
*The mystery of the Godhead finds full expression*
*in this prophecy of Isaiah.*
*The Christ is given the role of everlasting*
*Father in a very important relationship with the saints.*
*You remember the prophecy of John in the book of Revelation,*
*chapter 21:5-7.*

**"And he that sat upon the throne said, Behold, I make all things new. And he said unto me, Write: for these words are true and faithful.**

**And he said unto me, It is done. I am Alpha and Omega, the beginning and the end. I will give unto him that is athirst of the fountain of the water of life freely.**

**He that overcometh shall inherit all things; and I will be his
God, and he shall be My son."**
*The Lord God loves those who knows Him, and provides the most
important aspect we need.*
*We need to relate to Him as a Father,*
*He wants to relate us as a parent.*
*Of all the faiths, religions, philosophies, theories, and teaching,*
*none meets the needs of the man at the core of his being.*
*Only in Christ can the lost can find a Savior,*
*a Counselor, a Father and God!*

# December 30

## Psalm 127
### "Except the Lord"

**"Except the LORD build the house,**
**they labour in vain that build it: except the LORD keep the**
**city, the watchman waketh but in vain."**
**vs.1**

All the important players are spirits.
God is a spirit (John 4:24), the angels of heaven are spirits
(Hebrews 1:5), the devil is a spirit (Ephesians 2:2), and we are
spirits (I Thessalonians 5:23).
All the vain effort of fleshly pursuits fail.
Man's schemes and intrepid ideas eventually wither because the
finite can never surpass or compete with the infinite.
Except the Lord, the Father of Spirits (Hebrews 12:9), order the
course of lives, all is futile.
The events and experiences of good intended minds
can never ultimately survive, simply because it has not the hand
of the divine architect.
All of that can ever be accomplished without His hand of blessing.

*Never put trust in efforts of the flesh, instead, "walk in the spirit" (Galatians 5:16) as Paul admonishes, and then watch and rejoice in the perfect direction your life will take.*

# December 31

## Proverbs 7

### Sincere Sex Education Gone Bad

*The intent is noble and the advice is sound.*

*All of the observations are accurate and true, but overall, this object lesson of sex, seduction, and sensuality is useless.*

*Yes, completely **USELESS**.*

*David obviously loves his son Solomon, and prepares to direct him away from the very same weaknesses that he had.*

*But all that he said and warned his son about was ultimately useless.*

*Why? How?*

*The reason is blatantly clear.*

*Because even though all of his critiques were accurate and true, they were woefully inadequate.*

*How can I say that?*

*Because David, in all of his fatherly loving advice, made a huge mistake: he left out **God**.*

*Nowhere in this chapter do we read the only way to stay totally and wholly pure.*

*Nowhere in this chapter is God even mentioned!!!*

*Likewise, Christian bookstores are overrun with material pleading with young people to live sexually pure; books on how to date right; books on not dating at all; some books on the value*

*of arranged marriages.*

*But all too often it is merely good human advice, and note, a lot*

*of it is very good advice.*

*But it is human conventions, and ideas, at best sprinkled with a*

*few bible verses, but no bible centered plan and praxis is given.*

*Please listen very carefully:*

*If He can powerfully, miraculously save you, why not trust the*

*same Person to keep you?*

*It **can** be done; but only **His** way.*

*There are others who have faithfully waited, even amidst over-*

*whelming temptation, and God was completely faithful to them.*

*They maintained their sexually purity, and so can you.*

# Appendix

# Bible Reading Plans

*I* have purposefully omitted a bible reading schedule from each days' study, because I did not want to assume that everyone reads the word the same way.

There are many different plans to go through the word, each having great merit and success when partnered with those who are inclined by personality and learning style to match its' suggested way of reading the text.

So, in appreciation to that, I have offered a few suggestions hoping that the reader will try each until a good match is found. For the point is that everyone read through the bible at their own pace, as often as possible.

To expect everyone to follow the same approach is unfair and leaves many to get discouraged and quit, when if an alternative plan was available, the chances of completing the bible at least once a year is doable.

# Reading All Sixty Six Books, in Sixty Six Days

O f the many bible reading plans I know, this is the most ambitious.

Sixty six in sixty six makes it possible to complete the word in just over two months, so that one may read the bible nearly six times a year!

The plan is not for the reader to skim through the word. Genuine aggressive reading is *always* the intent, but for those who want to develop a consistent momentum this can word out well to their eternal benefit.

This is the schedule:

Every day read 5 of the Psalms and the chapter in the book of Proverbs that corresponds with the day of the month. I suggest that you read the Psalms in such a manner also. That is on the day of the month you read that Psalm also, then add 30 to that number four more times. So on the 8th day of the month you would read these Psalms: 8, 38, 68, 98, 128; and the 8th chapter of Proverbs. The only exception being on the 29th day of the month; on that day you'd read, 29, 59, 89, and the 149. Leaving Psalm 119 for the months that have 31 days; in those instances you'd only read that Psalm.

Now for the reading schedule for the rest of the bible you'd follow this plan:

1. Day one - Read the books of James, and I and II Thessalonians
2. Day two – Read the book of Mark
3. Day three – Read the book of Judges
4. Day four – Read the books of Daniel and Ezra
5. Day five – Read the books of Hosea, Joel, Amos, Jonah and Obadiah
6. Day six – Read the first 15 chapters of Acts.
7. Day seven – Read the last 13 chapters of Acts
8. Day eight – Read the books of I and II Corinthians
9. Day nine – Read the books of Ecclesiastes, Nehemiah and Song of Solomon
10. Day ten – Read the chapters 1 through 12 of Joshua
11. Day eleven – Read the book of Hebrews
12. Day twelve – Read chapters one through 15 of Genesis
13. Day thirteen – Read chapters 16 through 31 of Genesis
14. Day fourteen – Read chapters 32 through 50 of Genesis

15. Day fifteen – Read the books of I and II Peter, I, II, and III John and Jude

16. Day sixteen – Read the book of Esther and chapters 1 through 14 of Job

17. Day seventeen – Read chapters 13 through 24 of Joshua, Ruth

18. Day eighteen – Read chapters 1 through 15 of I Samuel

19. Day nineteen – Read chapters 17 through 31 of I Samuel

20. Day twenty – Read chapters 1 through 12 of II Samuel

21. Day twenty-one – Read chapters 13 through 27 of II Samuel

22. Day twenty- two – Read chapters 1 through 10 of Revelation

23. Day twenty-three – Read chapters 11 through 22 of Revelation

24. Day twenty-four – Read chapters 1 through 15 of Exodus

25. Day twenty-five – Read chapters 16 through 31 of Exodus

26. Day twenty-six – Read chapters 32 through 40 of Exodus

27. Day twenty-seven – Read chapters 15 through 30 of Job

28. Day twenty-eight – Read chapters 1 through 14 of Matthew

29. Day twenty-nine – Read chapters 15 through 28 of Matthew

30. Day thirty – Read chapters 1 through 15 of I Chronicles

31. Day thirty-one – Read chapters 1 through 11 of I Kings

32. Day thirty-two – Read chapters 12 through 22 of I Kings

33. Day thirty-three – Read chapters 1 through 13 of II Kings

34. Day thirty-four – Read chapters 14 through 25 of II Kings

35. Day thirty-five – Read the books of Ephesians, Philippians, Colossians and I Timothy

36. Day thirty-six – Read the books of Romans and II Timothy

37. Day thirty-seven – Read chapters 1 through 13 of Leviticus

38. Day thirty-eight – Read chapters 14 through 27 of Leviticus

39. Day thirty-nine – Read the books of Galatians, Titus, and Philemon

40. Day forty – Read chapters 1 through 13 of Jeremiah

41. Day forty-one – Read chapters 14 through25 of Jeremiah

42. Day forty-two – Read chapters 26 through 40 of Jeremiah

43. Day forty-three – Read chapters 41 through 52 of Jeremiah

44. Day forty-four – Read the books of Lamentations, Haggai, Micah and Nahum

45. Day forty-five – Read chapters 1 through 12 of Luke

46. Day forty-six – Read chapters 13 through 24 Luke

47. Day forty-seven – Read chapters 1 through 16 of Ezekiel

48. Day forty-eight – Read chapters 17 through 32 of Ezekiel

49. Day forty-nine – Read chapters 33 through 48 of Ezekiel

50. Day fifty – Read chapters 1 through 12 of Numbers

51. Day fifty-one – Read chapters 1 through10 of John

52. Day fifty-two – Read chapters 11 through 21 of John

53. Day fifty-three – Read chapters 31 through 42 of Job

54. Day fifty-four – Read chapters 1 through 16 of Isaiah

55. Day fifty-five – Read chapters 17 through 33 of Isaiah

56. Day fifty-six – Read chapters 34 through 50 of Isaiah

57. Day fifty-seven – Read chapters 51 through 66 of Isaiah

58. Day fifty-eight – Read the books of Zechariah, Zephaniah and Malachi

59. Day fifty-nine – Read chapters 1 through 17 of Deuteronomy

60. Day sixty – Read chapters 18 through 34 of Deuteronomy

61. Day sixty-one – Read chapters 16 through 29 of I Chronicles

62. Day sixty-two – Read chapters 13 through24 of Numbers

63. Day sixty-three – Read chapters 25 through 36 of Numbers

64. Day sixty-four – Read chapters 1 through 12 of II Chronicles

65. Day sixty-five – Read chapters 13 through 24 of II Chronicles

66. Day sixty-six – Read chapters 25 through 36 of II Chronicles

# Reading Chronologically

*T*o read the bible chronologically you must own a chronological study bible. I recommend the Reese' Chronological Bible. It is extremely well done and is consistent with a biblical timeline that seems to be accurate with sound theology and eschatology. However in many cases, the chapter divisions are not present so it may be more difficult to keep a flow accomplishment if this is your goal. But don't be disheartened, this is a wonderful and beneficial way of going through the word once a year. I highly recommend that at least once everyone should try this method of bible reading.

# Division Reading

$M$ost scholars will agree that the bible can be divided into ten sections. I think that this is the easiest way to read through the bible in a year. The idea being to read one division through a month, this will mean that there will some months when the reading is intense, aggressive and a bit overwhelming, while other months the reading will be extremely light. These are the divisions:

Law – Genesis through Deuteronomy

History – Joshua through Esther

Poetry – Job through Song of Solomon

Major Prophets – Isaiah through Daniel

Minor Prophets – Hosea through Malachi

Gospels – Matthew through John

Church History – Acts

Pauline Epistles – Romans through Hebrews

General Epistles – James – Jude

Prophecy – The Revelation

# Daily Chapter Reading

*T*his bible reading plan is probably the easiest to maintain throughout the year. Simply read 3 chapters a day in a book and do not wander. Start with Genesis and when completed, move to Matthew; then to Exodus, Luke and so on. You will complete the New Testament nearly three times before you complete the Old Testament. This is fine; just remember to take good notes as you go. You'll finish the bible in less than a year using this method.

If you increase to 10 chapters a day you will finish the bible 3 times in less than a year. Whichever plan you decide, stick to it! Become neither ambitious nor lazy!! Read your bible!!

CPSIA information can be obtained at www.ICGtesting.com
Printed in the USA
LVOW08s2306080716

495656LV00002BA/7/P